POWER HOLD 'EM STRATEGY

POWER HOLD'EM STRATEGY

DANIEL NEGREANU

CARDOZA PUBLISHING

Cardoza Publishing is the foremost gaming publisher in the world, with a library of over 200 up-to-date and easy-to-read books and strategies. These authoritative works are written by the top experts in their fields and with more than 10,000,000 books in print, represent the best-selling and most popular gaming books anywhere.

FIRST EDITION
Copyright © 2008 by Daniel Negreanu
- All Rights Reserved -

See free book offer on page 513!

Library of Congress Catalog Card No: 2008927150
ISBN: 1-58042-204-7
Todd Brunson photo ©Rob Gracie/GreasieWheels.com

Visit our web site: **www.cardozabooks.com**
or write for a full list of books and computer strategies.

CARDOZA PUBLISHING
P.O. Box 98115, Las Vegas, NV 89193
Phone (800)577-WINS
email: cardozabooks@aol.com
www.cardozabooks.com

I'd like to dedicate this book to the best parents in the world, Constantin and Annie Negreanu. They didn't always agree with my choices in life, but always supported me and believed I could accomplish anything I set my mind to.

TABLE OF CONTENTS

WINNING AT HIGH-LIMIT
CASH GAMES by Todd Brunson ················· 79

PLAYING NO-LIMIT
HOLD'EM ONLINE by Erick Lindgren ······139

SHORT-HANDED ONLINE NO-LIMIT HOLD'EM CASH GAMES by Paul Wasicka 185

MIXING IT UP by David Williams 217

SMALL BALL by Daniel Negreanu 287

PREFACE

Avery Cardoza

The book you're holding will forever change the way you think about no-limit hold'em. Seriously. You're about to read a treatise on beating the game of poker headlined by one of the most brilliant poker players in the world. Not smart, *brilliant*. And along with game-changing advice from Daniel, a select group of his friends, stars of the game in their own right, will give you their secrets as well.

How good is this book?

Let me put it simply. There are three books that I place in the pantheon of great poker books written in modern times. I'll call that time period the last 30 years, an era that was ushered in by the first book on my list. (I'm sure you can guess which one it is.) The books I elevate to this pedestal meet three critical criteria:

1. The strategies are so profound—even affecting the mindset of the game itself—that three readings

are not quite enough to absorb the book's scope and depth.

2. The material is revolutionary, elevating already published information to a level not previously expressed in print, and causing a profound impact on how players approach and play poker.

3. The text is accurate, presents incisive game-changing concepts, and is well-written, with no monkey-talk, platitudes, or inane math such as that professed by a few self-righteous egomaniacs.

So, what are the books? Not surprisingly, the first one is Doyle Brunson's *Super System*, the bible of poker and a must-read for any serious player, with nods to its worthy sequel, *Super System 2*. The second book on my list is the one you're holding, *Daniel Negreanu's Power Hold'em Strategy*. Once you finish reading its concepts and strategies, I don't think you will have any argument about this selection.

That puts two books on my list, neither of which is a controversial choice, leaving room for one other title...drumroll, please. Easy, now—not so fast!

The competition for that third slot is great indeed. World-class players and authors have published significant works—*Caro's Book of Poker Tells*, the *Harrington on Hold'em* series, and the *Cloutier/McEvoy Championship* series. These are all worthy aspirants to the throne but still, I don't quite squeeze them into the three-headed pantheon of the poker gods.

I'm tempted to put a new book near the top, the also-brilliant *Poker Tournament Formula 2* (and its companion guide, *Poker Tournament Formula*) by Arnold Snyder. This book incisively and accurately depicts the landscape of how tournaments really should be played, and debunks widely accepted icons and strategies in the process. But I'll have to see how this one passes the test of time. Snyder's tournament utility theories are opening the minds of a lot of tournament poker players.

So, what *is* that third book? I don't want to let you down after this buildup, but I'm going to leave that one slot in the top-three category open, for now anyway. Why? Because I suspect it will eventually be filled by Daniel's next big book. Or will the legend-to-be, Todd Brunson, who threatens to write his own *magnus opus*, steal that spot? Or might Snyder's groundbreaking work rise to that hallowed place? Yes, we'll have to wait for that one final anointment.

Meanwhile, the baton of the great poker books, initially carried by Doyle Brunson's game-changing *Super System*, has passed on to a new generation of hold'em players guided by *Daniel Negreanu's Power Hold'em Strategy*. It is this millennium's heir apparent to *Super System*. As Doyle did with his seminal work in 1978 (and later, with his updated *Super System 2* in 2005), Daniel has enlisted great players who have agreed to give away their powerful secrets to winning. The difference is that Daniel's book focuses *only* on no-limit hold'em, giving you 100 percent penetration into the "Cadillac of poker," as Doyle so aptly put it.

Helping carry the torch into the modern, aggressive and innovative world of no-limit hold'em are two esteemed *Super System 2* contributors, Todd Brunson and Daniel, accompanied by Paul Wasicka, Evelyn Ng, David Williams and Erick Lindgren. These great contributors have won countless tournaments, tens of millions of dollars in prize money, many millions more in cash games, and have achieved international fame through their poker playing.

I can promise you this—Daniel's book is going to open your eyes in awe. When he agreed to write under the Cardoza banner, I knew Daniel would fully commit himself to giving our readers something special. I just didn't realize it would be *this* special.

Strap yourself in, open up your mind, and get ready for a great read. The way you look at poker will be never be the same again.

INTRODUCTION

INTRODUCTION

Daniel Negreanu

By deciding to buy this book, you are taking the first step toward immensely expanding your poker knowledge. I put a lot of work into *Power Hold'em Strategy* and will share secrets with you that have helped me become the all-time money winner on the World Poker Tour, as well as consistently cash in the World Series of Poker and other tournaments worldwide.

In this book, you will find views on the play of hands that I guarantee will surprise you, as well as open up your mind to the advanced brand of poker that I play—small ball. Small-ball poker is designed to help you win in all forms of no-limit Texas hold'em by using a betting approach that limits your risk on each hand while promoting aggressive play.

Before you are ready to tackle the powerful small-ball chapter, however, I highly recommend that you review the entire book, starting with Evelyn Ng's chapter for beginning players. You'll learn an introductory approach to playing no-limit hold'em tournaments—not an optimal style of poker, mind you, but a

INTRODUCTION

great way for beginning players to quickly become competitive in tournaments by using an aggressive preflop strategy.

An outstanding group of professional players—people who have achieved tremendous success in no-limit hold'em tournaments and cash games—have contributed in-depth instructional chapters to this book. Todd Brunson shares his insights on how he succeeds playing in the biggest cash games in the world. My friends Erick Lindgren, Paul Wasicka and David Williams each tackle specific no-limit hold'em instruction in their insightful chapters.

Once you've digested their dynamic formulas for winning, you'll get to the small-ball chapter that I wrote. It has taken me more than a year to write these strategies. I have invested a great deal of thought and effort to make certain that I not only teach you how to be successful with a small-ball betting approach, but how to successfully defend against opponents who employ a similar strategy.

Obviously, this book is not a quick read! You'll find so much information to digest that you'll probably want to reread it several times, particularly the sections you find most important in helping plug leaks in your game.

I should also say that not all great players play alike. Sometimes they even disagree with each other on the best way to play certain hands. Each contributor to this book has been successful with his approach to hold'em, but as with anything, we don't always agree. I would challenge you to question the strategies you read and decide for yourself whether they will work with your game. Even if you ultimately find that the small-ball approach isn't for you, you'll gain a lot of value from understanding how small-ball players think.

Once you get into the nitty-gritty parts of my book, I predict that a few new light bulbs will start flashing in your mind illuminating advanced insights that will lead you to a far deeper understanding of how you can become a winning no-limit hold'em player.

BIG-BET
NO-LIMIT HOLD'EM:
A STRATEGY FOR NOVICE
TOURNAMENT PLAYERS

EVELYN NG

Evelyn Ng first attracted international attention in 2003 when millions of poker fans saw her play in the World Poker Tour's inaugural Ladies Night tournament. Though new to tournament poker at the time, the attractive and personable Canadian outlasted Jennifer Harman, Kathy Liebert and Annie Duke, finishing second to Clonie Gowan.

Ng later appeared at the 2005 Canadian Annual Poker Summit as the professional centerpiece. She also has acted as a color commentator for Game Show Network's *Poker Royale*, and for NBC's coverage of the Poker Superstars Invitational.

This poker celebrity started off by dealing in private clubs in Toronto, shifting to playing poker professionally, primarily in cash games. She moved to Las Vegas and is currently climbing up the tournament poker ladder, cashing for $73,230 in the 2006 WPT $25,000 Championship Event.

Ng's topic for this book outlines a strategy that beginners can use in no-limit hold'em tournaments. If you are a newcomer to tournament play, the strategy that she gives you is especially important because it is specifically designed to help you counter the aggressive moves of more experienced players. This gives you a much better chance of getting to the final table.

BIG-BET
NO-LIMIT HOLD'EM:
A STRATEGY FOR NOVICE
TOURNAMENT PLAYERS

Evelyn Ng

INTRODUCTION

Before I began playing no-limit hold'em tournaments, I had been playing limit hold'em cash games for years as a professional player. This was well before the poker boom. I never really had a reason to learn how to play no-limit hold'em because back then, the only hold'em games you'd find in a casino or cardroom were limit hold'em. After a novice player, Chris Moneymaker, won the World Series of Poker in 2003, interest in playing poker picked up. Then when the World Poker Tour hit television with its mini-cams that allowed you to see players' hole cards, things really changed. Suddenly, no-limit hold'em games were being spread everywhere and no-limit hold'em tournaments became the new craze.

The World Poker Tour gave me the opportunity to play in a unique event on television, a special ladies-only tournament with five other women: Jennifer Harman, Annie Duke, Kathy

Liebert, Maureen Feduniak and Clonie Gowan. Unfortunately, there was just one problem: I had never played no-limit hold'em!

Luckily for me, Daniel Negreanu, my good friend of many years, knew a thing or two about no-limit hold'em and he was gracious enough to help me develop a strategy that would give me a fighting chance against that tough group of players. In this chapter, I'd like to share with you "The System" that Daniel taught me for that event and beyond.

If you've had success playing no-limit hold'em cash games, but have never before played a no-limit tournament, read on! You'll pick up some valuable tips on playing a strategy that we've specially designed to help you last as long as possible when you begin playing no-limit tournaments. Otherwise, skip right along to the next chapter.

A SIMPLIFIED STRATEGY FOR NO-LIMIT HOLD'EM TOURNAMENTS

Tournament no-limit hold'em isn't the type of game you can jump into and play optimally right off the bat. Before you learn to run, you must learn to walk. Before you can advance to a competitive level in no-limit hold'em tournaments, you need to play a more simplified version of the game. One way to do that is by playing a style of poker that allows you to avoid putting yourself into situations where you will be forced to make difficult decisions. That's what I like about Daniel's simplified system of tournament play for novices: It makes the game so much easier when you begin playing no-limit hold'em tournaments.

The advice in this chapter is geared specifically to beginning players; it is not the ideal strategy for more accomplished players. Sometimes these suggestions may seem to contradict what is written in the other sections of the book that are geared towards advanced play. This chapter will have you focusing mostly on how to play before the flop, while the advanced sections shift the focus to decisions you'll be faced with after the flop. Understand that you won't necessarily be learning the optimal strategy for no-limit hold'em tournaments. Instead, you'll be using a strategy designed to help you advance deeper in tournament play by neutralizing your more experienced opponents' advantage over you.

You'll learn which hands to play before the flop and how to bet those hands in various scenarios. You'll also receive guidelines as to how you should proceed post-flop. Once you've learned how to use this strategy properly, and have become more comfortable playing tournament poker, you can take the next step and start playing a more advanced strategy for no-limit hold'em tournaments. Thankfully, you need go no further than the next few chapters in this book to find expert advice from Daniel and the other contributors.

The first step is understanding how to neutralize the edge enjoyed by more experienced opponents.

NEUTRALIZING EXPERIENCED OPPONENTS

Novice players can somewhat neutralize their more skilled opponents' advantage by making large raises that price them out of pots. By doing that, you force skilled players to pay a higher price to try to crack your hand or outplay you. An extreme example of this is to simply go all in whenever you play a hand. Going all in essentially forces your opponents to become robots. They can no longer outplay you, so they are left with simply waiting and hoping that they eventually get a strong enough hand to call you.

The first obstacle in defending against an all-in bet is being dealt a premium hand, but there is another obstacle as well—winning the pot with it! In hold'em, it is rare to find a situation where you are, for example, an 85-percent favorite or better before the flop. Even K♠ K♥ is only a 71 percent favorite over A♣ 6♦. And A♦ K♥ is a mere 61 percent favorite over 6♥ 7♠.

While moving all in before the flop would force your opponents to wait for premium hands before they dare call you, it's a bit more reckless than necessary. There are certain situations late in a tournament when the blinds are high in relation to the stacks where an all-in bet is certainly the way to go. But in the early and middle stages of deep-stack tournaments, you would be risking far more chips with an all-in bet than you need to.

Large raises accomplish an important goal for beginning tournament players: They force skilled opponents to wait for premium hands, and play a little more carefully against the raiser. That's ideal for you as a novice tournament player. Rather than putting yourself in tough situations after the flop where things get a little trickier, your goal is to win the blinds and antes without being called by any of your opponents.

PREFLOP

TOURNAMENT THEORY FOR NOVICE PLAYERS

An understanding of how much to bet is at the top of your list. Raising to three times the size of the big blind is considered to be a standard size raise in no-limit hold'em. If the blinds are $50/$100, a raise to $300 is the traditional raise size in tournament play. Anything more than that is considered to be a large raise, while raising less than three times the big blind is considered a small raise.

But not all experienced tournament players use that formula. If you've watched players like Daniel, Phil Ivey, David Williams, Todd Brunson and some of the other superstars in the game, you've noticed that their raise sizes are usually closer to two-and-a-half times the big blind. The reason that works for them is that they want to get involved in more flops and thereby force their opponents to make difficult decisions after the flop. And of course, they also risk fewer chips when they attempt to steal the blinds.

BET SIZING

How much you raise on the hands you play is where the strategy for novice players differs from traditional tournament protocol—and where it differs from small-ball tournament strategy, as well. Instead of the standard strategy, and rather than the small-ball strategy for raising, I suggest making your preflop raises four to five times the size of the blind.

For example, with blinds at $50/$100, if the size of your raise is $450 (4.5 times the size of the big blind), you are laying 3 to 1 odds ($450 to win $150) on your attempt to steal the blinds. A small-ball player who comes in for 2.5 times the big blind would only be laying 5-3 odds on his steal ($250 to win $150).

If the blinds are $200/$400 with nine $50 antes, a small-ball player will be risking $1,000 to win $1,050 (slightly better than even money) if he makes his standard two-and-a-half times the blind raise. As a novice player using the raising guidelines I suggest, you will be risking as much as $2,000 to win $1,050 (closer to 2 to 1).

What is the main reason that a novice player should raise more than a traditional tournament player and more than a small-ball player? Experienced traditional players and small-ball players don't mind being called; they want to play flops. You, the novice, would rather not get called because you want to avoid seeing flops.

So, when you find a hand you are going to play and no one has yet entered the pot, pick a number between four and five times the big blind and stick with it. I strongly recommend that you don't vary your raise sizes based on the strength of your hand. You don't want to develop any betting patterns that perceptive opponents may notice. For example, suppose you are making your raises with A-A and K-K slightly smaller than you are with your other hands because you want people to call you. Believe me, good players will catch on to what you're doing and will take advantage of you. You'll be giving away information without even realizing it. My philosophy is that you should always make them pay for any information about your style of play!

But as a novice, I suggest you start out by raising to five times the big blind. As you improve your tournament game, you can slowly lower that number to four-and-a-half and then to four times the big blind. When you become a superstar, you'll eventually take it even further to only two-and-a-half times the blind. But at the starting line, take it one step at a time.

Now let's take a look at some other guidelines for preflop betting in various situations.

WHEN PLAYERS HAVE ALREADY LIMPED INTO THE POT

If a player has already called in front of you, you have to make an even larger raise to force him out of the pot. What I don't want you to do is limp in behind this player. In fact, I don't want you to limp in at all before the flop (with the exception of those times when you're in the small blind, which we'll get to later).

Since your goal is to win pots preflop and avoid having to make tough decisions after the flop, limping in should not be part of your repertoire of plays. Limping gives you no chance to win the pot before the flop and, unless someone raises, guarantees that you'll be taking a flop in what may be a marginal situation for your hand. A beginning player should live and die by this motto: Raise or fold before the flop!

So, if no one has entered the pot in front of you before the flop, you should abide by the five times rule—raise to five times the big blind. If one or two limpers have entered the pot in front of you, make it seven times the size of the blind if you want to play the hand. If more than two limpers come into the pot in front of you, make your raise nine times the size of the big blind.

For example, with the blinds at $100/$200, suppose one player limps in for $200 in front of you. If you raise five times the size of the blind ($1,000), he is much more likely to call the extra $800 than he is to call a raise that is seven times the blind ($1,400) and costs him an extra $1,200. The larger raise amount should put enough pressure on your opponent to make him think twice about calling you. And that is the result you want!

I know for a fact that this approach really frustrates the more skilled players who want to keep the pots small preflop. They might even try to discourage you from making large raises before the flop, but don't let them get to you. Stick to your game plan, and I guarantee they'll hate you for it!

THE 5-7-9 TIMES RULE
The Preflop Raising Strategy for Novice
Tournament Players

Number of Limpers	Size of Raise
None	5x
One	7x
Two	9x

WHEN A PLAYER HAS RAISED IN FRONT OF YOU

Things get a little trickier when another player has raised in front of you. Since your motto is, "Raise or fold before the flop," you are going to rule out smooth calling raisers as well as limpers. Since you aren't going to be calling in any situations, the number of hands you can play when facing a raise is limited.

The raiser's table position is an important factor when deciding how to play a situation. To simplify things so that you don't have to worry too much about reading your opponents or playing a complicated guessing game, use the following approach: Play conservatively against raises from early position and become progressively more aggressive as you get closer to late position.

Let's look at an example. You are dealt the A♣ Q♦ on the button. A player raises from under the gun. I suggest you fold. Yes, fold! Despite the fact that you have a strong hand, a player who raises from early position generally has a stronger hand.

Now let's look at a similar scenario. This time, you are dealt the A♣ Q♦ in the small blind. A player raises to $300 from late position. You have the same exact hand but this time you definitely want to play. Why? Because your opponent is more likely to be stealing in this situation. The question is, how much should you raise? The answer to that brings up another one of our rules: A preflop reraise should be five times bigger than the raise you are facing.

In this example, the raise was to $300, so you would raise it to a total of $1,500 (5 x $300 equals $1,500). That amount should apply enough pressure on your opponent to ensure that he won't be calling just to try to outplay you after the flop. If he calls the raise—or worse, reraises you—it's highly likely that your A-Q is in trouble. The size of your raise will help make it easier for you to clearly define that. We'll talk about what to do if he calls your raise later on in this chapter, but for now let's lay out a set of rules to guide you when an opponent raises in front of you before the flop.

RAISING RULES FOR NOVICES
When You Hold A-Q

Opponent's Position	His Action	Your Action
Early Position	Raise	Fold
Late Position	Raise	Reraise

WHEN YOU ARE FACING A RERAISE

By playing a conservative, yet aggressive, style of poker, you won't be faced with as many reraises as a looser player would get. Your raises will demand more respect. Therefore, if a player does reraise you, his reraise usually signifies that he has a legitimately strong hand that *you* should respect. Unless you have a premium hand, you should fold in the face of a reraise unless it's an all-in reraise that won't cost you very many chips to call. A short-stacked, all-in player's range of hands is generally much wider than a typical player's. In other words, he'll play more hands because he often gets to the point of desperation, maybe even going all in with any hand that looks playable.

If you have a premium hand and someone reraises you, I would advise you not to get very fancy. Simply make a large reraise with any of the following hands: A-A, K-K, Q-Q, A-K, and J-J. Fold any other hand, including pairs lower than 10-10 and A-Q. Keep in mind that this strategy isn't optimal, but for new players like you who are just starting out on the tournament trail, playing this strategy is the safest way to last as long as possible in an event. This approach will give you a chance to win by being aggressive with your good hands and folding in all marginal situations.

Of course, reading your opponents plays a role in how you deal with any situation in poker. And as you improve as a tournament player, you can add calling to your repertoire of plays. But for the most part, this beginning strategy—Raise or Fold—is designed to make tournaments simpler to play by using a basic system that you won't have to think through in stressful situations, and a course of action that you don't need to veer from.

This beginning system makes you susceptible to being trapped by a skillful opponent; there's no question about that. For example, if you are dealt Q-Q and someone is dealt A-A or K-K, you aren't at the stage where you can get away from these traps. Instead, you'll just have to hope that you get lucky and outdraw your opponent.

A-A, K-K and Q-Q are easy hands for you to play. Naturally, you'll want to raise or reraise with them at every opportunity. J-J and A-K are hands that you might want to be slightly more cautious with, especially if you think that your opponent might have a stronger hand than yours. You may want to fold these hands in the face of a reraise. But I don't recommend that you fold unless you know enough about how your opponent plays to justify the idea that he probably had A-A or K-K.

THE 25-PERCENT RULE

The 25-percent rule is specifically designed for beginning tournament players. It will help you to avoid outthinking yourself or getting outplayed in marginal situations. The rule is simple: Anytime your standard raise represents 25 percent or more of your stack, you should go all in. Think it over carefully and you'll see why this rule is effective.

Let's look at an example of how it works. Suppose the blinds are $100/$200 and you are sitting on a stack of $3,700 in chips. Since your standard raise is 5 times the big blind or $1,000, making the raise would represent more than 25 percent of your stack. So, rather than making a bet of $1,000, you would be better served to go all in for the entire $3,700.

> **ANYTIME YOUR STANDARD RAISE REPRESENTS 25 PERCENT OR MORE OF YOUR STACK, YOU SHOULD GO ALL IN.**

The key reason for going all-in in this situation is that it will help you avoid any potential mathematical disasters if you get reraised before the flop. You see, if you make it $1,000 to go and a player reraises you all in, you'll be getting excellent pot odds to call—but what if you have a marginal hand? Instead of being put in a situation where *you* have to make a difficult decision, your move-in bet before the flop throws the decision back into your opponent's court. If he calls, you cannot be outplayed—you are going to see it through to the river, no matter what!

The same rule applies to reraises as well. For example, if a player makes it $600 to go with the blinds at $100/$200, a standard reraise for you would be to $3,000—five times the original bet. If your stack size is below $12,000 (25 percent of $12,000 is $3,000), then you should make a huge reraise and go all in for the whole amount. That may seem risky, but again, it will help you to avoid having to make tough decisions. Now suppose your stack size is $10,000 and you make it $3,000 to go. A player moves all in over the top of that bet. Since you have already invested 30 percent of your stack, you're getting huge pots odds to make the call.

I urge you to remember, however, that a player who reraises a reraise before the flop almost always has a very strong hand. Being a beginning tournament player, though, may make it difficult for you to discern how strong your opponent's hand is. You probably also will have trouble deciding whether or not you should call for your remaining $7,000 against the kinds of hands your opponent may have. By going all in before the flop rather than making your standard size of reraise, you can avoid this mathematical problem altogether. And then, just hope for the best!

I did really well using this betting strategy in the WPT ladies night tournament. When my opponents saw that I was raising with good hands, it discouraged them from trying to play back at me. I would win pots—though, admittedly, not huge ones. But that was okay with me, because I didn't want to get too sophisticated. This worked for me because I wasn't very good at getting fancy. Having a system in place going into the event made me feel a lot more comfortable at the tournament table. Further, Daniel's novice strategy was very effective for me, especially for that particular, high-pressure setting.

STARTING HAND GUIDELINES

Experienced players can play a variety of hands well, but as a new player, there are fewer hands that you can play profitably. Let's look at them by position.

EARLY POSITION

You don't want to play too loosely from early position as a beginning player. If you raise in first position, be sure you have a strong hand. As always, make your standard raise with any hand you play.

In no-limit hold'em tournaments, the presence or absence of antes influences your play to some degree. When there is no ante, you should play more conservatively than you do when there is an ante. Let me explain why this is true. In big-stack tournaments, you have to start posting an ante at a certain point in the event. Usually a $25 ante starts going in at the beginning of the second $100/$200 round—often around the fourth level of play—and it gradually increases throughout the remainder of the tournament.

After the antes start going, the fun begins, so to speak. You see, with more money in the pot, experienced players often loosen up their requirements for starting hands and start trying to steal the antes and blinds more often. This means that before the antes begin, the play is tighter than it is after the antes begin. For that reason, you should play fewer starting hands in the beginning, adding some additional hands after you start posting an ante.

Following is a general guideline for hands you should raise from early position. But if you don't have one of the hands listed in the charts, fold.

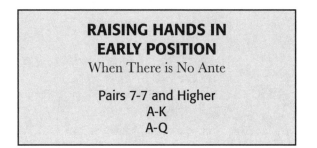

**RAISING HANDS IN
EARLY POSITION**
When There is No Ante

**Pairs 7-7 and Higher
A-K
A-Q**

> ## RAISING HANDS IN
> ## EARLY POSITION
> When There is an Ante
>
> All Pairs
> A-K
> A-Q
> A-J
> K-Q
> Two Suited Cards 10 and Higher

MIDDLE POSITION

In middle position you can play all the hands you play from early position with very few changes. The big difference between playing hands from early position and playing from middle position is that someone may have either called or raised in front of you. Here are some guidelines for dealing with middle position hands based on the action in front of you.

If **no one has entered the pot**, raise with the hands in the following chart. But if you don't have one of the hands listed in the charts, fold.

> ## RAISING HANDS IN
> ## MIDDLE POSITION
> When No One Has Entered the Pot
>
> All Pairs
> A-K
> A-Q
> A-J
> K-Q
> Two Suited Cards 10 and Higher

If someone has **limped** in front of you, raise with the hands in the following chart.

> ### RAISING HANDS IN MIDDLE POSITION
> When There is a Limper
>
> 7-7 to A-A
> A-K
> A-Q

If someone has **raised** in front of you, reraise with the hands in the following chart.

> ### RAISING HANDS IN MIDDLE POSITION
> When There is Already a Raise
>
> A-A
> K-K
> Q-Q
> J-J
> A-K

Does this strategy seem a little too conservative against a raise? Remember, the raise you are facing is against an early position player. The only time you might want to widen your list of reraising hands is when your opponent is a loose player who raises from early position with suited connectors as well as strong hands. Against players like Daniel, Erick Lindgren or Phil Ivey, you should reraise more often because they probably will give you more credit for a strong hand since you are playing conservatively. Also, small-ball players will often raise with speculative hands from any position, especially when antes are present.

The reason a novice needs to be a little more conservative against a raise, or even a limp, is because you won't be smooth calling any type of bet until you have more tournament experience. Once you've mastered Daniel's simple beginning system and you start to evolve as a player, you will add a few tools to your repertoire, such as smooth calling raises and limping in behind other limpers. But let's wait until the end of this section to talk about how to use those plays in accordance with your betting system.

LATE POSITION

Great players thrive in late position by playing more hands and being aggressive in marginal situations. Even as a novice, late position is the place where you can open up your game a little bit, though not a lot. Your approach to playing late position should be identical to playing middle position except that you'll add a few hands to your list. You will only be adding them, however, in situations where no one has yet entered the pot. If an opponent limps or raises preflop, you should play the same way you play from middle position, for the most part.

From late position, you can widen your range of raising hands to include some of the marginally good hands like 8-8, 9-9, or A-Q. When no one has entered the pot, raise with the hands in the following chart. But if you don't have one of the hands listed in the charts, fold.

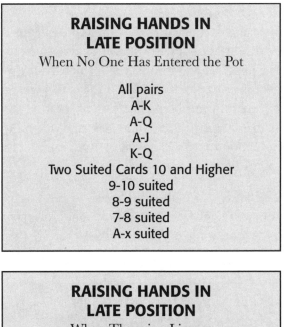

**RAISING HANDS IN
LATE POSITION**

When No One Has Entered the Pot

All pairs
A-K
A-Q
A-J
K-Q
Two Suited Cards 10 and Higher
9-10 suited
8-9 suited
7-8 suited
A-x suited

**RAISING HANDS IN
LATE POSITION**

When There is a Limper

7-7 to A-A
A-K
A-Q

If someone has **raised** in front of you, reraise with the hands in the following chart.

**RAISING HANDS IN
LATE POSITION**

When There is Already a Raise

A-A
K-K
Q-Q
J-J
A-K

PLAYING THE BLINDS

When you use this novice betting system, playing from the blinds can be a little tricky. There will be times where you may be seeing a flop in an unraised pot, which could put you in some dangerous situations. Against a raise, you would proceed as normal, but if everybody has just limped in, you'll have a decision to make from the small blind. With half of a bet already in the pot, there will be a few situations where it makes sense to call rather than raise or fold.

Play all the hands we've already discussed just like you would against limpers, regardless of your position. However, I suggest that you play a little more conservatively from the small blind and just call rather than raise with all of your hands except:

**RAISING HANDS IN
SMALL BLIND POSITION**

A-A
K-K
Q-Q
A-K
J-J
10-10
9-9
A-Q

With all the other playable hands that you would enter a pot with from late position, it's probably a safe play to go ahead and limp in from the small blind. There are also some hands that I suggest adding to your play list from the small blind when you have one-half the bet already in the pot:

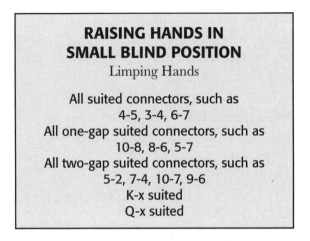

Adding these hands to your repertoire can be dangerous, but as long as you follow some strict post-flop guidelines, there is some value in playing them. A great player would call from the small blind with over 90 percent of the hands dealt to him in a limped pot because he is confident in his ability to avoid disaster after the flop. But as a beginning player, you should proceed cautiously from the blinds so that you don't go broke in a tricky situation that your betting system doesn't cover.

The betting system I have outlined for you is designed to help you avoid tricky and dangerous situations. If you are nervous about playing these hands, don't play them at first. Wait until you feel more comfortable at the table and have developed confidence in what you're doing. Folding these hands isn't a big mistake, especially for a new player who wants to avoid trouble.

SMALL BLIND VERSUS BIG BLIND

From the small blind, if every other player folds and it's just you and the big blind, you can widen the scope of your raising hands to include any ace, as well as any of the other playable hands mentioned for late position play with antes.

If you are in the big blind and the small blind just limps, you can also widen your reraising range somewhat to include any ace and any hands that you would play from late position with antes.

PLAYING A SHORT STACK

Your starting hand standards change as your stack dwindles to the point where the 25 percent rule applies. If your standard raise represents 25 percent or more of your stack, you can start being more aggressive by adding a few more hands to your repertoire in every scenario.

For example, if the blinds are $100/$200 and you are dealt the A♠ 7♠ under the gun, but only have $2,100 left in chips, you should go all in. Despite the fact that A♠ 7♠ isn't a hand in your recommended group of starting hands from early position, tough situations call for tough play. You are always better off going down with a fight than anteing yourself out of the tournament while sitting around waiting for a premium hand.

When you have a short stack and are the first player to enter the pot, I suggest that you go all in with any of the hands that you would enter the pot with from late position. Also, I prefer being aggressive against a raise if I suspect that my opponent is just trying to steal the blinds. Of course, it may take quite a bit of tournament experience before you develop a feel for this type of play. Just remember than when you're on a short stack, you have a lot to gain by being aggressive and little to lose.

PREFLOP SUMMARY

The whole idea behind this approach to preflop play is to give you a real shot at winning when you are a tournament novice. Hopefully, you also will get lucky enough to avoid traps, or suck out when you have the worst of it. By playing this aggressive preflop strategy, you can neutralize an experienced player's advantage over you by forcing better players to pay dearly to see the flop. That way, you essentially minimize a pro's opportunities to outplay you.

I'm not claiming that this is the best strategy. In fact, you'll often be taking large risks for minimal gain. But I believe that this approach to tournament play is the best way for a beginner to be competitive against tougher competition. Trying to play flops with better players and outmaneuvering them usually is a recipe for disaster.

In this section, I outlined a relatively basic and easy-to-learn system for playing no-limit hold'em tournaments. You learned the types of hands to play, and how to bet them. In the next section, we'll deal with the tougher task of learning how to apply this system to post-flop play.

FLOP

When things are going well for you as a beginning player, you won't have to worry too much about actually making decisions after the flop. But no one can avoid seeing the flop forever!

Eventually, you'll need to play a flop, so it's important to have a system for dealing with various situations you'll be facing. As was the case with the preflop strategy for beginners, what you'll read in this section isn't the best way to play no-limit hold'em tournaments. The biggest flaw with this approach is that because you'll be playing marginal situations aggressively, you'll often find yourself trapped in certain situations that pros might avoid. Just the same, it's a much better approach than one that will give you no chance to succeed.

For the sake of simplicity, let's categorize some important types of hands and situations you may find yourself in after the flop and discuss the best way for a novice to play each of them.

FLOPPING TOP PAIR OR AN OVERPAIR TO THE BOARD

Our starting-hand guidelines for beginning players are pretty strict. Therefore, when you flop top pair, you will always have a good kicker. Any time you flop top pair on the board or hold an overpair to the board—for example J-J on a board of 9-6-2—I suggest that you play your hand strongly. In fact, that's your approach with any hand that you get to the flop with. You will usually want to make a bold bet, one big enough to win the pot right on the flop. Let's take a look at an example.

Hand In Action

With the blinds at $100/$200, you raise to $1,000 from early position with J-J and a player on the button calls you. The flop comes 9♠ 6♦ 2♠ and it's up to you.

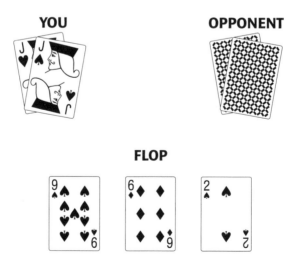

YOU

OPPONENT

FLOP

The advice that I suggest for beginning players in this situation is almost in direct contrast to what professional players may do. With $2,300 in the pot, a pro who wants to keep the pots small would likely bet around $1,200, or approximately 50 percent of the pot. But as a novice tournament player, I suggest that you make a pot-sized bet any time you bet on the flop. In this case, that amount would be $2,300.

The 25-percent rule applies to post-flop play as well. In this situation, if $2,300 represents more than 25 percent of your total stack size, then you should move all in.

Hopefully, when you bet on this flop, your opponent will just fold and allow you to rake in the pot so that you don't have to risk being outdrawn or outplayed. If your opponent calls, you'll have to reevaluate the situation on the turn. (We'll show you how to do that in the next part of this chapter).

You will have to face a difficult dilemma in this situation if your opponent elects to raise you. A raise could mean several things: He has 10-10, a flush draw, a straight draw, a set, Q-Q/K-K/A-A, or possibly, he could even be on a bluff. With so many variables coming into play after the flop, I think you can understand why your goal as a beginning player should be to win pots *without* seeing the flop. The correct play in this situation is dependant upon your read of your opponent.

This is the first time I've asked you to make a decision that is not entirely reliant on the system. I can't even give you a definitive answer as to the best way to play in this situation. But I can give you something even better: some guidelines that will cover all types of situations you might have to face on the flop. Here is a checklist of six questions you should ask yourself before making your ultimate decision.

Checklist for Dealing With a Flop Raise

1. Is my opponent aware that I'm a conservative player?
2. Is my opponent capable of bluffing?
3. What type of hands would this player call a large raise with before the flop?
4. Would he slowplay a pair of aces, kings, or queens before the flop in the hope of trapping me?
5. Would this player raise me with a draw?
6. If my opponent flopped a set, would he raise me on the flop? Or would he be more likely to wait for the turn to raise?

If you decide that your opponent is likely to have you beat and your best-case scenario is that he is on a draw, fold when he raises on the flop. In most cases, and especially in deep-stack tournaments, folding is your best option considering your conservative table image. If he's perceptive, your opponent has noticed that you play only premium hands. Therefore, if he raises you on a ragged flop, he probably has a hand that he wants to trap you with.

After answering all of these important questions, if you still aren't sure whether you are beat, or if you feel strongly that you have the best hand, your best course of action is a large reraise. For consistency's sake, make your reraise the size of the pot. In most tournaments, that will commit you to the pot or even move you all in. But don't worry about that. The strength of this aggressive, big-bet poker style is not its ability to avoid traps. Its strength is that it will always shift the pressure, the difficult decisions, away from you and put it squarely on your opponents.

FLOPPING TWO PAIR OR A SET

The way you choose to bet two pair or a set shouldn't be any different than the way you would bet top pair. A pot-sized bet with virtually any hand you bet post-flop will ensure that your betting amounts do not fall into patterns that your more perceptive opponents will notice.

Flopping two pair or a set is good enough for you, as a novice, to play for all your chips if necessary. More experienced players may be able to get away from traps when they are beaten, even with strong hands such as these. But it's very difficult for a beginner to recognize when it's right to make a big laydown, so it's better to just go with the hand.

If an opponent bets in front of you, make a pot-sized raise when you have two pair or a set, regardless of the texture of the flop. This simple, yet aggressive, betting strategy, does not recommend slowplaying. Instead, the strategy includes a betting approach that is consistent, regardless of the strength of your hole cards.

FLOPPING A STRAIGHT OR A FLUSH

The story is much the same when you flop a straight or a flush. Make a pot-sized bet on the flop and hope that one of your opponents raises. If you do get raised on the flop, the pot should be large by then. That is exactly what you want when you flop a made hand. Don't slowplay the hand. Reraise with another pot-sized raise.

FLOPPING A FULL HOUSE OR BETTER

As you can probably tell, the approach for novice tournament players is one that should be difficult for your opponents to read based on your betting patterns. They probably will have trouble figuring out your hand strength because you bet different hand strengths the same way, even when you flop quads or a full house.

Unless they know your strategy going into the tournament, chances are good that your opponents won't believe that you would bet the pot when you flop such a strong hand. For that reason, an opponent may try to bluff-raise you. In that case, it would actually be a good idea to slowplay by just calling the raise and hoping that your opponent bets the turn. With a hand this strong, there is no reason to fear getting outdrawn, so there is no real need to reraise on the flop.

The problem is that if you reraise, your bluffing opponent probably will fold. By just calling his raise, you allow the bluffer to continue to try to take the pot away from you. In other words, you'll make more money off his ill-timed bluff-raise.

MISSING WITH AN A-K

How you play A-K when you miss the flop is where a level of deception comes into play for you. Since you bet all your good hands by making pot-sized bets on the flop, it makes sense for you to make a similar bet when you hold A-K and you miss the flop completely. Suppose you have the A♥ K♦ and the flop comes 8-4-2.

Hand In Action

YOU

FLOP

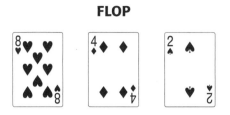

You make a pot-sized bet and an opponent calls—or, even worse, raises your bet. Now what do you do? I suggest that you should shut down completely unless you catch an ace or a king on the turn.

Betting the flop in this situation will help make you a bit more difficult to read. Suppose you only bet the pot on the flop when you have something strong, but when you miss the flop you make a different bet size. It won't take your opponents very long to pick up on that pattern. They will start folding when you bet the pot, but calling or raising when you make a different size of bet.

By consistently betting your hands this way, you put the load on your opponents to guess where you are in the hand. Do you have overcards or an overpair? Have you flopped two pair? Did you flop a full house? Adding deception to your game doesn't require any outlandish moves or bluffs. You simply do it by making sure that the range of hands you bet the flop with is wide enough that your opponents will have to guess what you are holding.

PLAYING A PAIR WHEN OVERCARDS ARE ON BOARD

Playing a pair when there are overcards on board is a tricky situation in which many beginners make significant mistakes. It's one of those marginal situations where your pair could be way out in front, or way behind if your opponent catches a piece of the flop.

You should approach these situations as you would when you miss with an A-K or when you flop a set—bet the size of the pot. If another player bets before you, you face a difficult decision. Unless you have reason to believe he is bluffing, you should fold. However, if you think you have the best hand, or want to find out, reraise the size of the pot. My advice, though, is that the safest play is to simply fold in these situations, and that's what you should do most often.

If you raise and your opponent calls or reraises, then you need to shut down completely. If you bet the flop and an opponent calls, you should also shutdown for the rest of the hand and hope that your opponent doesn't bet the turn or the river.

Let's look at an example. The blinds are at $100/$200 and you make it $1,000 from middle position with J-J. The big blind calls, so there is now $2,100 in the pot. The flop comes Q♣ 8♦ 3♣ and your opponent checks to you.

Hand in Action

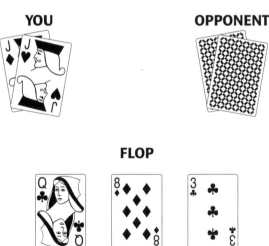

YOU   OPPONENT

FLOP

You lead out at the pot for $2,100. Your opponent calls. Now what do you do? Unless you catch a third jack on the turn, plan on just checking the rest of the way. If your opponent bets on the turn or the river, I suggest that you fold. Unless, of course, you have reason to believe that your opponent is bluffing or may even be betting a weaker hand such as A-8 for value. (Look for more instruction in the next part of this chapter for how you should play on the turn and river.)

PLAYING AGAINST MULTIPLE OPPONENTS

The higher the number of players that see a flop, the more likely it is that someone will hit the flop. When playing against multiple opponents, pay attention to the texture of the flop in deciding whether you should bet when you miss with your A-K/A-Q hands. And whether or not you should bet your pair when an overcard hits.

In an extreme example, imagine that you raised before the flop with the A♣ K♣ and three people called, making it a four-way pot. The flop comes 7♥ 8♥ 9♥.

Hand in Action

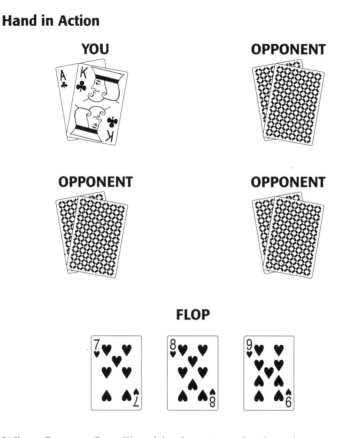

When I see a flop like this that completely misses my hand, I figure it probably has hit at least one of my opponents. Somebody probably has made a flush, a straight, or has a draw to one or the other. In a case like this, you're better off saving a bet by checking and then folding when the action comes back to you. Your observant opponents may pick up on the fact that when you check in multiway pots, you probably have nothing, but that's okay. As a beginning player, it is best to take a straightforward approach to multiway pots, bluffing slightly less often than you would against just one opponent.

Let's take a look at another example. You raise with J-J from first position. Two players and the big blind call behind you. The flop comes A♠ K♦ 4♠ and the big blind checks.

Hand in Action

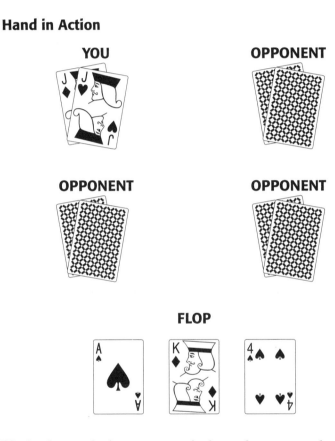

You've been playing conservatively, and now two players with position over you call your preflop raise, and the big blind defends. What does that tell you? It indicates that at least one of your opponents has an ace. And that's dangerous for you. Fold against any action.

When only one player is in the pot with you, you can bet the pot on the flop to represent a hand such as A-K. Your bet will help tell you where you stand in the hand. If your opponent calls, you would have to shut down and then fold if he bets the turn.

Of course, as I've said before, this is not the optimal (and eventual) strategy you'll be playing in no-limit hold'em tournaments. It is simply a strategy that you can put into action with very little knowledge of the game and be competitive. You will certainly be weak in some spots and overly aggressive in others. But my goal in sharing this system with you is to take the guesswork out of no-limit hold'em tournament play. As you improve, you are going to change your approach and strategy, but I highly recommend playing this way while you're learning the ropes. It worked for me in the beginning, and I believe it will work equally well for you.

PLAYING DRAWING HANDS

The way you'll play drawing hands will be another addition to your level of deception as a player. I recommend a very aggressive approach with drawing hands—pot-sized bets and even pot-sized reraises when you flop an open-ended straight draw or a flush draw.

The idea behind being aggressive with drawing hands is that they are high quality semibluffing opportunities, and since the beginning approach doesn't contain very much bluffing at all, plays like these are even more effective. Let's take a look at an example. With blinds at $50/$100, you raise to $500 with the A♥ Q♥. The player on the button calls. The flop comes 7♥ 4♥ 2♦.

Hand in Action

YOU   OPPONENT

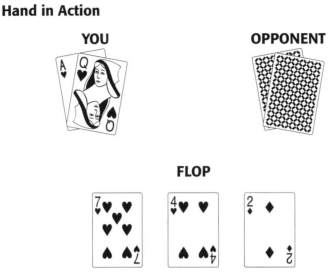

FLOP

You bet $1,300, the size of the pot, and your opponent raises you to $3,300. On this flop, even if your opponent has J♣ J♠, your hand is still favored to be the winner by the end of the hand. Any heart (nine outs), ace (three outs), or queen (three outs) would give you the best hand. Having 15 outs with two cards to come is a favorite over any hand. Even in the worst-case scenarios, when your opponent flops a set or slowplays K-K, you still aren't drawing dead.

The value in reraising the flop is that you can represent A-A and your opponent may fold his probable J-J. Even if he calls, it's not a bad result because you are the favorite. But if he folds, that's an even better result because you win the chips in the middle without having to hit your hand. There is also the possibility that your opponent has a hand like J♥ 10♥, which would mean you have him crushed!

The great thing about making semibluffs with drawing hands is that even when your bluff doesn't work (that is, your opponent doesn't fold), you still may have a good chance of winning a big pot if you hit.

FLOP PLAY SUMMARY

In situations where you'll see the flop, this betting system, even when people know what you are up to, has enough deceptive factors so that your opponents won't be able to play perfectly against you. When you make a pot-sized bet, they'll have no idea what that really means since you'd do it with top pair, two pair, a middle pair, a set, a flush, a straight, a full house or better, a draw, or even a hand that missed the flop completely.

Making pot-sized bets also allows you to define your opponent's hands more clearly, whereas a smaller bet might not give you enough information to make a good decision on the turn. Large bets will also help ensure that you charge your opponents a big price to continue after the flop.

On the flipside, though, large bets will often cause you to lose more chips than a more experienced player would lose in certain situations. But that's the price you'll have to pay in the beginning to be competitive against better players. Essentially, the flaws in this strategy are in overbetting hands in spots where a smaller bet would get the desired result with less risk to your stack.

TURN PLAY

This is the street where beginners are most vulnerable against more experienced opponents. Without question, the turn is the most difficult street to play in hold'em. But it is also the street where the risk/reward ratio is the highest, since pot sizes get much larger by the turn.

Before discussing the approach to playing the turn, let's review the importance of how your opponents perceive you. If they have been paying attention, they should have noticed that you are playing very few hands and will bet the flop aggressively whenever you are in a pot. Therefore, if a player is still with you until the turn card, he must have some kind of a hand; otherwise, he would have folded.

For example, suppose you semibluffed with J-J on the flop against a board of K♠ 9♦ 4♥.

Hand in Action

YOU

OPPONENT

FLOP

Your opponent called your semibluff bet on the flop. Now he bets the turn card. It is usually best for you to give him credit for at least a pair of kings and fold your hand. As a general rule, if you don't have top pair or better by the turn, or a good drawing hand, you should check and fold to a bet. Playing this way may make it possible for an experienced opponent to outplay you, but still, this approach is a solid strategy for new players.

You can add a trick to your repertoire on the turn, however, that will allow you to ward off predators. The best way to fight back against a player who is trying to outplay you on the turn is to try for the check-raise.

Let's take a look at an example. With the blinds at $25/$50, you make it $250 to go before the flop with Q-Q. The button calls you. The flop comes Q♣ 7♦ 2♠.

Hand in Action

YOU	OPPONENT

FLOP

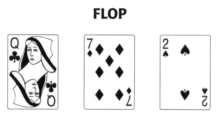

You bet $575, just like you would with all the hands you have played until that point. Your opponent calls. Since you have made trip queens, the situation looks like this:

1. Your opponent calls your bet on the flop so that he can try to steal the pot from you on the turn, or
2. He has a strong hand such as A-Q, K-K, A-A, 7-7, or 2-2, or
3. He has a medium pair that he thinks may be the best hand against your possible A-K.

Now, if the turn card is something similar to the 3♣, he'll see it as being no help to your hand. If you check, there is a good chance that he will bet in situations 1, 2 and 3. Once he bets, you can go for your big check-raise play which will force him to fold in situations 1 and 3. But if he is in situation 2, you might just be able to bust him for all of his chips.

Let's take a look at an example. The blinds are $50/$100 and you raise to $500 with the A♣ K♠ preflop. The player on the button calls you. The flop comes Q♠ 10♥ 3♠.

Hand in Action

YOU   **OPPONENT**

FLOP

You bet the size of the pot on the flop, $1,250. Your opponent calls. The turn is the J♦. Once again you bet the size of the pot, $3,750, and your opponent calls. On the river, the 2♦ hits. It is a complete blank.

YOU   **OPPONENT**

BOARD

You have the nuts and are hoping your opponent has a hand such as a set of queens.

There is $11,250 in the pot and your last bet was $3,750. If you bet the size of the pot again on the river, it is less likely that your opponent will call unless he has the same hand you have. So, here you could bet around $5,500 or $6,000, which is still a substantial bet in relation to the blinds.

You don't get a lot of opportunities to value bet the nuts on the river, so it's important that you get value for your nut hands when you make them. Of course, your opponent may have called a pot-sized bet on the river, in which case you would have won more chips. But more often than not, a pot-sized bet will scare him away. And without his donations, you will get no value out of your nut hand on the river.

WHEN TO CALL A RIVER BET

Knowing when to call a river bet can be tricky for a novice. The essence of poker often comes down to the simple question: Does he have a hand, or is he bluffing? The answer may be the most difficult aspect of tournament play for novices since it is difficult to be totally systematic in your approach. Here are a few guidelines for making these types of tough decisions.

1. **Don't Be a Hero**
   If all you can beat is a bluff, you should probably just fold your hand. One of the biggest mistakes I see beginners make is that they get lost in hands

by the river and have no idea what to do. For example, they have J-J and the final board reads A-10-9-6-6 and their opponent makes a sizeable river bet. It's a simple case of either:

a. Your opponent is bluffing or;

b. He is value betting a hand that has you beat.

There is no in-between in these situations since your opponent is very unlikely to be value betting a hand worse than your pair of jacks. As a general rule, when you find yourself in situations where you can only beat a bluff, let it go unless you have a read on your opponent and have strong reasons to believe that he is bluffing.

2. **Call with Top Pair or Better**

If you end up with top pair on the board, two pair, trips, or better, you should probably call your opponent—unless there is a four-card straight or a four-card flush on the board at the river. Great players can fold some very strong hands on the river when they know they are beat, but that is not going to be your forte as a beginner. If you've made it to the river and end up with a relatively strong hand, it usually makes sense for you to call a river bet with one of these hands since the pot will likely be very large.

River play can be tricky and that's why my advice for you as a novice player is to play very carefully at the end. Rather than get involved in too much sophisticated thought, I believe that it makes more sense for you to play this street as straightforwardly as possible. As you improve your tournament play, you'll be adding more strategies to your playbook. Until that time, I firmly believe that getting too clever will only cost you money in the long run.

ADJUSTING FOR SHORT-HANDED PLAY

Play becomes short-handed only during the very late stages of a tournament. As a novice player, you won't be making many final tables just yet. You'll be able to last a long time and get deep in tournaments while you're learning the ropes, but you'll have to get very lucky to make it as far as the final table.

Short-handed play is generally defined as six-handed or less. Playing short-handed requires some significant strategy adjustments, especially for novices who already are starting out with strict starting-hand requirements. Also, by that point in a tournament, the stack size to blind ratio is usually small. This means that players will be going all in more frequently rather than coming in with a standard-sized raise. This actually helps you as a novice because your approach of playing your hands aggressively before the flop becomes the norm in short-handed play. Your opponents often will not have enough chips to justify calling your raises to outplay you after the flop because it will cost them far too high a percentage of their stacks.

The most important thing for you to do at a short table is widen your starting-hand requirements. You also may be forced to reraise with hands that you probably would have folded at a full table earlier in the tournament. For example, if a player raises from under the gun in a nine-handed game, you would fold a hand such as the A♣ J♠ on the button. In a six-handed game, however, it's almost never a mistake for you to go all in with this type of hand before the flop. Aggressive play wins pots in short-handed play, which fits extremely well with the approach that you have been taking all along.

In short-handed play, hands like ace-rag, big picture cards, and pairs go up in value, while suited connectors go down in value. That's not to say that you shouldn't try to steal the blinds with something like 7♥ 8♥ from the button, but hands like A♥ 6♦ are more the types of hands that you would rather play in the late stages of a tournament. The ace becomes a powerful card heads-up because it allows you to be aggressive preflop. It also all but insures that if you end up in an all-in pot preflop, you probably won't be crushed.

The only hand that would totally crush your A-6 offsuit is exactly A-A. If your opponent had K-K or A-K, it spells trouble for you, but you would still be able to catch one of three outs (the three aces left in the deck) to win the pot. You could even catch runner-runner to make either a miracle straight or a flush. In other words, if your opponent has a big pair against you, that's not a good thing, but your hand certainly is not dead by any means.

A very aggressive short-handed strategy will make it easier for you to avoid playing flops entirely in short-handed play. You just need to get comfortable raising with hands such as A♣ 3♦ or K♥ J♣, or pairs such as 10-10 and 4-4, when you are the first player to enter the pot. If someone moves all in behind you and you have one of these marginal hands, you can fold, although you might call if:

1. The bet doesn't cost much more,
   or
2. You are already committed to the pot.

Since you'll be using the 25-percent rule even in these situations, you shouldn't run into this problem very often since the chances are good that you may be the first player who goes all in. However, if you have a monster stack of chips, you can comfortably fold those hands in the face of a reraise. You want to protect a big stack.

I believe that in short-handed play, a nothing-to-lose attitude is key to success. Be happy that you've made it this far—but really go for the win by seizing the moment. Why just try to inch up the pay scale when you have a chance to win it all?

In fact, if your opponents seem to just be waiting to move up the pay scale, choose an even more aggressive strategy than normal. Let them be meek while you boldly take the lead.

THE NEXT STAGE: LIMPING AND CALLING RAISES

Once you have soaked in all of this information, and have gotten the hang of tournament no-limit hold'em, you can start thinking about taking your game to the next level. The beginning strategy is limited for good reason—it keeps you out of trouble—but as you improve your play, you are going to enjoy playing more hands and seeing more flops.

Before you can progress from being a big-bet beginner to being a small-ball pro, you need to gradually add additional strategies to your play list. For example, if three people call in front of you, there is no doubt that you are getting good value to play a hand such as 9♠ 10♠. But under the strict betting system for beginners, you are forced to either raise or fold in all preflop situations. Of course, 9♠ 10♠ is not quite strong enough to raise with in this case, but with a small-ball approach it's also a hand that's too strong to simply fold.

The reason I advise novices to fold those types of hands is because I want you to first master the raise-or-fold system of playing preflop before adding new variables to your game. Once you've mastered the beginners' betting system, you can start limping into pots with some of the marginal hands that you would have folded as a rank beginner—hands such as 3-3, 4-4, 7♣ 8♣, K♠ Q♦ and A♠ 7♠. These are all hands that you may steal with from late position, but ones that I previously advised you to fold.

Once you become more comfortable with your post-flop play, you can start seeing some cheap flops with these types of hands in the hope of catching big. If you do happen to catch a good flop, then you can continue to use the beginning betting system by making a pot-sized bet.

Aside from limping into pots with some of these marginal hands, you can also try calling smaller raises with a wider range of hands rather than always reraising. For example, suppose someone raises and two people call in front of you. You look down at 3-3 in the big blind. I think it would be a shame to either fold or raise. Calling is a good play in this situation. By just calling, you can proceed to the flop in the hope of catching a set.

By adding a few options to your tournament strategy, your game will become more deceptive. You won't be playing quite as robotic as before, and that alone will make it more difficult for your opponents to read you. Once you've become more comfortable with this approach, you'll be ready for the next stage of your poker learning—making smaller raises and bets, playing more hands in more positions, bluffing more often, and playing more creatively with your premium hands.

CONCLUSION

As I mentioned earlier, this beginning section wasn't written to teach you the optimal way to play no-limit hold'em. It was designed to help make starting out on the tournament trail a little less intimidating as you become comfortable sitting at a tournament table and feeling like you belong there.

You've learned what hands to play and in what situations. I also gave you a betting system that covers various situations and left no stone unturned in your preflop betting strategy. As a hand progresses to the river, it becomes increasingly difficult to play in a systematic fashion, but I gave you some guidelines on how much to bet different types of hands in various scenarios.

BIG-BET NO-LIMIT HOLD'EM

Once you've mastered this simple approach to playing no-limit hold'em tournaments, you'll be able to lower your bet sizes and adopt a more sophisticated playing style. And you will gradually add more strategies to your playbook. I wish you luck as you continue your march to the final table!

WINNING AT HIGH-LIMIT CASH GAMES

TODD BRUNSON

Todd Brunson's tremendous success at tournament poker is all the more impressive because he didn't start playing tournaments regularly until recent years when tournament poker became exceptionally lucrative. Before the explosion of big-money tournaments, he primarily spent his time at the green felt playing high-stakes cash games. He and his father Doyle are noted for playing the highest cash games in the world, and regularly appear on GSN's *High Stakes Poker*.

A dominating presence at any poker table, Todd has been a consistent winner ever since he left his college career after three years of studying law at Texas Tech to play poker fulltime. He has 12 major tournament wins, including the 2004 Bellagio Festa al Lago championship. Todd won his first gold bracelet in the 2005 $2,500 Omaha eight-or-better event, and also won Fox Sports Network's *Poker Superstars Invitational*, season three. He has finished in the money in dozens of tournaments, including 13 WSOP and four World Poker Tour events.

His strength at no-limit hold'em is legendary, and his insights into seven-card stud eight-or-better are equally remarkable. Todd's dominance in high-stakes stud eight-or-better led his father to select him to write that section of *Super System 2*. He also writes an incisive column for *Card Player* magazine. Todd serves as captain of Team Brunson from DoylesRoom.com, where you will find him playing online.

His pivotal role in defeating Texas billionaire Andy Beal heads-up for millions of dollars in the "big game" is depicted in Michael Craig's book, *The Professor, the Banker and the Suicide King*.

Brunson's topic for this book is how to win at high-limit cash games. He demystifies the mindset and the strategies required to win at no-limit cash games. You'll find out why some players make short rebuys in cash games, while others prefer rebuying the maximum amount.

Todd's writing style is both educational and entertaining. He grabs you with his wit and captures your continued attention with his wisdom. Here is part of what he says about bluffing: "Bluffing may be the most overrated play in poker. Where I come from, a bluff is something you try to push a sheep over. A sheep won't allow itself to be pushed over a bluff. Neither will most poker players, at least not very often." You're in for a treat with Brunson's treatise on how to win no-limit cash games!

WINNING AT HIGH-LIMIT CASH GAMES

Todd Brunson

INTRODUCTION

I was honored when Daniel first approached me to be one of the contributors to this book. Even with the relative youth of the contributors, the success of the group over the past six or seven years is staggering: over $30 million and too many titles to count among us. I was thrilled to be included in the group of players he had assembled. That was my first reaction.

After I thought about it for a while, I realized all the knowledge that would be readily available to the general public. With all these secrets out, how could we continue our success? Anyone with a few dollars could pick up this book and become a great player in no time at all. Was this wonderful ride finally going to end?

After a little more thought, my father's books, *Super System* and *Super System 2*, came to mind. They also put a great deal of inside secrets and information in the hands of the general public, but did they ruin it for the already established pros? Quite the contrary! His books helped more players become confident enough in their game to step up and try their luck in the big tourneys. Tournaments became harder to win, but when you did win one, it was well worth the wait. I'm sure I don't have to tell you that paydays have skyrocketed over the past ten years. The more quality books out there, the more players—and the more players, the more money.

Besides, I'd already given my word to pen a chapter. If some of my explanations or examples seem too short, remember I only had one chapter. My book will come out right behind this one and will go into greater detail on many of the subjects I'll talk about here. Besides, with all this info from some of the best tournament players in the world, you should have more than enough to keep you busy for a while. Let's get started.

HOW MUCH TO BUY IN?

"How much should you buy in when you sit down in a cash game?" is a tough question. An even tougher one is, "How much should you rebuy if you go broke?" Or should you rebuy at all? There is no simple answer to these questions. Unfortunately, there's not even a good rule of thumb for everyone.

If you are new to the game and unfamiliar with the players, you may want to buy in small at first, possibly even the minimum allowed. If you think you're the best player in the game and your bankroll can stand it, you'll probably want to have the whole table covered; that is, have more chips than anyone else at the table. What to do if you're somewhere in between? You may want to have the worst players covered so that you can bust them if you get the chance.

Your table image has a lot to do with how many chips you need in front of you. If no one is intimidated by you as a player, you may need to have big stacks to force people to give you the respect you deserve. Obviously, this can backfire on you. (I told you there's no easy answer here!) It's a personal decision that only you can make. I'll tell you about a decision I recently had to make, and the thought process that was behind it. Maybe this example can help you decide next time you sit down in a no-limit cash game.

> **BUY-IN AMOUNT**
>
> **YOU MAY WANT TO HAVE THE WORST PLAYERS COVERED SO THAT YOU CAN BUST THEM IF YOU GET THE CHANCE.**

I played on the show *High Stakes Poker*, which airs on GSN (the Game Show Network). This is a normal high-stakes no-limit hold'em game with blinds of $200/$400 and a $100 ante. The buy-in was for a minimum of $100,000, and short rebuys of $50,000 were allowed. Players bought in anywhere from the minimum (most did, actually) to $400,000.

I had brought $500,000 with me and couldn't make up my mind how much to start with. Daniel solved this problem for me when he drew the seat two to my right, bought in for $1 million, and proceeded to play almost every hand dealt—and play them aggressively. I bought in for the minimum $100,000 and waited for a good hand to either trap Daniel, or let him stir up some action and run someone into me. If a marginal situation came that required me to make a difficult decision, my relatively small buy-in would allow me to simply move all in and not worry about it. After all, I couldn't be hurt too badly. I could simply rebuy if I missed my draw or my made-hand didn't hold up.

Now, had I lost my initial buy in, I would have had to make a decision about how much to rebuy. Should I rebuy the minimum or more? I faced an interesting and complex quandary. Let's take a look at the pros and cons of each option. Let me preface this first with a quick example of how winning influences the way an opponent might play against you.

HOW WINNING INFLUENCES RESULTS

For the sake of this discussion, let's say that you're winning. You're not winning a lot, just enough to keep ahead of the herd. Your table image is solid. Let's look at an example of how an opponent might play against you.

Hand in Action

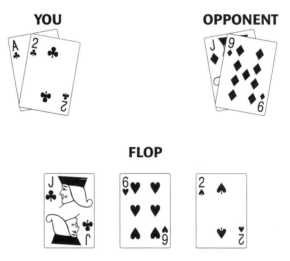

Your opponent raises preflop and bets $25,000 into a pot of about the same amount. You move all in for $90,000 total. Your opponent has to call $65,000 more to see a showdown. If you are even or if you are winning, he has a very hard call to make: There are few hands out there that he can beat. Trips or an overpair have him in bad shape. If you share top pair with him, you almost certainly have him dominated. He's got to hope that you have some stupid hand like second pair, which he probably won't put you on, or a flush draw.

If you do have the flush draw, he's only a little more than a 1.6 to 1 favorite if you have no overcards to accompany your draw. If you have one overcard, his advantage slips to slightly less than a measly 1.2 to 1. If you have two overcards, this percentage actually flips, making you a 1.2 to 1 favorite. If you have a pair with your flush draw, you're a small favorite.

What does all this add up to? If you're even or winning, your opponent will usually lay down his top pair/marginal kicker in a spot like this. He just can't be much of a favorite. However, he can be a huge dog.

Now let's try to figure out what will happen in the same hand when, instead of winning, you're stuck.

REBUYING SHORT WHEN YOU'RE LOSING

Let's say that you're stuck $300,000 and have just lost your latest short buy-in. If you rebuy the minimum again, the advantages of rebuying at $100,000 a pop are the same as before, only more so now. Why? Because when you're stuck a lot, your table image is no longer as strong as it was. Your opponents are less afraid of you and are less likely to lay down their hands to you. They know that you are much, much more likely to gamble, and your thinking may not be quite as logical as it once was. That is, they believe you're on tilt.

In the example above, the range of hands that your opponent can put you on increases dramatically as do the odds of his calling you. You need to slow down at this point. If he is right about your tilt factor, you may be making bad decisions. You'd

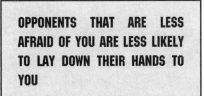

OPPONENTS THAT ARE LESS AFRAID OF YOU ARE LESS LIKELY TO LAY DOWN THEIR HANDS TO YOU

better either continue to buy in short, or just quit and live to play another day. If you decide to continue, short rebuys will keep you from getting hurt too badly on one play, and will make your decisions more simple. However, with your table image shot, your short stack won't earn you much respect and you're going to be called down a lot.

The solution may be to sit tight and wait for a good hand, knowing you'll probably get paid off when you make it. If this is your plan, don't let the rest of the table in on your intentions. Take a page from the Phil Hellmuth crybaby book and let everyone know how unlucky you are. Let the steam pour from your ears. Only *you* will know that you've shifted into low gear!

There is a significant drawback to this plan, however. You may wait all night for a good hand that never comes. And even if the good hand comes fairly quickly and you are lucky enough to double up, you're still not even. This leads us to our next alternative, making larger rebuys.

BUYING AND REBUYING LARGE

My father wrote in his original *Super System*, "You should always have at least as much money on the table as you are stuck." The reason is that, if you are lucky enough to double up, you will get even or be a winner. While this concept is 100-percent true, being the gambling optimist that he is, my father overlooks the downside to this philosophy: It can get you even, but it can get you even worse—buried, to be exact!

I don't want to sound too critical because I do believe this can be good advice for some, but not many have the discipline or the poker talent of Doyle Brunson. So, be careful when trying to emulate him.

RISK VERSUS REWARD

This system actually sounds like doubling up in blackjack when you're losing (a sure way to go broke), or doubling up on a stock every time it drops a few points (price leveraging), which almost all stock brokers and analysts warn against. Now you know the pros and cons, the advantages and dangers of each option. In the end, how much you buy in and rebuy is entirely up to you.

To each his own. Everyone has different strengths and weaknesses, so the answers can be different for you depending upon your situation. Base your choice on your personal abilities, keeping your weaknesses in mind. Weigh risk versus reward to help you make up your mind, then go with it. If it proves to be the wrong choice for one particular play, tweak your thought process accordingly and move on. Don't dwell on past mistakes—learn from them!

FIND YOUR OWN STYLE

Some players are hyper-aggressive, others are super-tight, and the rest fall somewhere in between. Who's correct? They all can be. That's one of the beauties of poker. Almost any style can be refined into a winning one.

Are you dying for action or do you have the patience of a monk? Find a style that accentuates your strengths, minimizes your weaknesses, and fits your personality—and make it your own. No two players play exactly the same way so don't even try to imitate another player. That's copyright infringement! All kidding aside, there's nothing wrong with adopting a few traits from each of your favorite players. Building on others' groundwork is how we grow as a society.

Fans often ask me how they can improve their game. The best answer is to watch good players. Try to figure out what they do. If you're working on one part of your game, watch a player who is strong in that area. Daniel and Michael "The Grinder" Mizrachi are great readers, Tuan Lee and David Williams are fearless, Scotty Nguyen and T.J. Cloutier have tremendous patience.

No matter what styles you emulate or borrow from, make aggression a mainstay of your approach if you want to be a winner on the green felt.

IDENTIFY YOUR OPPONENTS

Poker is just like any job. While you're on the clock you should be working, regardless of whether you're in a hand or not. There's a ton of information out there, just lying there waiting. Pick it up and use it. It's at your disposal! This is one of the reasons it's so important to pay attention to the game even when you're not involved in a hand.

Once you develop your own style, you should learn to read how your opponents play. You might even try rating their aggression or looseness on a scale of 1 to 10, with 1 being the tightest (Berry Johnston, Lyle Berman), and 10 being the loosest (Tuan Le or David Pham).

The tighter the player, the better the hand you'll need to enter a pot with him. If Tuan Le or David Pham enter a pot from any position, I'll probably at least call with a hand as bad as Q-10 or A-9 offsuit as long as I'm not afraid of getting jammed up between players. Conversely, if Berry Johnston or Lyle Berman enter a pot from anywhere except a steal position, I'm probably going to muck a hand as good as A-Q offsuit. Avoid playing with the rocks whenever possible. Mix it up and gamble with the maniacs, but don't be scared—that's what they want.

Being a loose player doesn't automatically make you an aggressive player. You can determine the looseness of a player by the percentage of hands he plays as well as the quality of the cards he turns over in showdowns. Remember, just because a player is tight doesn't mean he's not aggressive, and vice versa. I'm probably the tightest contributor in this book, but when I do enter a pot, I'm at least as aggressive as anyone else, if not more so. Aggression means that you bet or raise when you're in a pot. This isn't as easy to gauge as tightness or looseness, but by paying attention you should be able to get a good feel for the level of a player's aggression.

Tight and aggressive players are otherwise known as *rocks* (or sometimes *nits*). As I said, avoid them whenever you can. Loose and aggressive players are known as *hyper-aggressive* (or sometimes *maniacs*). You can gamble with these guys! Tight and passive, or better yet loose and passive (calling stations), are the bread and butter of a pro poker player.

TIGHT-PASSIVE PLAYERS

Tight-passive players have a hard time winning at poker. They may break even or win in really good games, but they won't survive in the long run. A few bursts of aggression, such as check-raising persistent value bettors, infused into their game can change this. Keep the heat on these guys, but back off immediately when they show any strength at all.

You can often gamble with tight-passive players because, while they usually start with a premium hand, they often give free cards and don't get full value out of their winning hands. They will often check a big hand on the end when a total blank comes and then make an absurd statement like, "Well, the pot's big enough for me."

These are the opponents you'll want to play suited connectors or small pairs against. If you both flop nothing, you'll probably be able to steal the pot from them. If you see that they're going to call you down, save your money. They will often be afraid enough of a bad flop to check, but not scared enough to muck.

Hand in Action

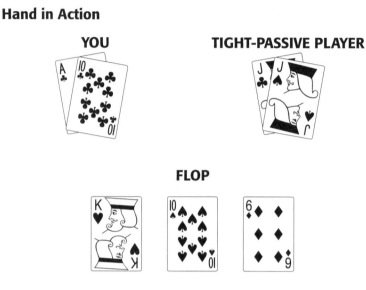

Let's say that a tight-passive player raised preflop and you called. He bets the flop and you call. On fourth street, he checks, you bet and he calls. Don't value bet on the end here. Pocket queens or jacks are the obvious hands that will beat you, but if he's tight-weak enough, he may even have K-J. It's not worth trying to get a call out of an A-Q or A-J. If your opponent entered the pot with a worse 10 than you have, he's probably not a weak-tight player. He's probably a member of our next category, the weak-loose player.

WEAK-LOOSE PLAYERS

The weak-loose player, the calling station, is your main target. If he were your opponent in the above example, you'd want to go ahead and value bet your hand on the end. Not only will he call with tens and a worse kicker, he will probably call with sixes in the hope that you were on some kind of draw. He wants to call no matter what he holds, and will rarely fold a pair for a reasonable sized bet. Hope springs eternal with calling stations. Value bet them to death!

It's important to identify calling stations immediately when you start a new table. Once you've identified these weak-loose players, get involved in as many cheap flops with them as possible. How do you take advantage of situations against them?

Never bluff a calling station. That's just throwing your money away. Don't follow through on a semi-bluff either. Take the free cards and keep the pot small until you make your hand. If you bet the nut flush draw on the flop and he calls, check the turn and take the free card. Remember, he's a calling station; he'll pay you off when the flush card hits. He'll also call you down when it doesn't, so save those extra bets!

Value bet all the way. Bet top pair with no kicker or second pair with a good kicker. When he calls, don't be alarmed. Remember, he's a calling station! Continue to bet even when somewhat scary cards fall. He may put you on a bluff because he knows you should be scared when an overcard falls, but continue to bet. Even bet the end when a flush card comes and he checks to you. Again, your bet will look like a bluff to him.

Just be careful when the calling station bets out or, especially, when he check-raises. Calling stations rarely, if ever, bluff. This is one more reason to pay attention when you're not in a hand. You need to know who bluffs and who doesn't.

When you find yourself with a big hand against the calling station, you can sometimes get extra money by overbetting the pot. If he falls for it once, you'll probably have him hooked. Don't try to get tricky by checking or betting small once he takes the bait. Reel him in! Continue to overbet the pot, and possibly move all in on the river or somewhere along the line.

The calling station has a hard time throwing away marginal hands. It may even be impossible for him to throw away an overpair. Take advantage of this! Value bet to get the most out of every hand. Just make sure you have a hand!

BLUFFING

Most people who rarely play, or have never played poker, believe the game is all about bluffing. They think bluffing is the cornerstone of strategy. Some people who play on a regular basis are also under this illusion. If you are one of these people, if you constantly try to bluff and pick off bluffs, you're going to have a difficult poker life in front of you.

Bluffing may be the most overrated play in poker. Where I come from, a bluff is something you try to push a sheep over. A sheep won't allow itself to be pushed over a bluff. Neither will most poker players, at least not very often. Some players can virtually never be bluffed: the calling station is at the top of this list.

The "idiot" is right behind the calling station on the Do Not Bluff list. A player must have some common sense to lay a hand down. Never try to bluff an idiot! This is true all the time, but especially true if the idiot is losing. Whenever you get the urge to bluff a stuck idiot, take your money and flush 95 percent of it down the toilet. Keep the other 5 percent. At the end of the year you will show a huge profit.

In fact, don't make a habit of bluffing any type of player that is losing a significant amount of money. Stuck players of any type always think their opponents have observed their bad luck and are trying to take advantage of it. Many other players do this too. Don't be one of them! Wait

> **NEVER TRY TO BLUFF AN IDIOT! THIS IS TRUE ALL THE TIME, BUT ESPECIALLY TRUE IF THE IDIOT IS LOSING.**

for a good hand against stuck players, then value bet them to death.

PLAYERS TO BLUFF

So, who should you bluff? Tight players are usually pretty good targets. Once they miss the flop, they often surrender without a fight. The loose-aggressive player is also a good one, but this fish can be much trickier to reel in.

The playing style of loose-aggressive players demands that they can't simply give up on a pot when they're challenged. They will often call raises with bottom pairs or inside straight draws that most players would muck right away when raised. They're often not getting proper pot odds to make these plays, but they steal so many pots that they occasionally can give up some equity to maintain their table image. They also usually believe they can outplay their opponent on a later street.

I'm not telling you *not* to bluff these guys, only to be careful when you do. It may take more then one shell to get the job done. They may call your raise with a weak hand, say, bottom pair or sometimes even no pair/no draw. But then, when they check to you on fourth street, you can't show weakness or they will pounce. Continue with the play and fire again.

If a loose-aggressive player calls you a second time, but you still sense weakness and believe in your first instinct, you must follow through. Finish what you started and fire that third barrel! You'll take the play away from him if he missed his draw, had no draw, or holds a small pair. Even if you misjudged the strength of his hand, it will be tough for him to call with second or even top pair. It will appear that you hold two pair or better.

Very few players can bluff on all three streets and good players know this. Even when they call you twice, they will often back off on that final bet. Notice that I said "good players." Idiots or novices are often oblivious to this fact. But of course, you shouldn't be bluffing these guys anyway.

If you try these plays too often, they won't work against *anyone*. As you're watching your opponents and putting them in categories, figuring out how they play, they're doing the same to you. Even idiots will notice that you've played five hands in a row and have been caught stone-cold bluffing in three of them.

TABLE IMAGE

Make sure you have a good table image before you try a bluff. If you've played five hands in a row, your table image is shot for the time being and you will appear to be on tilt. Sit back and wait for a hand; you probably won't get action until the waters calm anyway.

If you haven't played a hand in hours and a good but loose player raises in front of you in middle to late position, this may be your chance. Your table image should be good and the fruit ripe for the picking. Don't forget that I said "*good*, aggressive player." If he's a bad aggressive player, he may not be able to get away from a marginal hand and you'll just be burning up your chips.

BLUFF RERAISES

You probably don't want to risk all of your chips on a bluff very often, although sometimes that's what it takes. A reraise of two-and-a-half to three times your opponent's total bet should do. Let's say the blinds are $100/$200, and he makes it $500 to go. If you make it $1,250 to $1,500, that should be enough to make him consider laying down a marginal hand.

If he reraises you, don't fold immediately. Pretend that you have a tough decision to make so that he won't think you're trying to run over him. This will make it harder for the whole table to get a read on you. Never show a hand in this spot. You'll be giving away way too much information if you do. You'll be answering a question that it may have taken a player at your table years to figure out!

BROKEN AND COORDINATED FLOPS

Preflop raises are a little simpler then postflop raises, especially in tournaments. There aren't a whole lot of hands that an opponent can call you with preflop unless he really wants to gamble. After the flop, that number multiplies like horny rabbits. You need the right flop to try a bluff.

Look for a broken flop when bluffing—something like Q-7-3, K-8-3, or J-6-2, preferably offsuit. Look for a flop unlikely to give your opponents a straight draw, even a gutshot draw. It will also be tough for them to flop two pair with a ragged, disconnected flop.

Never bluff into multiple opponents when the flop contains both a jack and a 10. It's almost impossible that this combination misses everyone. You can be pretty sure that someone flopped something with a board that has those two connectors. This is especially true when the pot was raised preflop because of the likelihood the raiser was playing two big cards. Look at all the hands that get a piece of a J-10 flop, even when the third card is a deuce: A-A, A-K, A-Q, A-J, A-10, K-K, K-Q, K-J, K-10, K-9, Q-Q, Q-J, Q-10, Q-9, Q-8, J-J, J-10, J-9, J-8, J-7, J-6, J-5, J-4, J-3, J-2, 10-10, 10-9, 10-8, 10-7, 10-6, 10-5, 10-4, 10-3, 10-2, 9-8, 9-7, 8-7. 'Nuff said.

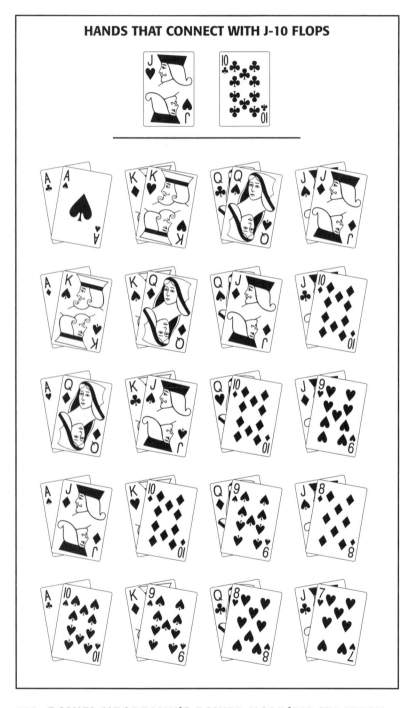

HANDS THAT CONNECT WITH J-10 FLOPS

The type of bluffing we've been talking about up to this point is called *dry bluffing*, that is, betting with no hand, like when you completely miss the flop. If you hold 7♠ 6♠ and the flop comes K-Q-2 with no spades and you bet, your bet is considered a dry bluff. I don't suggest dry bluffing very often, if at all.

This is not to say that you need the nuts to make a bet. You don't always even need a made hand. Betting with outs or betting on the come is perfectly acceptable and effective poker. This type of bluffing is known as a *semibluff*.

THE SEMIBLUFF

What is a semibluff? When you probably don't have the best hand at the moment, but you have the potential to improve to the best hand, you are semibluffing if you bet. By betting marginal hands, you give yourself an additional "out" or way to win the pot. Not only might you make your hand, but all of your opponents may fold before you even have to draw.

Remember the 7♠ 6♠ example? This time let's say that the K-Q-5 offsuit flop has two spades. If your opponent holds a hand such as A-Q, you're going to be about a 3 to 2 dog. That is, if you run the hands out hot and cold (no betting).

Hand in Action

YOU	OPPONENT

FLOP

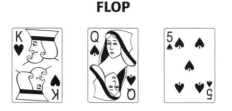

The beauty of poker, especially no-limit, is that you don't always have to have the best hand to win. I'll take the 7-6 over the A-Q all day long, and I'll at least turn the table on my opponent, making me a 3 to 2 favorite, probably more.

"How is this possible?" you ask, as you scratch your head in awe and disbelief. The semibluff!

You see, even though he holds the best hand, he's going to have a hard time calling big bets on the flop and turn. That is, if you have the proper table image. Even when he does call, you're going to make your hand about 40 percent of the time. It's something like, "He's damned if he do and damned if he don't."

Let's look at one more hand before we move on.

Hand in Action

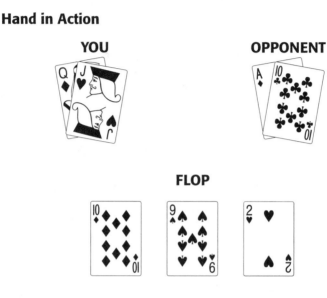

Unless one of you has some sort of flush potential, these two hands are about dead even. You could turn the Q-J into K-J or K-Q and you'd drop down to a little more than 3 to 2 underdog. With any of these hands and the proper table image, you can usually make your opponent lay down top pair. Unless, and this is the last time I'm going to warn you, you're up against a calling station or idiot.

In that case, wait until you make your hand and then...you know the drill!

VALUE BETTING

Getting maximum value out of each hand is important if you want to win at poker. Value betting is betting when you think you have the best hand. Often, it isn't clear if that's the case or not, but if you think you have the best cards and you bet them, you're value betting.

Players value bet all the time, but most of these decisions take place after the flop, on the turn and river. That's when you've gained the most knowledge about an opponent's hand by the action he's taken up to that point. Usually, a scare card will come at some point in the hand: A flush card will fall, a straight card, an overcard to your pair, or possibly even a connected card that could have hit your opponent's kicker, giving him two pair.

That's when you have to decide whether you should bet again with that scare card on the board. Some scare cards are scarier than others, of course. Let's look at an example.

Hand in Action

YOU	OPPONENT

FLOP

Let's say your opponent raised your bet on the flop and you just called, not wanting to gamble too much with a board like this. What's the scariest card that could possibly show up on the turn? No doubt about it, the Q♠.

BOARD

The Q♠ completes any flush draw, the bottom end of the open-end straight, several gutshots, and hits two straight draws as an overpair to yours. It is also likely to help your opponent if he holds top pair along with you, or has a pair of tens.

What do you do?

You would most likely have to fold to a bet at this point, unless you have a strong tell on your opponent. It is possible that you still have the best hand, but it's just too risky to call any reasonable sized bet.

PLAYING A SET

Folding to a bet wasn't a hard decision in that scenario, but what if you hold top set instead of top pair? If you don't have much money in, and the bet's not too large, you may just call to try to pair the board or simply in the hope that you still have the best hand. However, if you have a significant amount of money in the pot—and by significant, I mean around half your chips—and you are first to act, you can't always just give up. This is especially true if your opponent is highly aggressive. He may simply be taking advantage of the fact that a very scary card hit the board.

Checking at this point could induce a bluff, but the risk of a card coming that will beat your hand doesn't compensate for the danger of allowing a free card. So, what is your best play here?

It may be to simply move all in. The reason is, if your opponent was on a draw and made it, he's going to move all in once you check to him anyway. With half or more of your chips in the pot, you're still getting a good price to draw out if he has you beat. You're about a 3 to 1 dog to pair the board with one to come. Add to that the fact that you may still have him beat, and passing is no longer a viable option.

By moving in, you lose nothing since you were going to have to call him anyway to stay in the hand. And you're going broke anyway if he made his hand on the turn. If he didn't make it, and is pot-committed himself, you gain the bet by not letting him off the hook when the scare card hits. An added bonus to moving in here is that he may fold many straights fearing a bigger straight or a flush. You see, scare cards work in both directions.

To make this play, you must be fairly certain that you had the best hand to begin with. That's why I picked top set. If you had bottom set or two pair, this play may not be correct. If you're not sure whether you have the best hand, not only do you have to consider that you may have been drawn out on, you may never have had the best hand at all.

Besides value betting, what else can you do to get full value when you have a big hand? That's our next subject.

TRAPPING

"Not all trappers wear fur hats." I'm sure you've heard this saying before. It means that many poker players trap or slowplay a big hand. But here's another saying that's also true: "Not all poker players wear fur hats." This simply means that not all players slowplay their big hands. It's very important to figure out who does and who doesn't trap so that you'll know which players it's safe to bet into when they check.

Once you know the answer to that question, there is another one you must answer: "Should I wear a fur hat?" If you don't play poker very much, or if you constantly play against new opponents, you may be able to leave your fur hat in storage. However, if you play a few times a month or more with the same players, your opponents will be able to draw a bead on your play. Get your fur hat and dust it off 'cause you're going to need it!

Not only will you want to trap players to get full value from your hands, you'll need to put fear into them to prevent them from value betting marginal hands into you. When my opponent flops top pair with a marginal kicker against me, he may bet to find out where he is. But he will be very cautious if he knows me at all. He probably won't be value betting all three streets against me.

So how do you identify the trappers? You can tell a lot by the way they look; and no, I don't mean they'll be wearing a big white beard with a ten-gallon hat and chaps. Are they young? Young players are much more likely to trap with or without a hand. Maybe they lack patience or just haven't been beaten badly enough, often enough, to know real pain. We are all more reckless in our youth. Maybe it's lack of wisdom or just the thrill of living on the edge, but whatever the reason, young guys and gals like to raise, especially check-raise.

Is your opponent flashy? Loud? Hyper? Same thing. Be careful value betting against these players. Older, conservative-looking, quieter people usually like to bet their hands and play more straightforward poker. However, this isn't always true—just a rule of thumb—so be careful.

How do you know for sure? The bad news is that the only way to find out for sure is to pay for the information. The good news is that it doesn't have to be money that you pay to learn—

it can be attention. Stop gossiping, stop watching TV, and stop flirting (unless it's with me and you're hot), and take at least one earplug out from your Ipod, or turn the volume down. Pay attention!

Chances are that when a trapper is at your table, he will probably attempt to ply his trade on someone else before he tries it out on you. I say "probably" because there are usually seven or eight other players at the table besides you. Watch, observe, learn, remember—it's free, there for the taking. Those who don't learn from history are doomed to repeat it and make the same mistakes.

Now that we've talked a little bit about general principles of trapping and being trapped, let's look at some specific hands to avoid.

TRAP HANDS

A trap hand is one that is likely to flop you the second-best hand. The newer you are to the game, the more you should avoid calling raises with these types of hands preflop. An experienced player will often be able to make a read and lay down trouble or trap hands when he's beat. However, if you lack experience, you'll want to avoid these situations as much as possible. By avoiding trap hands, you can keep your tough decisions—and thus, your risk—to a minimum.

Often, but not always, the second-best hand will be dominated by the best hand.

TRAP HAND #1

A Dominated Hand

PLAYER ONE   **PLAYER TWO**

FLOP

TRAP HAND #2

A Small Favorite

PLAYER ONE   **PLAYER TWO**

FLOP

As we can see in example one, Player Two is completely dominated. He can only win with a jack, making him about a 10 to 1 dog. In example two, Player One again has the best hand, but this time he is only a small favorite. Player Two has a lot of outs—a 5, 7, 8, or a 10 will improve his hand. Player One can still improve should Player Two pick up an 8 and make two pair, or Player Two would actually be the favorite.

You don't have to be a 10 to 1 favorite to have someone dominated. While there is no official rule on the basic number, I would place it at about 2.5 to 1 or more. Domination usually occurs when you face an overpair or share a card—especially if you pair that card—with an inferior kicker. If you have a made hand and face a better made hand with no redraws, or have set under set, you are totally dominated and in deep guano.

TRAP HAND #3
Made Hand Facing Better Made Hand

PLAYER ONE   PLAYER TWO

FLOP

TRAP HAND #4

Set Over Set

PLAYER ONE   **PLAYER TWO**

FLOP

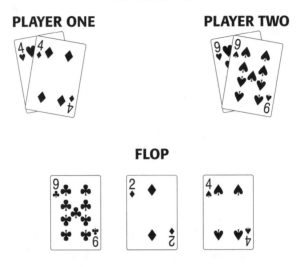

When you flop the bottom end of a straight, you should always be careful. Conversely, when you flop bottom set, you usually cannot get away from it unless both you and your opponent have a ton of chips and you know your opponent well. Generally, you'll just want to play the hand as though it's the nuts when no made hands (straights or flushes) are possible on the board. If you play full time (2,000 hours a year), you will only face set under set once or twice a year, so don't even worry about it.

TRAP HANDS AND DOMINATION

Following is a brief list of some of the worst trap hands alongside the hands that will dominate them, as well as a short explanation of the problems you may encounter with them if you get raised and are contemplating a call.

The Trap Hand	The Hands that Dominate It
K-Q Offsuit	A-A, K-K, Q-Q, A-K, A-Q
This is the most borderline trap hand of all. It should often be played, even if you are raised, depending on who the raiser is, his position, and the player's skill level	
K-J	A-A, K-K, Q-Q, J-J, A-K, A-J, K-Q
If the K-J is suited, along with its straight potential, being suited can make this trouble hand playable if you don't have to put too much money in preflop.	
K-10	A-A, K-K, Q-Q, J-J, 10-10, A-K, K-Q, K-J, A-10
Straight potential limited! Stay away!	
K-9	A-A, K-K, Q-Q, J-J, 10-10, 9-9, A-K, K-Q, K-J, K-10, A-9
Don't even think about it!	
A-J Offsuit	A-A, K-K, Q-Q, J-J, A-K, A-Q
Marginal. Read your opponent and make a judgment call.	
A-10	A-A, K-K, Q-Q, J-J, 10-10, A-K, A-Q, A-J
You must be up against a real maniac to call with this one. You might defend your blind from a raiser in steal position.	
A-9	A-A, K-K, Q-Q, J-J, 10-10, 9-9, A-K, A-Q, A-J, A-10
Loses to all premium hands containing an ace. No straight potential using both cards.	
Q-J	A-A, K-K, Q-Q, J-J, A-Q, A-J, K-Q, K-J
Some decent straight potential, but generally not enough to warrant a call.	
Q-10	A-A, K-K, Q-Q, J-J, 10-10, A-Q, K-Q A-10, K-10
The straight potential is starting to add up. Just be careful if you flop one pair.	
J-10	A-A, K-K, Q-Q, J-J, 10-10, A-J, K-J, Q-J, A-10, K-10, Q-10
Great straight potential, like the Q-10 noted above, but beware one pair with this hand!	

TRAP HAND: K-Q OFFSUIT

TRAP HAND

DOMINATING HANDS

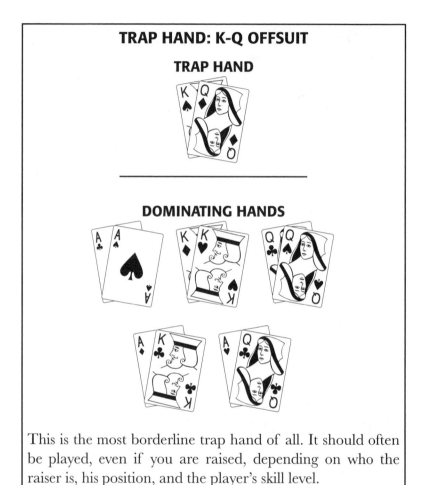

This is the most borderline trap hand of all. It should often be played, even if you are raised, depending on who the raiser is, his position, and the player's skill level.

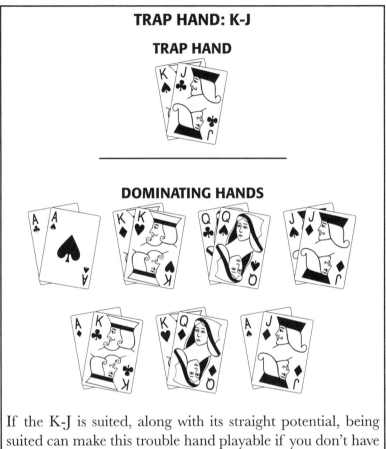

TRAP HAND: K-J

TRAP HAND

DOMINATING HANDS

If the K-J is suited, along with its straight potential, being suited can make this trouble hand playable if you don't have to put too much money in preflop.

TRAP HAND: K-10

TRAP HAND

DOMINATING HANDS

Straight potential limited! Stay away!

TRAP HAND: K-9

TRAP HAND

DOMINATING HANDS

Don't even think about it!

TRAP HAND: A-J OFFSUIT

TRAP HAND

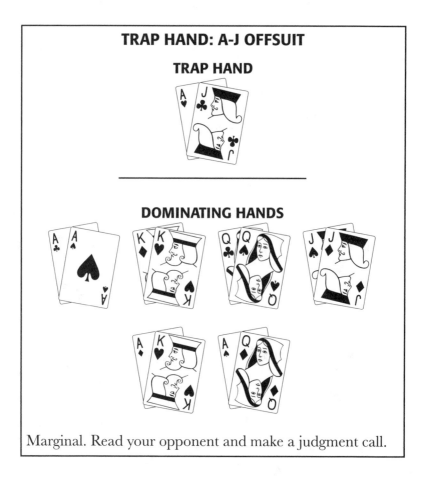

DOMINATING HANDS

Marginal. Read your opponent and make a judgment call.

TRAP HAND: A-10

TRAP HAND

DOMINATING HANDS

You must be up against a real maniac to call with this one. You might defend your blind from a raiser in steal position.

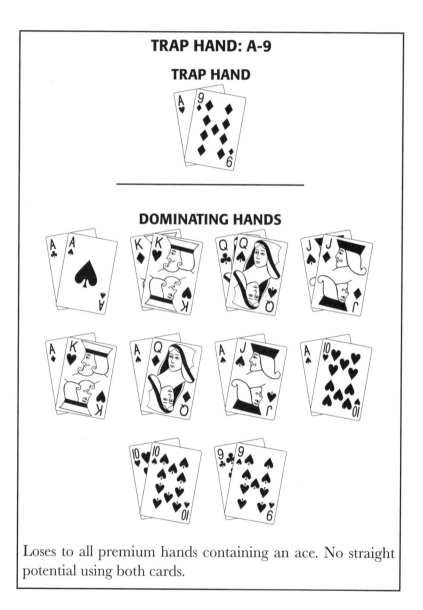

TRAP HAND: A-9

TRAP HAND

DOMINATING HANDS

Loses to all premium hands containing an ace. No straight potential using both cards.

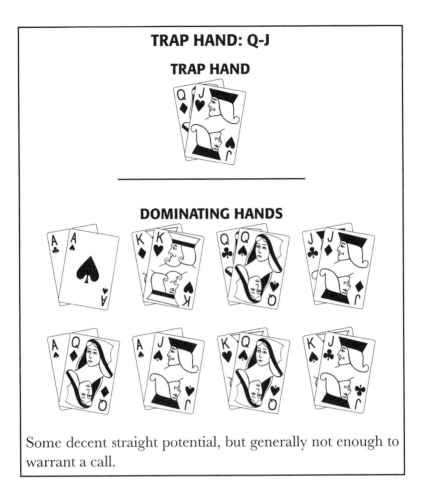

TRAP HAND: Q-J

TRAP HAND

DOMINATING HANDS

Some decent straight potential, but generally not enough to warrant a call.

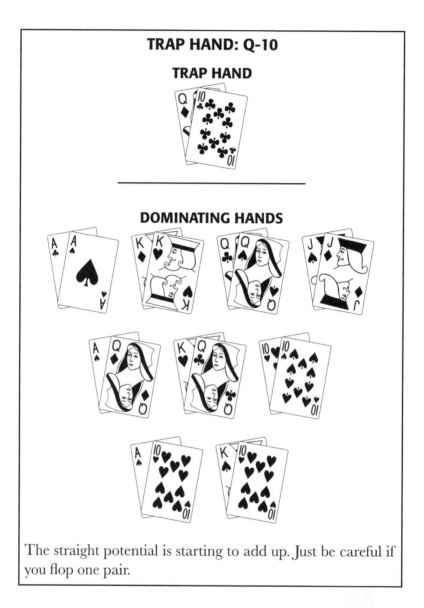

The straight potential is starting to add up. Just be careful if you flop one pair.

TRAP HAND: J-10

TRAP HAND

DOMINATING HANDS

Great straight potential, like the Q-10 noted above, but beware one pair with this hand!

Notice that I left A-Q off this list. Ten years ago, I would have named it as the number-one trouble hand of all. However, times change. With the advent of Internet poker and the flood of wild players that it has brought to the felt tables, I no longer consider A-Q a trap hand, but a premium one. Still, take care if a super tight player raises up front and you hold the newest member of the premium hands club.

> **TEN YEARS AGO, I WOULD HAVE NAMED IT AS THE NUMBER-ONE TROUBLE HAND OF ALL. I NO LONGER CONSIDER A-Q A TRAP HAND, BUT A PREMIUM ONE.**

I left many trap hands off the list, as they should simply never be played against a raise without really good cause. Any hand with a big card plus a medium or little card is just unplayable. One exception may be ace-little suited, but it is still marginal. You'll probably need multiple callers already in the pot to make calling correct.

Unplayable Raise Hands

Some hands you may be tempted to call raises with that I left off the main list are:

> K-8 suited or unsuited
> Q-9 suited or unsuited
> A-8 offsuit on down (A-7, A-6, and so on)
> J-9 offsuit
> J-8 suited or unsuited
> J-7 suited or unsuited

It may be okay to raise with these hands if no one else is already in, but never call raises with them. I know, never say "never." I'm sure many of you will read this and then see me do the opposite on TV. If you do, there's a reason I'm doing so. These are just general rules of thumb. Besides, as the great Doyle

Brunson told me over and over as I was growing up, "Do as I say, not as I do, you little SOB!"

DEALING WITH MEGA-LOSS

What if you're not playing any trap hands but still continue to lose at an alarming rate? We all have those days. Without money management skills, you can lose all your profits for the year in just a few days. You've got to know when to hold 'em, and know when to fold 'em. No, I'm not talking about the great Kenny Rogers song. I'm not even talking about a specific hand. So, what the hell am I talking about then? If you let me finish, I'll tell you!

Here it is in a nutshell: It's imperative that you learn money management skills if you want to stay afloat as a poker player. Like the song says: "You've got to know when to hold 'em, know when to fold 'em, know when to walk away, and know when to run." It's that "walk away" part that's so hard for some people. But as a poker player, you will have days when no matter how good the game and how good you play, you just cannot drag a single chip.

Why does this happen? Well, the left-minded logical experts will tell you that it's simply standard deviation compounded by the fact that your opponents are no longer afraid of you—and therefore, they are playing, correctly, more aggressively towards you. Add to that the fact that your once ironclad discipline may begin to break down after ten straight runner-runner flushes in a row beat your big pairs and sets.

The rightt-minded, free-thinking, open-minded or just plain loony experts will say that it's karma, the planets are out of alignment for your sign, your opponents are all on rushes, or that you're just plain unlucky.

Who's right? Who's wrong? Who knows? Who cares? All that matters is that you can't win a pot, and if you don't do something to stop the bleeding, you may go broke in a single session. Sound crazy? You don't think you can lose that much in one day while playing good? Yes, you can! I've seen it happen hundreds of times.

Whether it's standard deviation, bad karma, or bad play (or the slight chance that you may be getting cheated), the mega-loss must be dealt with. Many of you are shaking your head in agreement with me as you read this. But if it hasn't happened to you yet, beware, because it will. I'm not wishing bad luck on you, just trying to prepare you for when the eventual nightmare session hits.

Here are some solutions from both sides of the brain.

Left-Minded

The left-minded, logical person may recommend any of the following:

1. **Play fewer hands:** Less chance for bad beats.
2. **Value bet less:** Will decrease your standard deviation.
3. **Cut back on the semibluff:** Will help stop all the check-raising.
4. **Don't dry bluff:** If it didn't work before, wait 'til you see someone try it while on a mega-loss. While painful to watch, it's actually kinda' funny.

Right-Minded

The right-minded, free-thinking person may recommend any of these tidbits of advice:

1. **Walk around your chair.**
2. **Walk around the building:** Actually, there is some logic to this. Walking can burn off steam. (Ted Forrest actually does this.)
3. **Display lucky cardholders or pagan idols:** My father actually does this: Ever seen Casper?
4. **Don't play out of a rack:** I actually do this (or rather don't do this). Almost all top pros follow this superstition. I don't really believe it, but why tempt fate?
5. **Sacrifice a live chicken:** Cuco and Chau Giang actually do this.
6. **Go to a strip club:** A lot of players do this!

What if none of these suggestions work? When it comes down to it, there's only one real solution, no matter what side of the brain you listen to—quit for the day. To win the war, battles must be lost along the way. Swallow your pride, get up, and live to fight another day.

One of the nice things about tournaments is that they make this decision for you by not allowing you to rebuy after losing all your chips. Unless you sit down in a side game or a second chance tourney, you're done for the day. If you go far in a tournament, especially if you just miss the money or take a bad beat, I recommend that you stay away from the live games. I've bought several houses with the money that tournament specialists have dumped off to me after scoring in an event.

CASH GAMES VERSUS TOURNAMENT PLAY

It's usually dangerous to mix the two forms of poker, cash games and tournament. I'll usually concentrate on one or the other for a period of time. For example, during a recent World Series, I played a lot of events and only three side games (all three were on days I was knocked out of that day's event within a few hours). Not only was it time consuming to play both, but the style I needed to be playing for one was completely different from the other. It's easy to get the two confused if you do that.

It's much easier to stay in one mode or the other depending on which you choose. I can't count the number of times a player has done well in a tournament, walked straight over to a side game, and said, "Well, I'll just play an hour or two to relax after my big win." Famous last words! These guys either win a few thousand (no big deal, compared to the big payday they just cashed in the tourney) or lose big. It's just as easy to lose a few grand as to win it. And when they lose it, they'll sit there all night trying to get even, often losing the whole payday from the tournament (which could be hundreds of thousands or even millions of dollars). Seriously.

Why can't they win at a cash game after doing so well in a tournament? They probably are mad if they didn't win, even if they came in second. I don't care what they say on the outside, on the inside, they still know they lost. Even if they aren't upset, they're probably still in that final table, ultra-aggressive, do-or-die mode. It's one thing to play short-handed against players who are punch drunk from the marathon session they've put in (and who probably aren't top players anyway), but if you try that against fresh, seasoned pros in their own game, you're in for trouble. I hope I got that point across.

What are some other differences between tournament and live play? We discussed table image already, but it can be more difficult to establish your table image in a tourney so that you can play your game and make your plays.

Of course, the big difference between tournament play and live play is that you can't rebuy in a tournament; therefore, you must be much more careful with your chips. Let's say that a tight player bets the whole hand through. You missed a big draw but made middle pair along the way. On the end, the rock bets the size of the pot. You figure it's 10 to 1 against his bluffing and the pot's only laying you 2 to 1. This guy's so tight the whole table knows he's not bluffing. Easy decision, right?

Not necessarily. I mean, no one can fault you for folding, that's for sure. But what are the upsides to calling? For one, there's the obvious: You may have picked that 1-out-of-10 times this guy was bluffing and you'll win a nice-sized pot unexpectedly. You will look like a genius and everyone will slap you on the back and tell you how great you play. The rock will most certainly be terrified that you have a big tell on him and he'll be wary of you for a long time to come.

That one win will cover three out of the 10 times that scenario comes up. (You will get your money back the first time, win his bet the second time, and take down the pot the third time.) But what about the other seven times? All that money you lost didn't just go down the drain, you actually bought something with it—table image. Who's going to bluff you after you just called down that rock? "My God! If Todd called down Joe-never-bluffs with second pair, imagine what he'll call me down with? I better not try to bluff Todd tonight."

Use this play as early as possible to establish your table image for the day. Remember, it won't work on idiots or players who don't pay attention at the table when they are not involved in a pot. It is best used when a lot of good players are at the table who *will* take notice of your unorthodox play.

Now, should this play be used in tournaments or in live play? I think that it can be used to a certain degree in both. However, in the tourney you don't want to risk too many of your chips setting up your table image. Your table may break at any time and most of that advertising will be wasted. People may not remember what happened the next time they play with you, or they may think that's just the way you were playing that day.

The advantage to making this play in a tournament is that if you make it early, the limits will be lower and it may cost you a much smaller percentage of your chips than it would have cost in live play. Your table image can be set when the blinds are at $50/$100, and still be working when they go up to $2,000/$4,000. That is, if you're lucky enough to stay at a table that doesn't break at all, or one that doesn't break until the end. Or, if your table does break, you may wind up with several of the players from your earlier table, and they may gossip.

Still, I prefer to make this type of play in side games. If the game is good, you'll probably play with most, if not all, of the same players all night, possibly longer. You will probably be playing with them on more of a regular basis, too. And they probably will be a higher caliber of player, more likely to watch and learn, so that your advertising dollar goes further. (There aren't as many Internet types or satellite winners, who tend to be weaker cash-game players, in the bigger side games.) Now let's move on to the next subject.

ALL OR NOTHING

Have you ever seen a great player smooth call on the end with top full, a king-high flush, or some other near-nut hand? It looks amazing when you see it happen, and most people who aren't top players ask, "Why did he just call?" Often, the reason is that he figured his opponent either had the nuts, a hand he couldn't call a raise with, or possibly was on a stone-cold bluff. If his opponent has the nuts, he will lose money if he raises. And if his opponent doesn't have a strong enough hand to call a raise, or if he's bluffing, it does no good to raise, does it? Let's take a look at some situations that really happened.

If you watched *Poker Super Stars 3*—if you didn't, get off your lazy butt and go rent it!—you probably recall watching a very memorable match. It was the first match in the super sixteen. The line up: Phil Ivey, Carlos Mortenson, Daniel Negreanu and me. Not a bad foursome! In fact, I'll take the four of us against any other four players on the planet in a cross book if anyone out there wants to gamble.

Daniel and I got heads-up fairly quickly in the match, and although he had about a 2 to 1 chip lead on me, I still had plenty of chips compared to the blinds. In other words, this wasn't going to be an all-in-before-the-flop crapshoot. We were going to have plenty of play on every street, at least for a while.

The first of the memorable hands came down about five minutes into play.

Hand in Action: Daniel versus Todd #1

I held the Q♦ 7♦ and Daniel held the 10♦ 4♦. The flop comes 10-5-2, two diamonds.

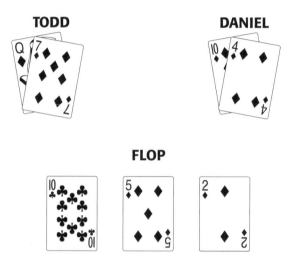

Obviously, a great flop for Daniel. Top pair with a flush draw matches up fairly well against most hands possible.

His top pair is about a 3 to 2 favorite over my bigger flush draw with one overcard. If I had had two overcards, I would have been about even money. If I held a 10 with a better kicker, it would also be about even money. If he were unlucky enough to run into a set—highly unlikely playing heads-up—he'd be about a 2.3 to 1 underdog. Against a smaller pair, a flush draw, or any straight draw, he's a huge favorite.

If you add up all the hands I could have, especially when you count up all the different straight draws, he is a huge favorite the vast majority of the time. So, after he bets the flop and gets flat called, he is confident enough in his hand to check the turn when a seemingly harmless offsuit 7 falls on the turn. This gives me second pair with a good kicker to go with my flush draw, meaning that I just drew out on two of the three pairs possible with this board. However, I correctly read that my hand may still be no good, and not wanting to get shut out of the pot by check-raising, I take the free card.

The final card….bingo! The ace of diamonds! This gives me the second nuts and Daniel the number-four nut hand. Amazingly, Kid Poker checks to me. His intense glare as I count my chips leads me to believe that he has a big hand also—and only one hand beats me. So I made my bet accordingly. A sick look on his face and a moan relieved any worries I had about my hand being no good.

Knowing that he had a big hand, I overbet the pot by about 50 percent, expecting him to call, which he did. Only thing is, it backfired on me. Daniel was most likely going for the check-raise, but when I bet so much, he correctly surmised that his hand was probably no good. So, he just called with the fourth nuts. (I hate that guy!)

As Daniel mucked his hand, he mumbled how he lost the minimum, and he's right. (Did I mention I hate him?) How did he lose the minimum, and why did he play his hand that way? Before we analyze it, let's look at another important hand in this match.

Hand in Action: Daniel versus Todd #2

I'm the big blind and Daniel limps in. I hold 5-2 and the flop comes 2-2-9 with two diamonds.

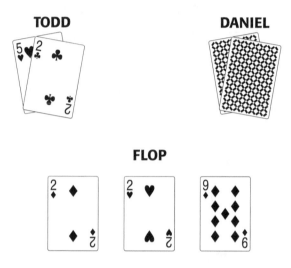

I check and Daniel bets the size of the pot. Now, I obviously have two choices: raise and most likely win the pot right there, or just call and take my chances. I decide to smooth call.

Off comes a third diamond and Daniel bets again. This time he underbets the pot. Is he fishing for a call, or just doesn't want to invest too much on another bluff? I pretend to check to see if I have a diamond. Then, again I just call.

The river comes a blank and Daniel fires again, this time around three-quarters of the pot. Now what are my options? This all-or-nothing hand is very similar to the first one. A raise on the river is out of the question. In the small chance that he's value betting a 9 or another pair he has made along the way, he's not going to pay me off. If he's bluffing, he's not going to call. If he has a deuce along with me, we'll either chop it or he'll have me beat with his kicker. As we can see, I'll only get called if I'm beaten. And I was: Daniel made the flush. A flush, a full house, or a deuce with a better kicker—all of them would've done the job. (I did say how much I hate him, right?)

Analyzing Both Hands

The second hand was similar to the first hand, in which we both made flushes. Originally, Daniel may have been going for the check-raise on the river, but when I bet so much, he knew that it was most likely an all-or-nothing situation. I was either bluffing, so a raise would be a waste of money, or I had a flush. Although his 10-high flush might have been good, I most likely had to have him beaten, given my big bet on the end. So he probably broke away from his original game plan, and called an audible to just call.

The play between the two hands on earlier streets was also similar for the same reasons. In the first hand, when Daniel checked the turn after I called him on the flop, he figured that he was either beaten or was a huge favorite. All or nothing. No harm in allowing a free card or trying to induce a bluff.

Likewise, in hand two, when I flopped three ducks I was either beaten by trips with a better kicker or a full house. Or, much more likely, Daniel had a 9, which gave him two pair and made me a better than 10 to 1 favorite. Or, as it actually turned out, he had a flush draw, making me a 3 to 1 favorite. The other possibility was that he was dry bluffing, in which case I probably couldn't lose unless I was struck by lightning and unable to turn over my hand on the end.

So, given the situation, I was either already beaten, a 10 to 1 favorite, a 3 to 1 favorite, or an almost total lock. All or nothing again! Under these circumstances, letting a free card come off usually isn't all that dangerous. It just happened to work out that the free cards had a big impact in both these examples, but still, giving a free card was the proper play.

THE BIG GAME

I'm about out of space, but the publisher and Daniel wanted me to talk about the Big Game a little bit, so here's what the no-limit aspect of our game has come to.

Most players don't realize that the Big Game—the high-stakes game usually played at the Bellagio by the top players in the world (my father, Phil Ivey, Chau Giang, and others)—is almost always a *mixed game*, meaning that we change the game every eight hands. The games we play are determined by who is in town and who starts the game. About half the time, the game is straight limit. At other times deuce-to-seven single draw no-limit, pot-limit Omaha, and no-limit hold'em are all a part of the mix.

When we play no-limit hold'em in the big game, we generally play $1,000/$2,000 blinds with a $1,000 ante. We play with a *cap*, meaning that we set an amount that is the most you can lose in a single hand. The cap we play with is usually $100,000, sometimes $150,000. If the player under the gun puts the live straddle on it (an optional third blind that is double the big blind), then the cap doubles to $200,000 or $300,000.

This structure leads to a very fast-paced, aggressive game, similar to the late stages of a World Poker Tour final table. Many pots come down to all-in contests before the flop, just like in tournaments. You may ask yourself, "Why would the world's greatest players assemble around a table on a regular basis and choose a form of poker with much of the skill filtered out?" Good question. I'm sorry I have no answer for you, except that top players crave action as much as oxygen!

This format guarantees action. Draw outs, bad beats and come-from-behind victories are a constant in our game—all the stuff that makes poker so painful, yet so enjoyable. Poker players love pain more then ice cream. There's nothing more satisfying than to watch a close friend lose a million dollars to a bad-beat runner-runner!

An old saying goes "The only thing better than playing poker and winning is playing poker and losing." Pretty sick, huh? Oh well, if we were normal we would all have jobs.

PLAYING NO-LIMIT
HOLD'EM ONLINE

ERICK LINDGREN

Erick Lindgren, "E-Dog" to his online opponents, is one of the most famous and successful poker players in the world. The 2003-2004 World Poker Tour Player of the Year, Erick has appeared at WPT final tables five times and delineated his formula for success in his book, *World Poker Tour: Making the Final Table*.

The handsome young poker star has always been an avid sports enthusiast, both as a player and a fan. In high school he earned acclaim as an All-League quarterback and MVP basketball shooting guard. His experience with the pigskin and the hoops has fueled his competitive fire to win every tournament he plays. "Play to win, not to survive!" is his motto. In addition to his aggressive approach, he is well known for his expert people skills and his advanced poker knowledge.

You'll find Lindgren playing online most often at FullTiltPoker. com. He also is a featured player in the "Activision World Series of Poker" and the "Stacked with Daniel Negreanu" video games. The winner of two WPT championships, including the Party Poker Million III tournament for a cool $1 million, Erick also won the 2007 Aussie Millions tournament for $795,259. Added to his impressive resume are more than 20 other final-table appearances, including his second-place finish in the $5,000 Short-Handed No-limit Hold'em event at the 2006 World Series of Poker.

Lindgren's topic for this book is how to play online no-limit hold'em for maximum results. What better teacher than the famous E-Dog himself? His expert advice, based on years of highly successful online cash-game and tournament play, will put you on the fast track to becoming a top Internet player. Particularly important are his 10 strategies for short-stack online tournaments. In sharp contrast to the slow pace of four-day, big-stack live tournaments, many online events give you a short time and a short stack to make your mark. E-Dog shows you the best strategies to race to the finish line in front of the pack.

PLAYING NO-LIMIT HOLD'EM ONLINE

Erick Lindgren

INTRODUCTION

Poker is poker no matter where or how you play the game, but the online version is a different animal with its own peculiarities, advantages and disadvantages. In this section, I will show you how to adjust your play for the online game so that you maximize your profit potential while minimizing risks.

Several differences between online poker and live poker are immediately apparent. First, of course, is not being able to sit across from your online opponents face-to-face. This anonymity makes it easy for players to click a button and push out bets. Second, it's very easy to come in and out of online games, so a lot of people play short sessions, often jumping from table to table. This ease in entering and exiting online games has created a distinct breed of Internet players—short buy-in artists looking for quick hits.

In this chapter, I will examine the distinctive elements of Internet poker, and show you how to attack the online game to turn its dynamics to your advantage. A lot of potential profit is waiting for you online. Let me point out a few tools that can help you harvest it.

HOW I STARTED ONLINE

I started my poker-playing career in 1995, playing live games in cardrooms. There weren't any no-limit games at the time—basically, I was a grinder trying to earn what I could at the tables. Later, I propped a $20/$40 game for a while, but in 1998 I reached a significant turning point in my career: I found Internet poker. I deposited money just to get a $50 bonus that was being offered on what was called Poker.com at the time.

In the beginning, I lost some money and I hated it. The software was terrible and they were raking $3 per hand even if you were playing heads-up. I thought that online poker was never going to work. Still, I kept at it.

I started with $3/$6 limit hold 'em, then moved up to $5/$10. But it was hard to make a living because they took such a big rake out of the pot, leaving me with very little profit for so much effort. So I hopped in the $20/$40 game, hoping the larger stakes would override the rake. I got lucky right away, and somehow beat a guy out of $2,000 bucks with my $200 bucks. I had only invested five bets—my bankroll!

After that lucky stroke, there was no turning back. I found that I could make a lot of money playing online poker and began devoting more and more time to it. Within three months I had three computers going and was playing up to eight games at once. I logged a ton of hands online and learned a lot about beating Internet poker along the way. In this chapter, I'm going to pass some winning secrets along to you.

ADVANTAGES OF PLAYING ONLINE

Playing poker on the Internet offers many benefits. Here are three of the important ones that really stand out to me.

1. YOU CAN EASILY JOIN A GAME

One advantage of playing online is that it's incredibly easy to just go to your computer, open up the site, and start playing right away. I like to play short sessions: half an hour here, fifteen minutes there, an hour there. I live in Las Vegas and it takes me that long to drive back and forth to the Bellagio. It's nice to avoid all that drive time by just hopping on my computer and starting to play.

The disadvantage of playing for only fifteen minutes is that you can't learn a lot about your opponents. However, you can play a solid game and make money. If you play a thirty-minute session, you're dealt as many hands as you would get in an hour or so in a live poker game. For people that don't have a lot of time, putting in that little half hour of power sessions is fine. In other words, online poker is convenient.

Another advantage is that you're fresh when you play quick sessions online, so you can play your best poker and optimize your profit potential. Better quality poker translates to better winning expectations. Over the long run, that puts more money in your online account.

One disadvantage to playing online—and many Internet players don't realize this—is that you can get fatigued pretty easily from staring at the monitor. For this reason, I think you should play short sessions, whatever amount of time is comfortable for you. Taking a break is easy online. When you start getting tired, just shut it down for a while and come back later. The game is always there!

2. YOU QUICKLY GAIN EXPERIENCE

With no live center dealer as in brick-and-mortar casinos, Internet poker is fast. You are dealt a lot more hands per hour online—more than double the number you would get in a live game (and that's when you're playing only one table!). Therefore, you quickly gain a lot of experience at what works and what doesn't in particular situations. You can detect patterns that opponents fall into, experience that you can carry over to your live games and tournaments. I can honestly say that I'm the player I am today because of all the experience I gained playing Internet poker.

3. YOU CAN LOCATE IDEAL OPPONENTS

Choosing your opponents, and having a large choice at that, is a big advantage online. You can select the type of game, players and stakes you want to play. You are able to build your bankroll quickly because every level possible is right there waiting for you at the click of your mouse.

Selecting the right table is important. The weaker the level of your opponents, the more money you should make at those stakes. A lot of sites have a "Friend Finder," or a tool that helps you find weak players that you have identified from previous play or observation. One way I check for a good game is to click on the "Average Pot" button. This shows me the tables where the best pots are being played. You can open up that game while you're on the waiting list and see how everyone is playing. You don't have to hop into a game right away; you can put in a little study time first. Sit there for a while as an observer and watch the play, determine what kinds of hands players are turning over, and then judge if it's the right game for you.

You might want to search out the games with large average pots, indicating that players are really mixing it up. Or if slower-paced games are more suited to your style, look for tables with smaller pots because you want a more conservative game.

> **LOOK FOR PLAYERS THAT DON'T KNOW THE GAME VERY WELL. LIKE AMBULANCE CHASERS, HOARDS OF PEOPLE CHASE THESE BAD PLAYERS AROUND THE ONLINE CARDROOM—AND YOU SHOULD PROBABLY BE ONE OF THEM.**

About the easiest way to find a good cash game is to keep notes on the players you want to track. There are certain players you want to be in your game, even if they are winners because they create action. You want loose players in the game because loose players lead to more pots for you to win—and bigger pots as well.

When a loose player, even a winning loose player, is in your game, a lot of pots are going to be played. Naturally, some players are going to lose big pots. If one guy continues to lose—whether you're in that pot or not—there is a good chance he is going to snap. You might be able to get a good piece of his action when he does.

You should also look for players that don't know the game very well. Like ambulance chasers, hoards of people chase these bad players around the online cardroom—and you should probably be one of them.

ASSESSING YOUR OPPONENTS

Admittedly, I've never used the poker-tracking online software that helps classify players, but it seems to be a good way to tell whether opponents are loose or tight by showing you how many pots they've played. This tracking tool will tell you how much money your opponents have won and whether they are winning or losing when you've been sitting at the same table with them. While the software only tracks hands and mines data when you are in the game, or if you leave your screen up, it is still pretty useful. One of the products out there that some players like is called Poker Tracker.

Just as you do in live games, you should be able to tell who the winners are pretty easily. They play some pretty solid hands, and they may even play some really bad hands, but no matter what the quality of their cards, they play their cards *correctly*. You cannot judge your opponent entirely by the kinds of cards he plays. In fact, if an opponent plays bad cards, there's actually a chance that he may be one of the better players, depending on the strategy he uses.

FOCUSING ONLINE

The most important prerequisite of making money online is focus. It's important to pay attention when you're playing, because it can cost you money if you aren't alert.

Focusing online is harder to do at home than focusing when you're playing in a live cardroom setting. You have to be very disciplined to maintain self-control when you're sitting in front of a computer.

When you are in a casino playing poker, the game is so much slower than online poker that it's easy to focus and be in the action. But if you lose your attention span online—whether people are in the room, you get a phone call, or whatever—you may sleepwalk through ten hands or miss them altogether. You may not pick up on something an opponent is doing that can give you a big edge. You might avoid making a big bet to take down a pot, or make the big bet when you'd be better off just folding. Or you could click on the wrong button and end up going all-in with a 7-2 offsuit. All of these bad things happen when you're playing at home and they cost you real money—believe me, I know! Keep in mind that those chips on your betting spot online are just as real as the ones in front of you in a live game. It's real money, *your* money.

A lot of factors go along with being a serious online poker player, essentials to making money in Internet poker. The most important of all is managing yourself, staying focused on your online game and not on the million distractions around your home environment. I might turn the TV off while I am playing online. I have seven TVs in my living room, so things can get especially distracting on a sports day. Playing poker online while sports games are showing on TV is a bad combination for me. I may be playing seven games and watching seven games! As a result, I've pushed the wrong button many times. Needless to say, that costs money.

> IF YOU WANT TO BE SUCCESSFUL, YOU **MUST** BE DISCIPLINED. IT'S THE FOUNDATION OF ANY SUCCESSFUL APPROACH TO INTERNET POKER.

I play poker to win money. It's my profession. Sure, I love what I do, it's challenging, and I often have a lot of fun. I'm not slaving away at a 9-to-5 job that I despise. And I love the convenience of playing at home, when I want and for as long as I want. But just the same, I'm playing online to make money. As I've stressed in this section, if you want to be successful, you must be disciplined. It's the foundation of any successful approach to Internet poker. If you intend to make money online, you need to take your poker time seriously.

BETTING PATTERNS

The number-one way to read your opponents' hands online is to detect their betting patterns. Obviously, you can't look your opponents in the eyes when you're playing online. You can't study their body language or physical mannerisms. You can't see how they react to the flop, your bets, or your withering stare after they've pushed a big bet into the pot. It's not like a live game where you can look into an opponent's eyes and scrutinize his expressions, or observe the way he sits or bets. You don't have any access to any of that information when you're playing Internet poker.

All you've really got to go on is how your opponents bet in specific situations: when they don't, when they do, how long it takes them, and how much they put in the center. But that's enough to really get to know their betting patterns.

So what exactly do you look for? You can figure out some players' patterns by how they vary their bets. Let's say that a guy bets 75 percent of the pot when he's bluffing and 60 percent when he really wants a call. Or maybe he bets only 50 percent when he really, really wants a call. Most players develop betting patterns that they fall into—it's your job to pick up on them as soon as possible and then use that information to your advantage.

You want to pay attention to how your opponents bet so that you can determine the quality of their hole cards. The basic online player will have the same basic betting patterns hand after hand after hand. It's very similar to a live game. Betting patterns are the number-one thing that I focus on in a live game, and they are absolutely the number-one focus that you must have online.

The amount of time a player takes to click his button and act upon his hand is one of the things you look for when reading an opponent's actions. When a player is bluffing, he sometimes will take a little longer to figure out the perfect bet to get you to fold. At other times, he might take longer to make his play because he knows what you have and is trying to figure out the perfect value bet. Of course, these patterns vary from player to player, so you need to study your opponents to see their tendencies.

The top players online have a great feel for betting patterns, a tremendous feel. It's almost like they can see you through the computer, because your betting patterns stick out so distinctly. They've played so many hands online and observed so many opponents, that after a while, they just seem to "see" your cards.

That's why it is so important to not only pay attention to your opponents, but to your own game as well! You want to avoid falling into patterns yourself that other players can pick up on. You must work on not being predictable, not doing the same thing over and over. Remember that your opponent's main source of information, just like yours, is to observe your betting patterns—the when, where and how much—to determine the why.

To protect against an opponent zeroing in on the strength or type of hand you hold, you need to do two things: maintain a consistent bet size when you enter the pot or raise, and vary the types of hands you play. Let's look at each.

MAINTAIN A CONSISTENT BET SIZE

Whether you're playing online or in live games, the key to avoiding tells is to be consistent in your bet size. You don't want the size of your bet or raise to announce the kind of hand you have. Some players mistakenly make different bet sizes depending on the strength of their hole cards. Pretty soon, other players pick up on these patterns, putting the predictable player at a big disadvantage.

Nobody should be able to tell whether you have aces, sixes, or even 7-6 suited by the way that you bet. You have to keep your opponents guessing. By playing a lot of hands and playing them the same way, they can't get a handle on what your bet means. They don't know if you're strong or weak. Your play becomes unreadable.

VARY THE TYPES OF HANDS YOU PLAY

How much maneuvering you do depends on whether you think your opponent is paying full attention, plus whether you're playing heads-up or short-handed. Against some players, I can just play like a robot and make the right bets for a situation and it works out. But other players are going to catch on to my robotic play and start folding hands I wish they wouldn't, or calling hands when I would prefer that they fold.

If that occurs, it's time to start changing your patterns so that your opponents can't read you. You need to shift gears right away, making sure your bets do not always make sense to your opponents. If you've been limping, mix some raises into your play. If you've been raising, limp a few times. If you've been playing fast, slow down a bit. Fold a little more often. Change up the way you've been playing to confuse your opponents and keep them off balance. Showing your opponent different looks will allow you to maximize your gains at the table.

PICKING UP BETTING PATTERNS

Right away, on the preflop, you want to find out who is tight and who is loose. Which opponents are making standard bets and playing good hands? Who is playing tighter up front and entering more pots towards the rear positions? If you see an opponent is playing good positional poker, you know that he is probably a pretty strong player.

Also be on the lookout for players that get out of line preflop. Let's say that I'm playing a $25/$50 no-limit game and I see a guy opening pots for $250 or $350. Obviously, he's betting way too much for the size of the blinds. Right there I'm thinking, "This guy is probably a tilter and he has too much gamble in him."

What am I going to do about it? Playing against tilters who overbet the pot restricts the number of hands I can play (unless I'm deep-stacked). Now that I have him classified, I'm going to wait until I pick up a good hand. When I get good cards, I can come over the top of him. Other players are going to want to come over the top of him, too, of course. Or I could just flat call and see what develops on the flop.

The correct preflop raise online (or live) is anywhere from two to three times the big blind. I'll also sometimes make it four times, to mix it up. I would never make it $300 preflop when the blinds are $25/$50.

ADVANCE PLAY BUTTONS

Although they are common in limit games, there are no "Advance Play" buttons in no-limit hold'em other than a few sites that have a "Bet Pot" button. Until it's a player's turn, he doesn't really know how much he's going to bet. There's nothing you are going to be able to pick up against a good player who just bets the pot constantly. He is going to turn it into a guessing game and force you to gamble.

How about the sites that have a Bet Pot button? That feature tends to dummy-up the play and make it more like a limit game in a weird way, since some players will just constantly bet the pot. In that case, you are going to struggle to get a read on your opponents. But what they do give up is not making the proper size of bets in different situations. Although opponents are very hard to read when they consistently use the Bet Pot button, their bets will be too much or too little a lot of the time.

BUY-IN STRATEGIES

In addition to the quality of your opponents, your strategy in cash games depends on whether you're playing a deep stack or a short stack. If you buy in for the max, you can play a lot of hands because you have chips to play with. You have room to maneuver. However, if you buy in for a smaller amount, you have to play tight for exactly the opposite reason—you don't have a lot of chips to play with.

Let's say you're playing a $25/$50 no-limit game with a minimum buy-in of $1,000 and a maximum of $5,000. That $1,000 buy-in for this game is light—it's not exactly deep stack poker.

How does playing with a short stack affect your strategy? Put simply, it changes everything. With just $1,000 in your stack, you can't take a lot of flops, because you don't have a big enough chip stack for that. Therefore, you're going to make more preflop decisions with that $1,000 stack. Suppose an opponent who has been raising a lot of pots makes a $175 pot-sized bet and you have A-Q. Since you will have a large portion of your chips committed to the pot if you just call his bet, you're probably better off moving all in with your $1,000. But if you have $5,000 behind you, there is no need to reraise to protect your stack with a hand like A-Q because you have plenty of chips. You can just call, take a flop, and see how the hand plays out.

One great read you can get on opponents online, even before a single hand is played, is the amount of chips a player buys in for. It not only gives you clues about how he might approach the game, but it often dictates what he can or cannot do. Let's look a little further into stack size and how it affects strategy.

SHORT STACK BUY-IN THEORIES AND STRATEGIES

There are two theories on buying in light for a game. One theory is that a $1,000 stack in a $25/$50 no-limit game can be very powerful. For example, suppose a player is raising every pot, jamming it up and playing way too loose. You could sit behind that aggressive player with $1,000, and when he makes it $175 and I call with an 8-6, you can shove in the full $1,000, especially when a guy like me who calls a lot of raises is already in the pot.

If you wait until you pick up an A-K, A-Q, A-J or even an A-10, you're going to win the pot a lot of the time. In this scenario, you've picked up $350 from both of us, plus $25 and $50 from the blinds. That's $425 in cash—not a bad haul! Now you can transfer to another game and do it all over again. I've seen lots of people do that, and it's actually a pretty solid online strategy.

There is a group of players who make a lot of money popping in and out of games like that. Some sites let you rathole chips, so a player can double up, leave and immediately come back for the minimum $1,000 buy-in. These short-stack, hit-and-run players are a pain in the neck, but at the same time, they help keep the games going.

The other theory about buying in light is that a player doesn't have much money and is taking a shot at a game that's over his head. If a player doesn't have enough chips for a game, he is going to play differently than he ordinarily would play.

Typically he will play tight, and you can take advantage of him.

Another type of short buy-in player is just trying to double up quickly. He always likes to start with $1,000, because one time he ran it up big and is hoping that luck hits him good again. If he busts out on a big play that doesn't work, he'll make his next buy-in for $1,000 to control how much he loses in one session.

And there's also the really tight minimum-buy-in player who waits for a hand so that he can move in, or tries to get in cheap so that he can flop a set. Meanwhile, he gets pushed around or blinded out while he waits for his move. These double-up, minimum buy-in players are generally losers.

However, you shouldn't make an immediate judgment on a player based on how much he buys-in for. There's no reason to rush to conclusions. Like everything else in poker, it's dangerous to jump to conclusions. A short buy-in could be a preset amount he has locked in, or a player could be buying in light for any number of other reasons. It might not be a lack of money, but rather a lack of money *in his account*. Online money is hard to get sometimes causing a player to come in lighter than he might like.

I don't worry too much about the short stacks at my tables. I'm just not focused on them. They are not going to affect me too much either way. I'm obviously dealing with a lot of other players, so I'd rather worry about my deep-stack opponents, the ones who have more chips for me to win from them.

BIG STACK BUY-IN THEORIES AND STRATEGIES

If a guy is buying for the max, he's obviously deep online. He has the money on the table because he's probably been winning, or he's a long-term pro and he keeps a lot of money in his account. I'd give him a little more credit.

Against a guy buying in for the max, you're going to have to calculate more pot odds or implied odds when you're in a pot against him. There is more strategy to consider. You're going to see more flops and be able to play more pots to the river. You'll be able to pretend you have hands and can bluff more often. I believe it's always better to play with a deep stack because you have more options; you're playing more poker.

To maximize my potential in a session, I'm going to focus on my opponents whose betting patterns matter, the players who have chips. If a guy with a $1,000 stack often pushes in behind me, I will track him and hopefully run some people through him. In other words, I am just going to call or raise with a big hand; and hopefully, he'll push and entice another player to call with a weaker hand. Then I'll have the option to reraise. So, I can bounce some stuff off of him if I know that a small stack goes all in pretty often. It gives me a few options to play some side pots against the third guy.

Let's say that you have pocket threes and see the flop three-way with an all-in short-stack opponent and a third player. The board comes Q-10-9, and the third player checks.

Hand in Action

3RD PLAYER

ALL-IN PLAYER

YOU

FLOP

You might want to shoot a bet into the pot to see if you can get him to fold something better than you have, maybe a pocket pair higher than yours. That way, you can get heads up against the original raiser, who is all-in. Who knows what the all-in player has? But when the third player checks, he's given you the right to take the pot. So, I recommend taking any side pots you can in online cash games. If it looks like your opponent has given up, fire in a bet!

When your opponent has the minimum buy-in amount, you don't have the implied odds for a big pot, and you'll be less likely to make moves on him. Why bet risky chips against a player when you can win only $1,000 from him, when you can make that same move against a player with $5,000 available to grab?

I'm a deep-stack player, so I am going to rebuy any time I'm below the max. I don't want to miss an opportunity if a big hand comes up and I can get all of my opponent's chips. That's why I like to top it right off. If you allow yourself to get short, your strategy changes and you must adapt to playing short-stacked throughout your session. It's much better to top off your stack, especially if you are playing against weaker players, even if they are running good. You need to have enough money on the table so that if you double up, you will get even from your losses and come ahead.

I like *chipping up*, earning chips bit by bit. At the same time, I never want to miss a chance to win a big pot if I flop a set against an opponent that will play with me. That's why I think you should buy in for the maximum. If you are not an underdog to the game, I don't see why you wouldn't take advantage of adding more chips if you have the chance to do so.

UNDERSTAND YOUR LIMITS

> I NEVER WANT TO MISS A CHANCE TO WIN A BIG POT IF I FLOP A SET AGAINST AN OPPONENT THAT WILL PLAY WITH ME. THAT'S WHY I THINK YOU SHOULD BUY IN FOR THE MAXIMUM.

Keep in mind that big swings of luck are possible, so you either have to be very comfortable buying in for the maximum in your game, or you should play at a smaller game. Remember, the online game moves fast. You get dealt lots of hands per hour and the play is more aggressive than a live cash game. You can't think in terms of just one buy-in because you might lose it quickly in no-limit hold'em. All it takes is one hand and all your chips are gone—and that can happen several times in a short span of time. I've lost as many as twenty buy-ins in a single game, but that's part of the risk. While you may not want to put that much money at risk, you should be comfortable enough to lose three or four buy-ins for one session. If it's not your day, take a break and try again when you're rested and those losses aren't on your mind.

STRATEGY AND TACTICS

BIG BETS AND BLUFFS

One of the scariest plays in live poker is putting a lot of money on the line with no hand to back those chips. Making a big bluff. The rush you get from it is amazing, but at the same time, making a big bluff is pretty scary, even intimidating. After all, big money is on the line!

However, many players who are super passive in a live cash game turn into different animals online. They become bold enough to make the big bluff they wouldn't dare if opponents were looking them squarely in the eyes. The biggest difference you'll find playing poker online compared to playing live games is that people are not embarrassed to bluff. It's easy to scroll the bar and up the bet amount. There is no intimidation before a bet is made or embarrassment after a bluff is called and a big bet is lost.

A lot of times in a live game, you might see players just check a pot down, but you hardly ever see that online. As long as there are chips in the middle, players are aggressively going after them, trying to take the pot. It's so easy to bluff online: All a player has to do is click his mouse and make that bet. Now the pressure is on you to put up your chips or fold and leave the chips in the middle for your opponent to pick up.

That's the big difference between live play and Internet poker—the fear factor goes away, leading to lot more aggressive play online.

POSITION AND JUNK HANDS

Position is important in hold'em, especially online because of the more aggressive nature of the game. Position gives you leverage to control hands. However, as in a live game, you want to make your aggressive plays when you're sitting near the button.

I won't do a lot of preflop bluffing, especially when another player raises in front of me. Reraising on the preflop is not a big part of my game—I want to see flops. If a player in a blind position reraises, but not enough to push me out, I have a potentially lucrative situation. A lot of players put in that blind reraise in a super-aggressive game.

In a more passive game, I may reraise. In fact, I am more likely to reraise with a hand like 6-5 or 8-4 just to bluff and make my opponent think that I am capable of reraising with nothing. If I hit my hand, he's playing out of position from the blind, and I have an excellent opportunity to win a bunch of his chips.

In position, you could consider playing bad opening cards preflop. *But always in position.* For example, would I play an 8-5 offsuit? If the circumstances are right—that is, I have position and I have chips—I'll play all sorts of hands. Of course, other factors enter into the equation, but you always want to have enough chips that an opponent will think twice before trying to blow you out of a pot with a raise. That's one of the main reasons I like to play a deep-stack game online and always buy in for the maximum. I try to see a lot of flops; and with my deep stack, I can pick and choose spots where I can put a bet out there to try to take the pot.

If you're going to play a lot of hands, you need to steal a decent amount of the time to make it profitable. That's one of the reasons why a deep stack, which allows you to liberally make these plays, works to your advantage.

SEEING FLOPS

I play a similar style online with my starting cards as I do in live games. I play a lot of hands and focus on position. My goal is to outplay my opponents when the three-card board hits. A lot of preflop play is guesswork, so I don't want to build the pots too big and give an opponent the opportunity to take me out with a big bet. By playing a wide range of hands and keeping my bets consistent, my opponents don't know what hands to put me on.

I don't see any problem limping with a lot of hands because I want to see the flop. However, I limp more often in late position. Every time I call in position preflop, when the flop comes, the other players have to decide whether it helped me, or if I'm slowplaying. By calling, I haven't defined my hand at all, so my opponents are kept guessing. They don't know what to do.

Sometimes, a player sitting behind me gets sick of my calling and takes a shot at the pot with a huge bet. His big bet gives me a chance to take him out if I've limped in preflop with a huge hand like aces or kings. Plays like these are made possible by keeping my betting patterns consistent. My opponents don't know if I'm holding aces or another junk hand that may or may not have hit the flop. It makes it very difficult for them to put me on a hand and make the proper bets and adjustments against me.

MANIPULATING THE POT

Calling and seeing flops also leaves opponents open to a tactic that you can use very successfully online: manipulating the size of the pot. Let's say that I flop a straight in a tournament or make it on the turn. I can let my opponent bet the flop and the turn, and I can call. On the river, if he bets again, which a lot of aggressive online players will do, I can put in my action raise if I know that he is apt to pay off. If the pot is too small on the turn but I've made my big hand, I'll want to put in a little raise there instead of waiting until the river. By making the pot bigger on the turn, my river bet can be even bigger.

This tactic is called *manipulating the pot.* You have a big hand and you want to make sure that you can get in a big bet on the river. You want to get paid for your good hand, so you need to figure out if the pot is big enough. If it's already a huge pot, feel free to check your hand on the turn if you're first to act. Let your opponent bet. But let's say that your opponent in a $25/$50 game has $3,000 left on the turn and he bets $1,400. Or he bets $1,000, so that he has $2,000 left. The pot is big enough that you could slowplay the turn and let him move into you on the river. And that's all good.

But let's say that you've made the nuts and the pot is just $400. Your opponent has $5,000 and you have $5,000. He bets $300. You probably want to put in a little raise to make the pot bigger so that you'll have a chance to bet $1,500 or $2,000 on the river and get paid.

Manipulating the pot is a very standard play in poker games—online and live. You want to build the pot up when you have a better hand and draw cheaply when you don't.

DEFENDING AGAINST OVERBETS

Many top players online like to bet $14,000 into a $3,000 pot and then when you fold, they'll show you a 7-high. And then the next time when you call, they'll show you four of a kind. They make these huge overbets, which is a really interesting tactic. The strong part of this strategy is that the overbets keep you guessing. And of course, they generally take down the pot, which gives your opponents a big edge on those plays.

This is not the way I approach the game because a big overbet like that—$14,000 into a $3,000 pot—is going to take a long, long time to get back if you get called and lose. The risk is just too big for an uncertain reward. And the temptation of making your next move bigger, committing even greater sums to the pot, makes the risk of playing deeper into the hand even greater.

If your opponent frequently makes these moves, you've got to believe that he's able to alternate between bluffing and playing straight. (Of course, what he does also depends on what he thinks you are going to do.) Essentially, either he's bluffing or he's not. If you make the call and lose, it takes a long time to recoup because of the bet size in relation to the pot. But in reality, a call is not as bad as it first seems. It's almost a 50/50 bet for you; you're calling $14,000 to win $17,000. But still, that $14,000 is a very tough call to come up with, especially in the constricted time that you have online. It's a big, big bet.

When you play somebody who overbets, you generally want to fold, unless you're sure they're bluffing or your hand is big enough to make the call. Sometimes, if a guy is running over you with big bets, you have to make a stand to equalize the game and fight fire with fire. Just pick your spot carefully, then blast away.

GETTING INTO YOUR OPPONENT'S HEAD

Throughout every deal, I try to put my opponent on a hand. I always ask myself: What's he got? What's he think I have? I'm running these questions through my head, and I'm also thinking back to his play on the flop and turn, and how he originally entered the pot in the first round of betting before the flop.

When you play a hand through in your mind, you can often put your opponent on a hand, which will help you play the river correctly.

TOUGH RIVER DECISIONS

River play is basically determining how much to value bet if you think that your opponent is bluffing, or how much to bet when you believe you have the better hand. And of course, getting out of the pot if you're beaten and your opponent is trying to bait you in deeper with the superior hand. To make the best play on the river comes back to paying attention online so that you can learn about your opponent—what hands he likes to play in what positions, what plays he's capable of making, and what his betting patterns tell you about the cards he likely holds.

Things get tough on the river when your opponent blows out a big bet and puts you to the test. You've got all those chips sitting out there. In that case, you have to go over the hand and his play. You have to think about it and decide whether his bet makes sense. You may come to the conclusion that he probably would have bet a lot less if he wanted to get called. Sometimes you'll just have to call some of those bets—there is nothing you can do about it.

Online, this is a more difficult play than it is in live games. You can't see your opponent, and your strategy decision is going to depend completely on how well you can read his betting patterns.

To come up with the right analysis, use your instincts. Try to picture your opponent in your head. Get a feel for his emotional state and how he is thinking. Is he winning? Is he losing? Is he content or does he really want this pot? You are putting a lot of factors into this thought process. It's a big decision: You are going to win or lose that day based on how you play that big hand, so you have to be alert to all the possible clues that can steer you to the right decision.

Sometimes it seems like you can tell when a player starts clicking his action buttons a little more rapidly. He starts playing a little faster and he's raising more. You can feel when a guy is becoming emotionally involved. Once that occurs, he is more likely to bluff you. Hopefully, you get to pick up a hand where you can induce the bluff and win a bunch of chips, maybe all of them.

PROTECTING THE BABIES

Sometimes you'll be sitting on the river with a hand that has little chance of winning in a showdown, but there's a bunch of chips sitting in the middle, many of which came from your stack. You'll need a bluff to take down the pot. Doyle Brunson says in *Super System* that you don't want to leave your babies out in the middle. What he means is that if you suspect that your opponent might give them up to a big bet, you should consider pushing some chips out there—bluffing—to protect your chips that are sitting in the middle.

This is a good point to consider when you're on the river with a busted hand—don't give up on the pot just yet. Winning at no-limit is about taking good, calculated gambles. If you've been paying attention to your opponent and have a good feel for his limits, you may be able to make a play at the pot.

USE YOUR INSTINCTS

If you pay attention to the game, you'll start getting a feel for your opponents and that will help you come to some understanding of how they're thinking, and consequently, what you should do in various situations. If you watch their betting patterns and the time it takes them to make their decisions, you develop a feel for where they're at in a hand and who they are as a player. Your instincts will kick in and help you come to the best decision in a big play. Don't play solely by your instincts, but then again, don't ignore them either.

Some players I know consistently change their names online. It typically takes me about ten minutes to figure out who those players are, just from their betting patterns. And there are a couple of other guys online who make such strange bets that you can tell in a few minutes that they're in your game. One player I know starts cussing in the chat box, so he immediately gives himself away. But you don't want to let your opponents know that you know who they are, though their identity eventually comes out in a lot of cases.

TAKING NOTES

Note taking is an important aspect to your game if you want to get better. When I got my start as an online poker player, I would take notes on a pad because at that time, they didn't have the note-taking feature online. There are so many players you end up playing against online, it is virtually impossible to keep track of them. Playing online isn't like sitting in a live game where you can visually identify a player, and the memories come rushing back when you see him again. And when you're playing live, there are only so many players that come in and out of a game. Players stay longer at live games—you might not have a single player change seats for hours or even a whole session.

Longevity at a table is something you just won't see online. When you're playing Internet poker, players shuffle in and out of games so rapidly—and you'll probably play like that as well—that you might compete against as many as 50 or even 100 players over a single playing session. That's too many players to remember, especially when you consider that the only visual difference between one player and the next is a bunch of letters on the screen and a generic icon shared by thousands of players.

A big part of your game is knowing how your opponents play and adjusting your game to take advantage of this knowledge. You need a way to remember players you've gained some history with. That's why taking notes online is so valuable.

If you want to be really proactive about it, you should log pot size, opponent's bets and hands (like top pair or queen kicker), and take notes on the dynamics of the situation—what he bet on the end, if there was a safe or scary board, and so forth. Describe the hands and, even more importantly, the situation. Figure out as much as you can about how much your opponent bets in each situation, because he is likely to follow those patterns in future hands. The information you collect gives you a big edge against that player if you have your notes at your fingertips.

Even more important than knowing your opponents in a game is finding the ones you like to play against. That's where the real profit lies online. And that's where note taking really benefits you.

PREFLOP TOURNAMENT TACTICS

THE 2X PREFLOP RAISE

In a tournament, I'm more likely to raise two times the blind when I enter the pot. It is a bit of an unusual bet, but it's something that I have done for a while. Many top players have adopted this style and rarely bet three times the blind as their opening raise.

You get to play a lot of hands this way and see a lot of flops. If an opponent reraises you, there's not as much meat in the pot, so it's easy for you to release your hand, or as I like to do, call and see if I can hit the flop. And if you are playing loose, it makes more sense. You open yourself up to the reraise when you are playing a lot of pots, because obviously you don't have good hands every time.

By making a two-times-the-blind opening raise, you have less risk and still have all the gain. Your raise can force opponents out, and with large tournaments that are a bit of a crapshoot, you want to win as many antes and blinds as you can. If the structure is bad in a tournament, meaning the blinds increase too rapidly and you aren't given enough chips to play at an unhurried pace, this is a powerful strategy. You want players to drop so you can keep collecting those antes and blinds. If you could win the blinds every hand, you'd win the tournament!

In tournaments with a good structure, I always raise in the hope that players will call my raise no matter what I have, especially the players in the blinds, as I want to play heads-up with just them. I don't want players sitting behind me to call because I want to have position throughout the hand. If a player or two calls, I'll deal with it, of course, but I really want the blinds to defend their bets.

When the blinds call, you play the player, which works as well online as it does in live games. When people defend and play out of position, it's a mistake.

By playing a lot of pots and only doubling the blinds, you frustrate your opponents. Compare this to the player that makes it four times the big blind. If you come over the top and take the pot away from him, you win a good amount of chips. On the other hand, if you reraised me and I had just made it two times the blind, you are not winning much if you take me out of the hand. And I have reduced the cost of seeing the flop and the risk of a player coming over the top of me.

DEFENDING AGAINST THE 2X RAISE

Let's look at this situation from the other side. What do you do if you are in the blind and a player in late position keeps raising your blind by pushing two times the big-blind bet into the pot?

How I play against that player depends on whether my opponent is an amateur or a top player. If the raiser who does it every time is a pro that I respect, I'm not going to defend with my bad hands, even with all the antes and blinds out there. It's just not worth it because he's got position. Against a great player, being out of position is too big a disadvantage. But against a weaker player that I can push around and maneuver more to my liking, I'm not going to throw away every hand because I can compensate by outplaying him.

If you're not a top-level player yourself, you should throw away those blinds against preflop raisers who are strong players. You shouldn't be a blind defender. It's too dangerous, too many chips are at stake. You not only have to put up those chips to see the flop, but the good player is going to come after you on the flop as well, and he's going to outplay you.

> **IF YOU'RE NOT A TOP-LEVEL PLAYER YOURSELF, YOU SHOULD THROW AWAY THOSE BLINDS AGAINST PREFLOP RAISERS WHO ARE STRONG PLAYERS.**

If a bad player is doing it, that's different. Don't be afraid to get into the pot. And don't be timid about throwing your opponent some rope, especially online in no-limit hold'em. You can even check-call your top pair down to the river. A lot of players raise to find out where they are. Against an aggressive player, that's a mistake. If you are playing against an aggressive player, just call him down, especially if there is some kind of draw out there. There is no reason to check-raise and then let him bluff you out with a big reraise. Just give him the rope. Your best play is to call and let him bluff in the end when you've got a better hand. On the river, there are no more cards to come and your opponents can't suck out. You are 100 percent the winner, so all you have to do is induce the bluff.

The aggressive player may be able to read you, because he is certainly going to put you on a pair. But at the same time, he is not going to care. He is going to say, "You can't call if I bet this much." That's why you need to read your opponent's betting patterns to decide whether it's a value bet or a bluff he is making.

10 STRATEGIES FOR SHORT-STACKED TOURNAMENTS

Online short-stacked tournaments are much different than the long, slow, main-event tournaments that take upwards of three days to complete. In these quicker online tournaments, you don't have a lot of chips to work with and have to play faster than when the structure is slow. The tournament has to end in a relatively quick timeframe, so the sites speed up the structure forcing competitors to play fast to stay alive—or get blinded out. Here are a few tips to look out for in these tournaments.

1. USING THE RERAISE

Once the antes start going in, start reraising with pretty good hands before the blinds and antes eat you up. You need to get chips into your stack quickly or you won't last very long. You should still follow a solid tournament strategy, but play at a much faster speed than you would otherwise.

You want to quickly figure out whose blinds you can steal and notice if anybody else is also alert to it. Let's say that a player keeps stealing the big blind's bets. If you see a player try to steal two times in a row, he's probably coming back for a third time. Let's say the stealer is in the middle position, you are in the cutoff, and the stealer raises the blind again. That might be a good chance to reraise the stealer with a good-sized bet. Make it look like you want to get called—don't just put in a huge reraise that is out of proportion and screams, "Bluff!" It's very hard to call a reraise out of position. And by pegging the stealer, you put yourself in a really good place to take the chips he's donated to your pot.

However, it is important to take position into account when you're restealing. If you're in the blind yourself, you could be in a lot of trouble if you get called, because you'll be out of position on the other betting rounds if your opponent plays back at you. But if you're in position, it makes it a lot harder for the raiser to call because you're the one that holds the advantage.

Reraising in these tournaments is a powerful tactic. It takes a tremendous amount of luck to win an online tournament because of the short timeframe, so you can't be afraid to take advantage of opportunities that present themselves. You can't be afraid to gamble if the situation is right for you. As the blinds go up and players start getting out of line too often, reraise it. Take some shots. You are not going to win an online tournament without doing some gambling.

2. TARGET WEAK PLAYERS

Pick any major Sunday tournament on any poker site. Players qualify all week long for pennies on the dollar; it only costs them a few bucks to get in. These are guys who won't pony up $200 for a tournament, so you can't give them much credit for being good players.

In these tournaments, try to figure out who the really bad players are as quickly as possible. Look for players who are making weird-sized bets that don't make any sense. Maybe they show a really bad hand they entered the pot with from an early position, or you see them go all in early with two sixes when there's no good poker logic to it. Pick a target and look for opportunities. Try to play as many pots as you can with the bad players.

3. LOOK TO FLOP BIG

Try to see some flops early and give yourself a chance to flop big and bust your opponents. For example, you should play any pocket pair in the hope of flopping a set against one of the guys who think that top pair is golden. In most online tournaments, you get $2,500 chips and start at blind levels of about $10/$20. This is a good chance to limp in and try to make a few hands, because typically, a lot of players are limping in as well. Hands like suited connectors and all sorts of junk hands can mint chips for you if you can get in cheap enough.

Give yourself a chance to get lucky and win some big pots with good hands that you can double through with.

4. GETTING NEAR THE MONEY

As the tournament gets deeper, you want to see if a player is just trying to get in the money because he wants some cash. One thing people do online that you don't see so much in live games is just sit there when it's their turn and let their timers blink. Blink, blink, blink. They sit there because they're just trying to get in the money. It holds the game up a lot. That's the downside for you, but you also have an advantage: You can steal these players' blinds because they're clearly just trying to move up the ladder. You don't even need to look at your cards, you can just take a shot at their blinds.

5. TIGHTEN UP WHEN YOU'RE LOSING

Once you get a little low on chips—let's say you lose a few small pots or a medium-sized one—it's time to lock it up and play tight.

Let's say that you started with $2,500 and your stack drops down to $2,000. Start playing tight, bear down, and play only premium hands. Your goal is to pick up a few chips and stay even until you are dealt a big hand. You want to steal blinds here and there so that you can hold your own until a hand you can play comes along. Essentially, you just want to play dead.

These short-stack online tournaments are actually a lot like World Series preliminary events, because you are so short of chips that playing rock-solid, tight poker is the correct strategy. As soon as you grow your stack, it's time to splash around some chips and play a lot of pots. You can go back to limping in to see three more cards to try to connect with a hidden hand. Or return to raising two times the big blind and either taking the pot down right there, or seeing what happens on the flop.

6. POSITION FOR THE BIG MONEY

All the money is on top of the payscale, so you need to position yourself to get into the top three. That's where the real money is. Although seventh- or eighth-place money may look great to you, it's going to be chump change compared to the top places.

Go for first place. One of the ways to do that is to start reraising players that are raising too much. Wait for spots where you can pick out someone who looks weak. Study your opponents' betting patterns and pounce when the right opportunity arises. Look for an aggressive player who thinks he can get away with raising hand after hand—until you start hammering back and chopping him down. Keep raising and keep pissing him off. A consistent raiser is less likely to call reraises if he thinks you're a good player. He'll give you credit for a good hand unless you bang him back once too often. Meanwhile, you'll collect some of his chips.

7. DON'T TAKE UNNECESSARY RISKS EARLY

Don't stick your neck out early in a tournament. You don't know enough about your opponents yet to properly gauge your play. If you are trying to win the tournament, you want to play some hands and try to get lucky early. If your chip stack dwindles, play tight.

8. PLAYING THE MIDDLE STAGES

In the middle stages, start stealing antes and blinds to keep your stack about even until you have a big hand. And when you get that big hand, don't be afraid to gamble with it. You can flat call a raiser when you have two aces or two kings preflop and try to trap him on the flop. The key is to make sure that you don't blow him out of the hand and get only the minimum. You need more chips than that to win.

Slowplaying aces can be a good thing. Here's an example. The blinds are $300/$600 and your stack is $15,000. A middle-position player makes it $1,600 to go. You have pocket aces. Why not just reraise him to $2,800 or $3,000? Don't let him get off cheap. Let him in there. If he beats you, he beats you—but make sure you get action on those aces. Don't play scared.

That two-times-the-big-blind raise is enough of a raise to get more chips in the pot, but not so much to make an opponent afraid to call it. The minimum reraise is actually a very effective play that's been brought in from live poker to online. It's like a nuisance reraise. It's almost impossible to fold against because you are getting such tremendous odds. If an opponent has K-Q and flops a king or a queen, he's going to have a hard time getting away from the hand. If you get aces, you are a big favorite over any hand, and you want to get paid for them. You need to get action on your big hands. That's the bottom line. Don't be afraid to gamble. Don't be afraid of those beats because you aren't going to lose the tournament by not gambling.

Your opponent might flop a set, but that's a risk you have to take. You cannot win in these tournaments online without gambling. You can't afford to shut people out when you have a premium pair. You have to take risks and allow your opponents to build pots for you. You want to win big pots—do not settle for the small ones.

9. PLAYING THE LATE STAGES

As a tournament gets near the money or the final table, I am looking to see if there is anybody that just wants to move up and play this game. If a guy is just folding, folding, folding, you need to attack his blinds. If a guy's playing too many pots, you need to reraise him. You've got to take a shot. Again, you don't have much time to play here with these fast structures; you need to make sure you are the aggressor.

Pick on the weak, pick on the strong. That's how to make money online in tournaments. Think of it this way: It's finishing versus cashing. You are going for the big money. All the money is up top, so once you've cashed, go for the gold!

10. STAGES OF THE TOURNAMENT: SUMMARY

Here's a general guide to tournament strategy.

a. **Early:** It's cheap to get in, so see lots of flops; look for trapping hands
b. **Middle:** The blinds and antes cost more, so play tight and look for opportunities.
c. **Late:** Position yourself for the top three spots where the big money is. Take more chances, reraise more often. Don't be afraid to put someone else's tournament life on the line with an all-in bet— make them come to you.

ONLINE CHEATING?

Many people have concerns about playing in a big game online with a lot of players. I play a lot of pot-limit Omaha, which would be the best game to collude in if players wanted to, but I don't worry about collusion too much because I've never done anything but win. I don't see cheating as being a big factor. Even if two players are sharing hole cards through instant messenger or something, it's not going to make a big difference if you play a good game. But then again, the possibility of online collusion is the price you pay to play in your pajamas.

It's not a perfect world. If you do see something goofy, like the same guys always in the same game, especially at the lower limits when there are four $5/$10 games, you might be a little suspicious. But just because people play together—either because they're friends or they just like playing against each other—doesn't mean anything fishy is going on. Just be aware that collusion is always possible.

Personally, I don't think friends should play in the same online game. It's not because I think anything is going on, it just makes me suspicious when I can't see my opponents with my own eyes. I've always avoided playing with my friends. Why would I want their money when there are all those other people online? Let me take the food off *their* table.

WHEN TO STOP PLAYING ONLINE

My advice on when to end an online session is simple: Play until you're not happy to be playing anymore, then just quit. Easy enough. Don't worry about whether you are stuck or how profitable the game looks. There are always profitable games to be found; that's the beauty of Internet poker. Plenty of choice all the time, day or night, Sunday through Saturday.

Let's say, for example, that you have limited yourself to losing three buy-ins in an online session, which is a lot for an average person. At that point, you have to realize that this might not be your day. Regardless of how you feel otherwise, losing three buy-ins will probably cloud your head, so you should stop playing and do something else.

Most of us pros think we are pretty good players and we enjoy the game. But let's say that an opponent got lucky against you or you think he's a donkey. Now it's going to be hard for you to walk away from that game, because the "sucker" has all the chips. Every pro's A-game is pretty good, but the bottom line is that you need to be careful that you are not playing your B, C, or D game.

When you think that you're not playing well, I don't care how bad your opponent is, you should quit. If you are not playing well, a bad player might take your money. Psychologically, it might be hard for some people to quit in a game that looks soft, even against opponents who are terrible. But if everything is working against you, what can you do? Of course, you're also saying to yourself, "There is no way I am going to let this guy go." You're just tied into that game.

> **EVERY PRO'S A-GAME IS PRETTY GOOD, BUT THE BOTTOM LINE IS THAT YOU NEED TO BE CAREFUL THAT YOU ARE NOT PLAYING YOUR B, C, OR D GAME.**

Whenever you're losing, you should be more apt to quit, because your opponent feels lucky and he feels good about himself. If he thinks you are a bad player, no matter how badly he plays, he's feeling pretty happy about beating you out of your chips. Because of all that, he is playing better. And most likely, you're playing worse because you're losing.

When the shoe is on the other foot and I'm the one winning, I always want to give my opponent a chance to bury himself. I'm playing and feeling good, he probably isn't. Here's a situation where I can probably take him for a lot more than he's already lost.

Play longer when you're winning and shorter when you're losing. That's my advice.

MY BEST HAND

One of the best hands I ever played was a few years ago versus Daniel Negreanu in a tournament when we were down to three-handed play. I got dealt Q-10 and raised, another player called, and Daniel called.

The flop came J-8-3.

Hand in Action

OPPONENT   **DANIEL**

ERICK

FLOP

It wasn't the best flop for my hand, but I had position. The first player checked, Daniel checked, and I bet. The first player folded and Daniel reraised about half his chips. He was trying to send the signal, "I've got a pair, I'm committed, I'm going with this hand."

Daniel and I talk a lot of strategy and my goal that day was to make a big bluff on him at some point, one that didn't make any sense. I looked at his chips and played the hand back in my head and got into his head as well. I thought there was a chance he'd fold. This felt like the right time to make my move, so I pushed in on him, giving him almost 5 to 1 on the call.

There was a time clock and he had ninety seconds left to act with one extension. He was certain that I had jacks or even Q-J, giving him only two outs for his remaining chips. I put him on exactly what he had, an 8. Unfortunately, as he told me later, he had Q-8—so my queen was no good—and I would need a 9 or a 10 to win if he called.

He ran out of time and folded. It was a terrible fold for him. Losing those chips probably cost him the tournament. Daniel would probably say it was the worst laydown of his career. I told him my cards after he busted out two hands later. He wasn't too happy with himself afterwards.

I was able to pull of this bluff and trick one of the best players in the world by mixing up my play really well.

CONCLUSION

You should always play your best game, no matter what. Just go in, play your strategy, and stick with it. It doesn't matter how long you play, 15 minutes or three hours. Online, the game never ends, and profitable opportunities are always waiting for you.

SHORT-HANDED ONLINE NO-LIMIT HOLD'EM CASH GAMES

PAUL WASICKA

When a player as young and new to the high-stakes tournament scene as Paul Wasicka wins $6 million in his first stab at the World Series of Poker championship event in 2006, the poker establishment tends to label him a flash in the pan. Not so with Wasicka.

Before making his impressive second-place finish to Jamie Gold in a field of 8,773 in the 2006 title event, Paul had already captured the notice of major tournament players by placing in three preliminary no-limit hold'em tournaments at the WSOP. To erase any lingering doubts about his durability, the 26-year-old won the NBC National Heads-Up Poker Championship in 2007 by mowing down a talented field of well-known players and reaping $500,000 in prize money.

Before he decided to pursue poker fulltime, Paul worked as a restaurant manager and bartender in Colorado, where he lives. After completing his 9-to-5 work shifts, Paul honed his poker skills by putting in long hours on Internet poker sites using his online nickname KwickFish. Since becoming a name in the poker world, he has worked for a far bigger restaurant chain, Kentucky Fried Chicken, appearing in a KFC national commercial. The poker star also is an instructor for the World Series of Poker Academy. As of spring 2008, Paul holds fifth place on the WSOP all-time money list.

Wasicka's topic for this book deals with how to win the shorthanded no-limit hold'em cash games that are so popular among online players. It is his prowess at the short game that led Paul to his ninth-place finish in the Heads-Up No-Limit Hold'em $5,000 buy-in tournament at the 2006 WSOP, and his follow-up victory in the televised National Heads-Up Poker Championship, where he outlasted the best and most famous players in the world while capturing the title. In this important chapter, Wasicka shares the many insights and advanced strategies he has developed along his path to success in big-league tournament poker.

SHORT-HANDED ONLINE NO-LIMIT HOLD'EM CASH GAMES

Paul Wasicka

INTRODUCTION

This chapter deals exclusively with short-handed online no-limit hold'em cash games. Short-handed means playing at a table of no more than a total of six players. There are short-handed tournaments as well, but those are a lot less prevalent than cash games, so I won't be covering them here.

The beauty, as well as the curse, of short-handed games is that they're action-packed. With so much play, they can be incredibly fun and quite profitable. Tread carefully though. Also called "6-max" tables, these games are some of the most volatile out there.

Since fewer players are at a six-max table, hand values go way up. Also, the blinds come around more frequently so it usually isn't worthwhile to just sit around and wait for premium cards. You'll have to expand your range of playable hands. For example, a K-J is mediocre at best in a full ring game, but at a short-handed table, it's definitely a hand you'll want to play. But that's what makes short-handed games so much fun—the action!

In poker, decisions often are based on personal preference. When I say something isn't profitable, that simply means it doesn't work for me. A number of playing styles can be successful in short-handed games. In the pages that follow, I've outlined some strategies that work for me, but this isn't to say that my style is the only profitable one out there.

BANKROLL MANAGEMENT

Bankroll management is arguably the most important thing in poker. Many great players go bust because they have poor bankroll management and fail to adjust for the extreme volatility of higher stakes short-handed games. Short-handed games are much more volatile than ring games so you'll need a bigger bankroll than at a full table. Most online short-handed games have a maximum buy-in of 100 big blinds. For example, if you're playing a $1/$2 game, the most you can sit down with is $200. Depending on how risky you are with your bankroll, you'll need about 35 buy-ins at whatever stakes you play to have a sufficient bankroll; 50 buy-ins would be ideal. So if you're playing $1/$2 no-limit games, your bankroll should be between $7,000 and $10,000. If at any point your bankroll falls below 35 buy-ins, I'd recommend you drop down a level, although some people are comfortable assuming more risk. Any amount lower than 20 buy-ins is dangerous.

Another bankroll consideration is the number of tables you're playing at once. Playing multiple games simultaneously means sitting down with a much larger percentage of your bankroll at risk. That feeling of vulnerability can have a negative impact on you while you're playing. I recommend starting with one table and only adding another one once you are comfortable with the table dynamics.

One nice feature on some sites is the addition of a time bank to cash game play. If you have a tough decision, you can opt to use some or all of your one minute mulligan (for lack of a better word). I love this feature and use it all the time when I'm trying to replay a hand to make the correct decision.

WINNING FUNDAMENTALS

PLAYING FEWER TABLES

You really should limit the number of short-handed tables you play to no more than four. I actually recommend no more than three, because it's important to watch hands that you aren't involved in. I usually sit at three tables and spend any extra time scouting other tables to see if I want to move. Maximizing profits is a fine balance between seeing as many hands per hour as possible and having the concentration and time to gain information on your opponents.

PLAYING REGULARLY

When you're playing online, it is important to play regularly. In the absence of a live game where you can look for physical tells, it's absolutely vital to know your opponents. Figure out who the regulars are and start looking for patterns. After a while, you should be able to describe each player's style including his strengths and weaknesses. This knowledge will help you to stay away from playing with the best players.

TIME OF DAY

A lot of professional poker players like to keep regular hours during the day, so a noon session might not be optimal if you're looking for weaker competition. Action frequently picks up around dinnertime on Friday or Saturday nights and continues through the weekend. Another good time to play is early Saturday or Sunday morning when you can catch people who have been playing all night and may not be at the top of their game. Every now and then, you'll see an increase in action after a major sporting event. These can be some of your most profitable days.

TAKING NOTES

When you're playing online, you should be taking notes. Keeping a book is one of the most important factors in becoming a successful online poker player. Since you're playing short-handed, you'll quickly get a feel for how people are playing. Write it down. Most sites have a note-taking feature that makes it easy. Keep in mind that most notes are saved to your actual computer so that if you play on multiple computers, you won't have access to notes stored elsewhere.

When you take notes, be specific. Don't just write, "This player is an idiot." Write, "Thinks my overbet on the river is the goods" or "Capable of a float out of position against an aggressive player." Make sure you note which cards each player is raising with (and in what position) so you'll be able to remember that person's range.

When you see an opponent make a play that doesn't make sense, try to figure out that player's motivation. Does he have a history with the other player? Is he setting up an image? Or is he just getting frustrated? The whys are just as important as the play itself. If I've only seen a person make one questionable play, I'll note my thoughts but I'll include question marks until that player repeats his or her behavior. For example, if someone has to show down a squeeze play that went awry, then I'm not going to assume that he is always squeezing with bad hands. I'll write something like, "Likes to squeeze??" Once I see the behavior repeated, I'll remove the question marks and start adjusting my play accordingly.

WHEN YOU SEE AN OPPONENT MAKE A PLAY THAT DOESN'T MAKE SENSE, TRY TO FIGURE OUT THAT PLAYER'S MOTIVATION.

It's also important to update your notes. I'll frequently play with someone who has major holes in his game, but then six weeks or three months later, he becomes a solid player.

Finally, if you're in a big pot with someone, check your notes on that opponent. Notes are only good if you read them. I've made the mistake of bluffing in a spot that should have worked until I read my notes that said, "Completely incapable of folding, even in obvious spots."

TABLE SELECTION

Before you enter a cash game, carefully select a good table. Good table selection is especially important in short-handed action because each person plays a more significant role in making up the table dynamic. Having two short stacks in a ring game, for example, isn't nearly as annoying as having two short stacks at a six-max table.

Begin your session by looking through all the available tables. If nothing looks good, consider starting your own game or not playing at all.

Another important consideration is your spot at the table. In general, it's good to sit to the left of short stacks, loose players, and people you know to be solid. When two seats are open next to each other, always take the left-most one so that a new player—whom you may know nothing about—won't have position on you.

MULTIPLE SITES

Good games come and go at different sites all the time. Pay attention to these opportunities. If you can build a bankroll on a few different sites, you'll give yourself the most flexibility when it comes to scouting all the games. A great way to do this is with transfers. Virtually all poker sites allow free player-to-player transfers. You can transfer money to a friend on Poker Site A in exchange for his sending you money on Site B. This way, when a juicy game suddenly materializes, you won't be hamstrung by having all your money sitting in the wrong site.

NO EGO

When it comes to poker, an ego will only cost you money. It's easy to feel bulletproof in your own house, safely tucked behind a big computer screen. And it's tempting to believe that you can outplay anyone, but keep in mind that the best poker players aren't the ones who try to outplay everyone. The best players are the ones who win the most money. Period.

Sometimes, for whatever reason, a session just doesn't go your way. Maybe you make a few moves that don't work, people stop respecting your raises, or you realize that you're not playing your best. When this happens, it's extremely important to live to fight another day. There's no point in turning a bad session into a devastating one. Since you're playing online, there will always be a game waiting for you when you're ready to play.

> THE BEST POKER PLAYERS AREN'T THE ONES WHO TRY TO OUTPLAY EVERYONE. THE BEST PLAYERS ARE THE ONES WHO WIN THE MOST MONEY.

Sometimes all you need is a fifteen-minute break. If you decide that your equity is still there, it's okay to sit back down. But don't hesitate to walk away. Even the top pros have losing sessions. Some of my best sessions have been ones where I lost, but I didn't lose nearly as much as I should have, given the circumstances. It's hard to not be results-oriented, but the only thing that matters in the long run is how well you play.

ONLINE TILT

Going on tilt online can be a lot easier than it is in live games. For one thing, you're in the privacy of your own home so it's easier to go berserk when something unfortunate happens. For this reason, I sometimes like playing in coffeeshops. Most importantly, it's often a lot harder to walk away when you are losing online because, unlike live play where you have to reach into your wallet to reload, all you have to do online is click one little button.

ACTUAL GAME STRATEGY

ADAPTATION

If you ever have to show your hand, it's essential that you immediately adjust your play. The only information about you that your opponents have to go on is what they've seen on the screen. Intelligent opponents will constantly make adjustments based on the information they've received about your play, so it's important to remember what they know of you. When you have to show a bluff, immediately say to yourself, "Okay, this guy just saw me check-raise with nothing. The next time I check-raise, I'd better have a hand." This is especially important the shorter-handed you play, because as fewer players are at the table, the match becomes more of a personal grudge match and less about hand values.

NO GARBAGE

No matter which strategy I use, when I build a pot, my hand will almost always have post-flop potential. For me, hands like

K-2 and 10-4 simply are not profitable. I don't hit miracle flops with these trash hands often enough to make playing them worthwhile. Furthermore, anytime I catch even a little piece of the board with them, I never know where I stand, and my cards are often dominated.

For instance, let's say that you raise with K-7 suited. This is a bad hand. Okay, now imagine that an opponent calls. The flop comes K-Q-9.

Hand in Action

YOU

OPPONENT

FLOP

You're not going to want to fold because you have top pair. But at the same time, you don't want to get it all in. You have a terrible hand because you don't know whether you want your opponent to call, raise or fold. Many players might raise you in a situation like this with an inferior hand such as Q-J to force you to make a very tough decision. If you don't have a desired outcome formulated in your mind, it's difficult to act. Knowing where you stand is an essential part of maximizing profits and minimizing losses.

STEALING BLINDS

Unlike a tournament where stealing blinds is crucial, it really isn't necessary in cash games. If you're sitting with $2,000 at a $10/$20 table, winning $30 in blind money is relatively insignificant. The real reason to raise in a cash game is to build a pot because you have a hand with a lot of post-flop potential.

BLUFFING

Your bluffs are going to get called a lot more when you play short-handed. Unlike ring games, players are not as willing to let go of any pair at the six-max tables. Therefore, use caution when trying to bluff someone out of a pot. Using this knowledge, it becomes that much more important to value bet when you are confident that you have your opponent beat. Ironically, a lot of times your opponent will be more likely to call you the bigger you bet, depending on your table image, so play around with the amounts of your value bets to see what is most effective. Often, I like to make my value bet 1.5 times the size of the pot.

If you are caught bluffing, you can make it a good thing as long as you are in the right frame of mind. Instead of being upset at your opponent for calling, or at yourself for making the play, think of how are you going to adjust your play and use a new table image to your advantage. Most sessions, I look forward to the time when my bluff gets called because that means I'll start getting a lot more liberal calls from my opponents, who will start calling down huge bets with mediocre hands. I've been called all in many times with hands as weak as king high before.

AGGRESSION

When you're playing any form of poker, it's important to be aggressive, even more so at short-handed tables. You want to put maximum pressure on your opponents. You don't want your opponents to win a pot when all they have is middle pair. Force them to either wake up with a hand or fold. You also don't want a player with a weak hand catching up because you likely are going to have to pay them off. Make it tough on your opponents. If you put someone on a hand that can't call a raise, you need to make the necessary move. The old poker mantra bears repeating, "There are two ways to win a pot: Have the best hand, or bet and force the other person to fold."

Since online games tend to be more aggressive than live ones, it's important to know the tactics of counteraggression. The best way to do this is by focusing on playing position, trapping, and being aggressive yourself. I like to battle preflop aggression with aggression of my own. Very rarely will I flat call a loose-aggressive player, especially out of position. I'm usually going to either reraise or fold because it's really hard to put a loose-aggressive player on a hand. Post-flop, I'll either trap or take a stand, depending on the vulnerability of my hand. Obviously, it depends on the player, but I rarely make a big fold short-handed.

PLAYING STRATEGIES AND HAND RANGES

A WORD ABOUT STRATEGIES

I'm not going to lay out the perfect six-max strategy because it doesn't exist. I will offer some general tactics that can be profitable in the right situations, and briefly list the strengths and weaknesses of each one. I think it's important to incorporate all of these strategies into your game.

THE BLUDGEONER

Bludgeoning means doing three things: attack, attack, attack! This is an aggressive style where you're not going to fold any pair or draw. When you have K-Q and the flop comes J-9-4, you feel like you've just flopped the nuts.

Bludgeoning is about stealing pots. As a bludgeoner, you're going to be betting big. The "Bet Pot" button is your friend. You're going to be frustrating people and getting them to start calling you with very marginal hands. You're never going to make a big laydown. It's a fun style to play!

If you have A-K and the flop comes 3-4-5, there's no way you're folding. Likewise, if you have K-10 on a J-10-4 board, folding won't cross your mind. Often you'll bet, hoping someone raises so that you can go all in. You're trying to force your opponent out of his comfort zone. It's a volatile style, but it can be extremely effective.

The Strengths of Bludgeoning

Bludgeoning can be very successful because you accumulate chips quickly. A typical hand: someone raises to $60. You make it $200. He calls and then folds to your continuation bet. Do this repeatedly and you'll have a stack in no time. You'll also be frustrating the other players. They'll either have to hit hands against you or start gambling, and a lot of people don't want to do that.

When you're bludgeoning the table, it's important to know when to put on the brakes. Most players have a boiling point. They get frustrated and start putting in a lot of chips with mediocre hands. When this happens, you need to stop stealing pots and only bet when you have a big draw or a hand you're willing to go with.

A bludgeoner is usually stealing, not bluffing. In other words, when all the chips go in, he often has a good hand. Since people usually associate a bludgeoner with a bluffer, bludgeoners almost always get paid when they hit. Therefore, when you decide to use this strategy, you should not bluff or slowplay.

Weaknesses

An obvious weakness of this strategy is that since it's very aggressive, you're going to experience a lot more variance than if you were playing more conservatively. When you go through a cold streak of cards, it can be frustrating and difficult to refrain from going on tilt.

When to Bludgeon

This style works best when your opponents are scared or playing passively. It also works well against calling stations because you won't be bluffing—remember? Bludgeoning doesn't work well against other aggressive players because they play back frequently. When your steals are working, bludgeoning can be very effective, but when people start playing back at you, you'll need to adapt.

GETTING CRAFTY

The next tactic is being crafty. Finesse players do everything possible to disguise their hands. For example, they might limp with A-A, or run a squeeze play with 7-9 suited. Crafty players make a lot of semi-bluffs. They take small stabs at lots of pots. People playing this style don't throw their weight around: they call more frequently, make odd bets preflop, and often try to trap their opponents. A typical bet ranges from one-third to two-thirds of the pot. Crafty players are the type that will float (call a raise with nothing) or mini-raise the river on a bluff. They might bet $20 into a $500 pot trying to induce a bluff.

The best crafty players make moves based on what their opponent has. In other words, hand reading is one of their biggest strengths. They are also good at knowing what their opponent will do in certain situations. They sense when an opponent thinks that a river bet twice the size of the pot is a bluff. If you're going to play this style, you should sit as deep as possible to allow yourself the total arsenal of moves. This allows you to play the big stacks and short stacks at the table differently.

Be careful. If you play this style, you are going to be bluffing a lot, but it's important to keep yourself in check. Some bluffing is good, but you don't want to bluff so frequently that you lose all credibility.

Because this style of play focuses on outplaying your opponent, you can be tempted to expand your range of starting hands. Undisciplined players start deviating from the game that was working for them. It's easy to allow your starting hand requirements to deteriorate from playing only solid hands to playing almost any two cards. Keep in mind that it's almost never profitable to play complete garbage.

Strengths

The benefit of crafty play is that it's extremely difficult for opponents to put you on a hand. Unless they have the absolute nuts, there's always a chance that they're drawing dead. Crafty players will get it all in much less frequently than bludgeoners. Typically, when all the money goes in, crafty players are going to have either a huge hand or a very strong belief that the other person has absolutely nothing.

Weaknesses

The biggest drawback of this strategy is that sometimes opponents are too inexperienced to know what's going on. A crafty player will often try to tell a story, but sometimes opponents just don't get it. It's not that they don't believe, it's that they aren't picking up what you're putting down. You can wind up making moves in pots that would work on good players but fall flat against inexperienced players.

When to Get Crafty

Getting crafty is most effective against very aggressive players whom you think bluff too often. The best time to rebluff aggressive opponents is when your reads become increasingly accurate. Crafty players struggle against calling stations because their game revolves around bluffing. Remember, we're talking about playing short-handed. You want opponents to fold as often as possible because you will usually have a weak hand. By definition, calling stations don't fold often, so bluffing regularly will invite disaster. Also, being crafty against a very tight player can be dangerous because tight players typically have good hands that they aren't willing to fold. You can't convince anyone to fold the nuts!

THE META-GAME STYLE

The meta-game style focuses on the game behind the game. Most of the time, the cards really don't mean much. You're primarily playing your opponent by exploiting the circumstances. This style can be extremely effective online because people aren't expecting it. The cornerstone of the meta-game strategy is in applying precedent to specific situations. Knowing that other players are looking for patterns, you establish one and then use it to your advantage. You want players thinking, "He always bets pot on a bluff," or "He only three-bets preflop with huge hands."

The meta-game style involves taking detailed notes on your opponents, and knowing what makes them uncomfortable. You need in-depth information on their tendencies. The meta-game requires looking for patterns in hand histories. This style is the most manipulative. You want to live inside your opponent's head and use both your patterns and his patterns against him. You're in a psychological battle.

The difference between a crafty player and a meta-game player is that crafty players take advantage when they think their opponent is weak, while meta-game players create a strategy based on perception. A meta-game player is very conscious of the flow of a match.

With a meta-game strategy, it's especially important to know what you've shown down and what your opponent thinks of you. It may not matter that you've only been playing the top ten percent of hands. If you hit a rush of cards, even though you've only been playing premium hands, your opponent may incorrectly assume that you are playing like a maniac. Winning the meta-game comes down to understanding what your opponents know about you and what they are capable of—and then using their "knowledge" against them.

Strengths

Your opponent will have no clue what you're doing. He'll have no idea why you check-raised one time but min-reraised the next time. Once he thinks he's put it together, you've already adapted and moved on to a new approach.

Weakness

Sometimes you set something up and you run into a hand. If you're too busy running mind games, you might miss the fact that your opponent has a monster hand. If he calls on the flop and calls on the turn, that doesn't necessarily mean that he will fold to a third barrel just because you've shown him huge hands in the past. Sometimes he simply has a hand.

When to Play Meta-Games

Meta-games are successful against aggressive players and really high-level players. They only work if opponents are paying attention to what has happened in the session. The shorter-handed the game, the better. This style is best suited for heads-up play, but it can be effective in all short-handed situations. Meta-game strategy isn't successful against people who just play their cards regardless of past action. It also doesn't work well against calling stations.

HANDLING THE OTHER PLAYERS AT YOUR TABLE

SHORT-STACKERS

I don't short-stack and I don't consider short-stacking to actually be playing poker, but it's a common feature of the six-max landscape that you should be aware of. Basically, short-stackers are players looking to flip a slightly weighted coin. Their whole game consists of getting all the money in preflop. Their basic strategy is to sit down with around one-fifth of the maximum buy-in, wait until they have a decent hand and there's some money in the pot, and then shove in their stack. They are looking for a small edge and running that situation as frequently as possible. They are merely playing percentages, trying to eke out expected value (EV) wherever possible. It is difficult to be profitable using short-stacking as a strategy against knowledgeable opponents. It's consistent and thus a predictable approach, which is the antithesis of good poker strategy.

However, a number of good players don't really know how to handle a short-stacker. When a short stack goes all-in, people make mistakes by saying things like, "Oh, it's only $50," and then calling with a mediocre hand.

Not all short-stackers act the same, but they usually operate with a specific set of guidelines. As with any player, the best way to beat them is to figure out their hand ranges and use those parameters against them. Some short-stackers are relatively tight. Others play a much larger range of hands. Some will raise 100 percent of the time in the small blind if everyone folds to them. If I know that a short-stacker does this, I'll reraise 100 percent of the time from the big blind. Even if I get called when I have a terrible hand, the short-stacker knows he can't continue to relentlessly attack my blind. That, in and of itself, has long term value.

Short-stackers value position heavily. They can't afford to siphon many chips, so they are much more likely to play premium hands under the gun. Likewise, they'll respect your position. In other words, if you raise under the gun and a short-stack goes all in behind you, he is much more likely to have a premium hand than if you are in later position.

The shorter my opponent is sitting, the less I'll make my open raise because it's very common that a short-stacker will either shove all in or fold. A lot of the time, I won't have a hand that I can call all in with, so by decreasing my opening raise, I save a little bit of money if I have to fold. Run that scenario 500 times and you're looking at a significant savings.

The best way to counter a short-stack is to beat them at their own game. Often you'll see short-stackers min-raise preflop. Don't assume they're weak and just shove your chips in. If they min-raise and you have a hand you're willing to go with, min-raise them back. This forces them to commit extra chips to the pot, given the pot odds. They will either be forced to make a bad fold, in which case you take down the pot uncontested (which is ideal), or go all in, which would also be good. You're fine with their call because you're going with the hand no matter what comes on the flop.

For example, suppose you have A-Q at a $10/$20 table. A short-stacker sitting with $400 in front of you makes it $40. A lot of times in situations like this, I'll make it $80. If my opponent goes all in, I'm happy to call. If he just calls, I'll either pot-commit myself or go all in on the flop, depending on the texture of the board. Keep in mind there's already $190 in the pot and he has only has $320 behind him.

Conversely, you may have a decent hand, but one that you don't really want to go all in with preflop. The short-stacker min-raises and you flat call with K-Q. I like a call here because short-stackers aren't good at playing post-flop poker. If they were, they would be sitting deeper.

Once I've called, I'm very likely to check-raise all-in on just about any flop. With $80 in the pot, you can expect a short-stacker to bet around $50 to $60 whether he has a hand or not. Most of the time he'll have nothing. You have plenty of fold equity and you'll usually have enough outs to make this play profitable in the long run, even if you do get called. This isn't the only strategy against a short-stack, but the lesson here is to take a short-stacker out of his or her comfort zone. Put the pressure on the short stack and expose yourself as little as necessary preflop.

> SHORT-STACKERS AREN'T GOOD AT PLAYING POST-FLOP POKER. IF THEY WERE, THEY WOULD BE SITTING DEEPER.

ISOLATING A SHORT STACK

A lot of times, someone will limp and a short stack will raise behind him. If I have a decent hand that I'm willing to go with against the short stack (something like 7-7), I'll make a small reraise. I'm obviously committed to getting it in against the short stack, but if the limper goes all in for a full stack I can still fold. I would also run this play with a huge hand so the limper can't assume that I'll fold to a shove.

YOUR OPPONENT IS A MANIAC

It's important to be the aggressor at a table, but what if you're playing with a complete maniac, someone who doesn't know about the fold button? Being maniacal can actually be very profitable. These players put extreme amounts of pressure on their opponents, and it's not uncommon to see them run over a table for periods of time.

It takes a stomach to play against someone like this, but if you've got discipline and nerve, you're going to get paid. The way to counter someone who raises and reraises everything is to play into his expectations. Play passively and feed him some rope. Playing passively doesn't mean folding. It just means not raising.

Here's a good example. At a $10/$20 game, I raised preflop with 10-9 suited and got called by a huge maniac in the big blind. The flop came 10-6-4 rainbow.

Hand in Action

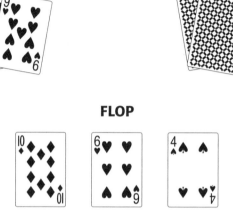

PAUL   OPPONENT

FLOP

The maniac checked, I bet two-thirds the pot, and he called. The turn was a king and he bet the pot into me. Rather than raising to protect my hand, I called. I wanted to induce a bluff on the river. If you are unsure what your opponent has, but know that you aren't going to fold, it's really important to add equity to your hand by selling weakness to induce a bluff for the times that your opponent has nothing. The river was an ace and again he bet the pot into me and I insta-called. He showed J-7. No pair, no draw.

The best way to combat maniacs is to reraise them preflop. Maniacs make their money by taking control of a hand and being able to represent anything postflop. They usually have nothing when they raise preflop. When you reraise a maniac preflop, you're taking control away from him and forcing him to narrow his range if he continues with the hand.

For instance, suppose he raises preflop, you reraise and he calls. The flop comes A♣ 9♣ 4♦. You continuation bet with your 10-10 and he raises. You shouldn't dream of folding here given his range of hands. He "knows" that you will fold if you don't have the ace, which is likely. You're pretty sure that he doesn't have a big ace because he probably would have re-reraised you preflop. He either has a mediocre ace, a flush draw, a middle pair, or absolutely nothing. Given his range of hands, coupled with how much money is already in the pot, this is an easy call.

> **THE BEST WAY TO COMBAT MANIACS IS TO RERAISE THEM PREFLOP.**

If you have a hand post-flop, you should think about how vulnerable you are. If I have top pair, I'll probably call down a maniac and let them do the betting for me. If I have a more vulnerable hand, such as bottom pair or middle pair, I'm more likely to reraise to find out where I'm at. Be careful when raising a maniac too often with weak hands because he is likely to push back even if he doesn't have any sort of hand.

The most important thing to remember is that you should never bluff maniacs. They are the most likely player to rebluff and push back with weak hands. They rarely fold; their game plan is to put pressure on their opponents. If you try to bully them, you're just asking for trouble.

TIGHT PLAYERS
You'll definitely encounter people who play tight at short-handed tables. I don't think it's an ideal strategy, but that's besides the point. Tight-weak players, also known as nits, wait for premium hands and hope to get paid off. They have very few moves and are usually very easy to run over.

Tight-aggressive players also have a small preflop range, but they are definitely capable of some moves. They know how to take advantage of their tight image by bluffing when they don't hit in the right situations.

Since tight players have such a small preflop range of hands that they play, it's often easy to put them on a hand. Against them, you want to play position heavily and stay away from trap hands, such as K-Q, A-10, Q-J. Suited connectors are ideal. If a tight player raises, I'll often reraise with a 10-9 suited. The raise disguises my hand, and if the right board comes, you will be in great shape to win a big pot. Ace-high flops are ideal against tight players because they will often be scared of the ace.

Be careful not to overplay hands against tight players postflop. If you raise preflop and a nit calls you, and he also calls your continuation bet, you should definitely proceed with caution.

PLAYERS WHO ARE BETTER THAN YOU

There is a good chance that at some point you'll run into someone who's better than you—or if that stings too much to admit, perhaps someone who's "equally good." Just avoid this player. If you like to play heads-up poker, don't sit at the same table with him. If you are playing six-max tables, you might not be able to avoid him entirely, but tread carefully when you're in pots together. I've seen players online blow through many buy-ins because they refused to admit that someone else had figured them out.

PLAYERS WHO ARE WORSE THAN YOU

When you realize you're playing against someone who is fundamentally flawed, you can do one of two things. The first is to see as many flops as cheaply as possible, and just wait to trap him. However, I usually prefer the second approach, which is to build pots with the weak player by isolating him preflop. Hopefully, he will donate his stack to you instead of the other vultures at the table drooling to get those chips.

ONLINE TELLS

Online tells are less concrete than live tells but they do exist. They generally fall into two categories: patterns and timing. Pattern tells are very specific to each player and they change as people improve. Online players tend to find a style that suits them and have a habit of playing very predictably. The best way to discover pattern tells is to check hand histories anytime a showdown happens. You want to know what each player did and why. Obviously, the more often you get to see opponents' cards, the better.

> YOU DON'T WANT TO BE GIVING OFF TELLS, SO IT'S IMPORTANT TO TAKE THE SAME AMOUNT OF TIME TO MAKE YOUR DECISIONS.

You'll pick up timing tells after you've played many hands with a person. When your opponent is just a little too quick to reraise you preflop, he may have a good hand. Likewise, when he bets out quickly on a flop, chances are the flop didn't improve his hand. If it had, he would have needed at least a second to think about his play. Keep in mind that a quick bet on the flop doesn't necessarily mean that he doesn't have a hand. It simply means that the flop probably didn't *improve* his hand, which may or may not already be good.

You don't want to be giving off tells yourself, so it's important to take the same amount of time to make your decisions. If someone raises and you know you're going to fold, you should still take some time before you do so. That way, when you're in a marginal situation that requires some time to think, you won't give anything away.

SPECIFIC SITUATIONS

FLOPPING A SET

I'll bet the flop when I hit top set only under three circumstances: if I've recently been caught betting into someone without a hand; if I have made a few unsuccessful continuation bets recently; or if I know that my opponent is either a calling station or overly aggressive.

PERCEPTION

Be aware of what your opponent has seen of your play, and use that information against him. For example, if I haven't been reraising preflop very often, I'm not going to wait until I have A-A to do it. Poker is always about deception, so the first time I reraise preflop, I'm probably not going to have a monster. I will, however, make sure that I reraise with a hand that has potential.

SQUEEZING

Squeezing occurs when one player raises, at least one other player calls, and then someone else reraises. For example, if someone raises to $60 at a $10/$20 table and two players call, you can make it $260 and possibly pick up the pot uncontested. Squeezing is generally a high EV play. This play is most effective when the initial raiser is very loose. You must be careful about your timing, though, because if the players at your table have been squeezing fairly often, good players will start trapping with their big hands.

In live play, people don't squeeze as often because players tend to be deeper stacked and less likely to fold preflop. Squeezing is a bully play that usually works best when the average stack is around 100 big blinds. As always, if you've squeezed once or twice, you'd better have something when you do it the third time.

SMALL POCKET PAIRS

Set mining, calling a raise in the hope of flopping a set, is better suited to nine-handed play than short-handed games. There are a few occasions to set mine in six-max games, but it really depends on your opponents. If you think an opponent will ship his or her stack, then you might consider set mining, but generally I like to raise and reraise preflop with small pocket pairs. It also depends on how much squeezing is going on at the table. If a lot of people are squeezing, then you definitely should not try to set mine.

Also, small pocket pairs are much easier to play in position. If you're out of position, don't call a raise and hope to flop a set because if you don't hit, you'll be in a tough spot. You probably have the best hand but you don't want to call a big bet to find out. It's just a bad situation.

THINKING AHEAD

It's important to anticipate what will happen in any situation. That way you won't be intimidated when it does happen. Thinking ahead is especially important when you are changing your strategy so that you know what you'll do before it happens. Anticipate the possible consequences of your actions before you act. If you bet, is your opponent likely to raise? If so, how much? What will you do in response to his raise?

IF IT'S WORTH PLAYING, IT'S WORTH RAISING

It's okay to mix in a limp every now and then, but in short-handed games, you generally want to be opening the pot with a raise. Raising preflop prevents the blinds from flopping miracle hands, makes people pay to play against you, and narrows the range of your opponents' hands.

CONCLUSION

There is no perfect six-max style because playing styles and table dynamics change so frequently. Just remember to figure out what your opponents are doing and find the best way to exploit their tendencies. In this chapter, I've outlined several successful ways to maximize your profits and minimize your losses online against different types of players.

I've given you rough sketches of players you're likely to encounter and strategies that have worked well for me. Just remember that each player is different, and nothing works forever. Practice good table selection and intelligent bankroll management. Then mix in elements of the different styles I've outlined for you. Using these tools, I'm confident that you will enjoy lots of success playing short-handed poker online.

MIXING IT UP

DAVID WILLIAMS

David Williams burst onto the poker scene in 2004 when he won $3.5 million for his runner-up finish at the World Series of Poker championship tournament. The young, college-educated poker player survived most of the final day as a short stack, but kept up the good fight against Greg Raymer, the eventual World Champion, and his other opponents with a solid and aggressive strategy.

To push aside any misgivings that his incredible performance was a one-time wonder on the tournament trail, David followed his big score at the WSOP by finishing second to Daniel Negreanu just four months later at the World Poker Tour Borgata main event. Later that year, the poker whiz won his first tournament, the Five-Diamond World Poker Classic $1,500 Limit Hold'em event at the Bellagio in Las Vegas.

With his good looks and easygoing nature, David is a media favorite wherever he plays. *Card Player* magazine featured him on its cover, and both *Playboy* and *All In* magazines described him as the "future of poker." He plays poker online at his sponsor site, Bodog.com, and conducts seminars for the Playboy Poker Camp. In addition to his tournament victories, Williams has placed high in World Poker Tour tournaments at the Mirage in Las Vegas and the Bay 101 in San Jose.

Williams' topic for this book, how to mix up your play in no-limit hold'em, provides great advice on how to confuse your opponents and keep them guessing about the value of your hand. In the Anatomy of a Hand segments, the brainy Williams analyzes the play of pivotal no-limit hands to illustrate the merits of varying your play, thus increasing your chances of winning against crafty opponents.

MIXING IT UP

David Williams

INTRODUCTION

Top players have two things in common. First, they're aggressive. They take the action to their opponents. They put bets, raises and reraises on the table, forcing the other players to respond to their initiative. They win a lot of little pots that way. Second, they are unpredictable. They *mix it up*. They enter the pot as easily with A-K as with 6-4, so that when opponents play with them, they're not sure where they're at in the hand. As a result, opponents make errors, often critical ones, for all their chips.

Mixing it up is the subject of this section. You'll see how powerful it is to play unpredictably. In 2004, when I won $3.5 million and second place in the main event of the World Series of Poker, it completely changed my life and made many dreams come true. I owe it all to the very same principles I talk about in this chapter—mixing it up. Even though, at the time, I was primarily a tight player, I was aggressive about it. When I played a hand, I could do things differently than the image my opponents had of me, and I won key pots that way.

THE POWER OF BEING UNPREDICTABLE

To make money at poker, you have to mix it up, which pretty much means that you need to be unpredictable. When you are competing against good players—which you are going to do most of the time in big cash games and certain big tournaments—being unpredictable makes it hard for them to play against you. Mixing up your play confuses your opponents and makes it difficult for them to figure out the right moves to make against you. When they can't put you on any certain hand and don't know for sure where you're at, any fancy plays they contemplate against you become risky and expensive—so much so that you may induce them into making big mistakes.

When you're unpredictable, you make opponents *think*. Often, their problem is that they don't know what to think! You've confused them by mixing up your play—calling, raising, reraising, re-reraising and check-raising with all sorts of hands in all sorts of positions and situations. Inevitably, when your opponents don't know what to do, they make bad plays and unintentionally put chips into your stack.

Your unpredictable play can intimidate some opponents to the point that they won't want to risk a mistake playing a marginal hand against you. As a result, they will only give you action with strong hands. Thus, when you face resistance from these types of players, you can be fairly certain they have the goods. They've become predictable.

THE PROBLEM WITH BEING PREDICTABLE

A predictable player is the easiest to play against, because you can almost always put him on a hand. You can figure out how he might bet. You can raise him without having to risk going up against a wide range of hands. If he doesn't have it, he is going to lay his hand down, and when he puts the betting back to you, you pretty much know he has a big hand. He plays by a pattern, and if you pay attention to that pattern, you'll profit from using that knowledge against him.

It is not just the weak and passive players that are easy to read—the crazy player also fits into that category. You know that he is always going to raise. You can count on him. You can limp in with your big hands, because you know he is going to put chips into the pot for you. And of course, when you're sitting there with pocket aces or another monster hand, it's a good thing to have him in the game.

Being predictable makes it easier to play against an opponent. I'll make some crazy plays on opponents I can read. Sometimes I'll make sure they see my crazy play, or I'll make sure they don't, and then I'll do something totally opposite of what I've led them to believe I'll do.

You cannot allow yourself to fall into a pattern by doing the same thing over and over again. If everyone knows where you're at in a hand, it's like your cards are face up. You can't really win. In the long run, you might get some play from people who aren't paying attention, but good players will know that you have fallen into a pattern—you do this when you have it, you do that when you don't. Being predictable cuts way down on the profit you can make on your big hands. Way down. You won't get any value on your big hands, and you won't get any free cards on your weak hands. These holes in your game put you at the mercy of your opponents.

ANATOMY OF A HAND

Here's an example of how unpredictable play leads to profits. I was playing in a loose cash game where everyone had a pretty deep stack. One player raised preflop, about three times the big blind, and got a caller. The play came around to me in late position. I also called, holding the 6♥ 2♥.

The Flop

The flop came J-8-6 with two diamonds.

Hand in Action

DAVID

JOE

PREFLOP RAISER

FLOP

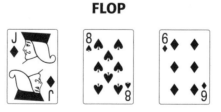

The preflop raiser bets out $2,000, and my opponent—let's call him Joe—just calls. Now, obviously, I didn't think my

6♥ 2♥ was the best hand, but I didn't think either of my two opponents' hands was very strong either.

I decided to raise to take the pot right there. Here's my thinking: The first player who bet out usually did that with marginal hands. By watching his play, I knew that when he got raised, he'd usually dump his cards. He was betting to see if his weak jack was good on the J-8-6 flop, or maybe he had A-8 and was betting out knowing that if he got raised, he could dump it. Then when Joe just flat-called his bet, he let me know that either he had a very big hand, or he didn't believe the guy either—but he didn't have the guts to raise.

My opponents didn't know where I was at because I do a lot of weird things at the table. And whether this move worked out or didn't work at all, I knew it would throw them off and give me future value. Weird plays add to the image I want to set up with my opponents. I don't want players to ever know what I am doing or what I have. And that's how I go about maximizing the profit I make from a poker game.

But how much should I raise? I considered raising $10,000, but I thought it was kind of risky to put that much in on the hope that both my opponents had nothing. If I get reraised or called, I've invested $10,000 in this pot—a lot of chips for my hand.

After weighing my options, thinking through my hand, and factoring in who my opponents were, I decided that the best course of action was to raise $3,000 and make it $5,000 to go. It was a small enough raise that I could dump my hand if I got reraised, only losing $5,000. Also, it confused my opponents. By raising only $3,000, it looked like I didn't want them to fold, like I'm trapping them. My small raise made it hard for either of my opponents to figure out what I was doing. They certainly couldn't figure me for a 6-2.

Sure enough, as I expected, the player who originally opened for $2,000 just looked at his hand and threw it away—he didn't even think. So I was probably right about him—he probably had a weak jack or an 8. He didn't feel like playing with a possible call behind him or another reraise.

It was on Joe. With the opener gone, we were heads-up. He stared at me for a while, thinking and thinking. He didn't know what to do. He had already made a comment about my playing unpredictably, so I knew I had him where I wanted him—confused. Finally, he decided to just call, which I was fine with, because it showed that he wasn't too confident in his hand. It also confirmed that he didn't know what to think. He even had a confused, "What's going on here?" look on his face.

I'm pretty sure that he would have raised me if he thought that he had a good hand. But I thought I was in a good spot, because he didn't know where I was in the hand. I was happy to have position and figured that I was going to have to fire another barrel to take the pot. As long as the turn card didn't help him, I thought a big bet would win the pot for me on the turn.

The Turn

The turn was a miracle 6♣. Now I've made trip sixes and am thinking, "Now I don't have to bluff. I can try to get value out of the best hand."

As soon as the 6♣ hit, Joe quickly grabbed two $5,000 chips and pushed them into the pot. He didn't put too much thought into this play, so I didn't really think he had jacks full, eights full, or anything like that, because then he might have done some Hollywooding. He might have thought about how to extract the most chips out of me, or at least see if I looked as though I was going to bet if he checked. It appeared to be more of a defensive bet. Maybe he had a weak hand in the middle, one that wasn't really bad, but wasn't awesome either.

In any case, he wanted to make sure that I didn't get a free card. It seemed as though he had the A-J and wanted to make sure that a bet went in on the turn. The diamond card didn't come, so I knew that his possible flush draw was not there, and he wanted to make sure that I didn't get a cheap flush card on the river.

I decided that I was going to at least call; there's no way I'm folding trip sixes. But do I want to raise? I can raise here, but I'll only get called if he has a 6 himself with a better kicker and he was just trying to get tricky. Or maybe has a full house, which I didn't think he had.

I decided not to raise because if he just had an A-J, I thought he would throw it away. If I just called, maybe an ace would come on the river and he'd go off for a lot of money. Or maybe another 6 would come and he would think his jacks full was the best hand. So I called for $10,000. I had position and was going to see what he did on the river.

The River

The river card was a diamond, that's the first thing I noticed. Maybe the flush got there and he had been betting a diamond draw. But the J♦ was out. I look at the river a little closer—it's the 2♦.

Hand in Action

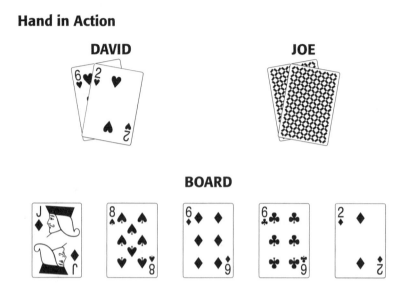

I've filled up with sixes full of deuces! Joe shook his head and checked. I didn't think he would check a flush. And I didn't think he would check a full either, because he would want to make sure he got paid for it. So I was pretty sure I had the best hand. It's possible that he had a 6, maybe an 8-6, but the diamond had to scare him a little bit because it looked like I had a flush.

We both had about $30,000 left and I'm thinking, "How much should I bet? How much can I get out of him?" One option was to move all in for $30,000. The pot had about $30,000 in it, so that would be a normal bet in this spot. If he had something, he would call. I could also underbet for $10,000, $12,000 or $15,000 to try to make sure that I got paid. But I figured he would know that I probably was not going to bluff small, that I would have something if I made those bets.

I wanted him to think I was bluffing. A small bet would look like I had made my flush and was only betting a small amount because the board was paired, and I didn't want him to raise in case he had a full house.

I decided the best option was to go for the full $30,000. I Hollywooded for a while and finally said, "I'm all in," making a big production of it. I really wanted him to think I didn't have anything and was just trying to pick up all that free money.

Joe really was confused. He thought for about five minutes. He looked at me and said, "You could have a flush draw, but I don't think you'd raise me to $5,000 with a draw. You could call with an 8. I've seen that before, but you couldn't have eights full and I don't think you have jacks full. Wait, I think you have eights full; that makes sense. You could have raised me on the turn, and you probably would have raised more on the flop."

My opponent was on the verge of putting a lot of money in bad because he couldn't put me on a hand. And playing my 6-2 the way I did, who could?

Finally, someone said, "Come on, Joe, we've got a game and we can't sit here forever."

Joe was still looking at me and said, "I don't think you have a flush."

I sat there praying to get called because I knew he didn't have me beat. I was bummed at the diamond, because if it had been the black deuce instead, I think he would have called me for sure.

Finally, Joe turned up a Q-J.

Hand in Action

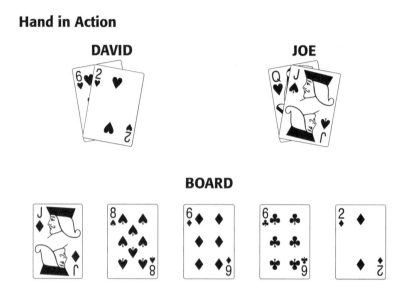

DAVID

JOE

BOARD

He has a pair of jacks. "I can't do it," he moans as he folds his cards and I rake in a nice pot.

Post Mortem

Joe had actually contemplated putting in $30,000 more with Q-J because he couldn't figure out what I had. Had I been a predictable player, someone who did the same thing all the time, either of these two possibilities would have gone through his head:

1. He knows I'm a rock and there's no way he could even consider that a Q-J would be good.
2. He knows I'm a total maniac and the Q-J has got to be good.

Even though I didn't get called, the fact that he even thought about it showed that the next time he had the chance in a similar situation, he might call. I ended up showing Joe my 6-2. "How the hell are you in this pot with this hand?" he asked. Normally I wouldn't show a hand like that, but I wanted to further confuse him, to show him that I can have anything at any time, make any move—I can raise him $3,000 with a garbage hand and I can raise him $3,000 with the nuts.

I didn't have to raise $3,000 more on the flop—it was one of those marginal situations that could go either way. I could have just dumped the 6-2 and moved on with my life, although I would have been a little sick to watch the hand play out. I also could have raised him a little bit, as I did. Those were the best choices. It was one of those situations where I could make either play, but I thought there was value mixing it up and confusing my opponent to the point that he didn't know where I was.

Had I raised and they both had folded on the flop, I was fully intending to turn over the 6-2 and show them that I could raise with bottom pair and no kicker. I wanted them to think, "This guy's got bottom pair, no kicker!" There may not be a lot of value in that situation, because most of the time I'm probably going to be behind and lose the pot, but it creates a new element they have to think about. *That's* the value.

In poker, you don't only play with the cards in front of you, you play for future hands and future pots—you build or play off impressions you've created from earlier hands. The next time, I might be able to raise with top set and my opponents would give me two things—credit for a garbage hand and lots of chips. I may lose $5,000 or so now, but I create a situation that allows me to win back more later.

> IN POKER, YOU DON'T ONLY PLAY WITH THE CARDS IN FRONT OF YOU, YOU PLAY FOR FUTURE HANDS AND FUTURE POTS—YOU BUILD OR PLAY OFF IMPRESSIONS YOU'VE CREATED FROM EARLIER HANDS.

By playing so many hands in so many different ways, your opponents cannot figure out what kind of hand you hold. Sometimes you'll have it, sometimes you won't. Sometimes you'll make a big bet, and sometimes a little bet. Your opponents won't know if you're going to call with bottom pair or if you're holding top set. Being unpredictable gets you a lot of value and confuses your opponents as to how to play against you. As a result, they end up making mistakes.

Joe got up and walked away from the table for a while. Finally, he came back and said, "Man, I never can figure out what you're doing, what you have, or what you're going to do. I don't like playing with you, I don't know what's going on."

And that's exactly how you want your opponents to feel.

SETTING THE GROUNDWORK FOR TRAPS

Most players have patterns they follow. They do the same thing and play the same hand the same kind of way. Top players don't have patterns, but the average player doesn't notice that. They'll just see what they see, and think you play just like they do. So if you can burn an image in their heads about how you play hands, you can set them up to make mistakes. You can trap them and take all their chips if the right situation presents itself. To illustrate this point, here is a profitable trapping move I played in a hand not too long ago.

A TRAP IN ACTION

We were playing $100/$200 no-limit hold'em, and I picked up two nines under the gun. The player to my right had a $400 straddle so it was up to me. I considered raising, but if somebody behind me called, I wouldn't know where I was at. I wanted to follow through with a continuation bet on the flop, but if it came king-something-something (or big card-something-something) and I got raised, I wouldn't know if the raiser had a king or if he didn't have a king on that board. I wouldn't know what to do. That's the problem with playing out of position.

I decided that the best plan of action was to limp in for the $400 and try to see a flop without a raise. If the flop came scary, I could just lay it down with no further cost. If I hit a 9 for my set, I could check and try to trap somebody.

We pick up another caller, and then the small blind raises it $1,500, about the size of the pot. The big blind folds, the straddle folds, and now it's on me. I really want to see if this guy has two aces or whatever, because he'll move in on me if I reraise him. If he's making a move with A-J or some garbage hand, I want him to fold it and to give me the pot and the money.

So I raise him $5,000 more, making it $6,500. The other caller folds and it's back on the raiser. He calls without hesitation. My first impression is that he doesn't have aces or kings. And I believe he's an inexperienced player who doesn't know how to trap. If he had aces or kings he would have pushed on me. I think my boy probably has a hand such as two tens, or maybe two sevens or two eights. Maybe he even has A-J, but I doubt it. I don't think he would call $5,000 more with A-J out of position. I put him on some kind of pocket pair.

There's $14,000 in the pot. I've got position on the small-blind raiser, so I figure I can make moves on him.

The flop comes A♥ 2♦ 7♠.

Hand in Action

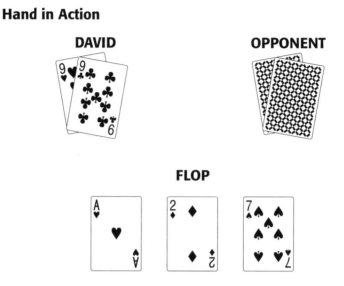

DAVID

OPPONENT

FLOP

He looks at his hand, kind of frowns, and checks. I'm thinking, "Okay, he must have two tens, two eights, something like that." I ask him how much he has left. He counts his money out and tells me he's got $15,000.

I bet the $15,000, all his chips. I'm not going to bet $10,000 and then fold for $3,000 to $5,000 more if he pushes the rest of his chips in. I decided that moving him in was the best course of action. If he's got even two kings, it's hard for him to call. With the ace out there and my reraise, I figure he's going to dump his hand, move on, and I'll pick up the money.

Well, the guy insta-calls and I'm like, "Damn, what is this hand?" He turns over A-Q. I have only two outs in the deck. I turn over my nines to make sure my opponent and the rest of the table see that I'm capable of moving in with any hand. I don't think my opponent made a good play, calling $5,000 more with A-Q out of position. More often than not, he's not going to connect with the flop and will have to fold to any continuation bet I fire into the pot. And after I limp and reraise, most likely I'm going to have aces, but to his credit, he didn't put me on that.

The fact that I just moved in and dumped $20,000 and didn't even have an ace formed an impression. He's thinking, "This guy is a bluffer." That's his image of me.

Sure, he picked up a big chunk of change off me, but I thought about what he thought of me, and was able to turn that against him just one orbit later. Here is how that hand played out.

PLAYING OFF A PREVIOUS HAND

I limp under the gun with a pair of threes. Two players call, and he makes it $1,200 from the small blind. I call and the other two guys also call. The flop comes 3-2-K. I've flopped a set!

Hand in Action

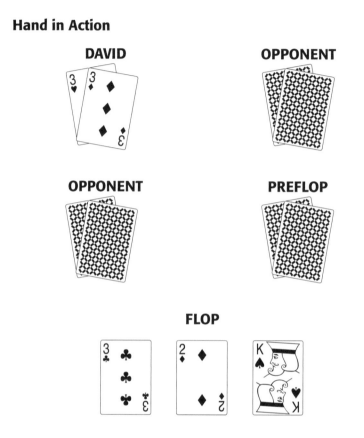

DAVID

OPPONENT

OPPONENT

PREFLOP

FLOP

The raiser pushes out a continuation bet for $3,000. I look at my options—calling and raising—thinking how to get more of his chips. Against a lot of players I might try to trap and just call, because if he has two queens, he might just throw them away. But I know what this guy thinks of me based on the hand we played previously, so I casually grab $13,000, making a $10,000 raise, and dump it in the pot. I'm counting on him to recreate that previous hand where I didn't even have an ace on an A-2-7 flop—I only had those two measly nines.

Everybody else folds and it's back on the preflop raiser. He looks at me and quickly shoves in around $40,000, all the money in front of him. I know what he's thinking: I must have two tens, or some crappy hand and I'm just making another move.

I called his all-in with little to no fear. He needed two kings underneath, the only hand that would beat me. He turns up A-K, one pair, pretty much the same hand as the A-Q he held before. I turn over my set. I've got him almost drawing dead. The turn comes a 7.

Hand in Action

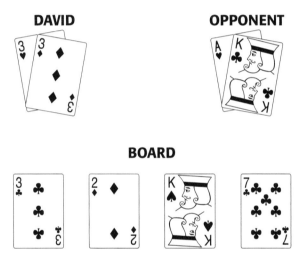

DAVID

OPPONENT

BOARD

Now he *is* drawing dead and I rake in a huge pot. Busted, he's looking at the empty felt in front of him, scratching his head. "I didn't know what you had. I had A-K, what was I going to do? I couldn't put you on anything."

The lesson here is that I used my image, my unpredictable play, to set him up. What happened on that earlier hand dictated how I played out this hand. I could tell by how this man played—what he had done previously—that he was going to put it all in with that king-high flop. Most players in that situation are not going to raise with a set. They're going to straggle along, just call, and set a trap. But the hand we played a few minutes earlier was still fresh in his mind. It was an important hand to him. He had doubled his chip stack and was all pumped up.

I made that move, raising $10,000 on the flop, strictly based on our recent history. I got the money back I had lost on the earlier hand plus all his original money. If you add up these two hands, I pretty much won the first one—it just took me a roundabout way to get those chips back that I had loaned him for a few hands!

UNDERSTANDING YOUR IMAGE

In the hand above, I showed how image can be used to induce an opponent into making a critical mistake for all his chips. Let's talk a bit more about image and the profit you can get from exploiting the information you create in your opponent's mind.

If you're going to make sketchy moves, such as playing a 6-2, it's important that you pay attention to the kind of image you are creating, and the kinds of situations and hand histories you are setting up with opponents. If you know that you and a particular opponent have played this kind of pot and you've done this against him, he's going to figure that you will do that kind of thing again. If you can do something totally different, you can really throw him off his game and trap him. You can manipulate him to get the result you want. Whether you want to find out something cheap, or fold your hand, or you want to get a lot of money in the middle and try to double up, you can use the history you have with that opponent to take his chips.

A lot of players talk about noticing what your opponents have done—he's done this, he's done that—but one of the key things that people forget is noticing what your opponents think about what you've done. You need to take poker psychology to that next level. You can't just consider what opponents could possibly have, or what patterns they've shown, or the kind of hands they are playing: You also want to consider what they think of your play and play off of their perception. Think out each hand, not only what hand he could have, but how the two of you have played hands together previously. What did he do? What did you do? What does he think you did? When you are thinking about his perceptions of you and playing off that, you have a huge advantage. That's where you can really use past history.

When you confuse an opponent, he can't figure out what you have. You may have played a lot of hands, but you haven't necessarily played that many hands against *him*. Against each individual player, you may only play one or two significant pots, or pots that he's paid attention to. Those pots are going to be in his head. You want to focus on the important hands, process the relevant information, and analyze what those hands meant to your opponent. And then you surprise him by doing something totally unexpected.

The hand I described in which I had pocket threes against big slick shows how profitable it is to be unpredictable. When my opponent bet $3,000, I had a decision to make. Did I want to call? Did I want to move in for $40,000? Did I want to raise him just enough to get him to move in on me? It was clear that I didn't want to raise half my stack, because then he would know that I was to call. I wanted to raise it enough that he thought I could fold my hand. That's why I dropped my chips in casually (in the same style as the previous hand we played), so that he'd think I had that same type of hand again.

Always think about all the elements of previous hands you've played with an opponent before you decide what the right move is. That way you can figure out the best way to get him to make a mistake. That's the key.

ENVIRONMENT, PERCEPTION AND IMAGE

Positioning yourself for player-to-player matchups on individual hands is important, but image extends to *all* the players at your table. Whenever you play, the table is full of opponents and you have to take that into consideration on every hand. That's part of the feel you need to develop to get the most out of your current environment and the image you've created. Thus, it's important to be aware of how the people around you are playing—who is in charge, who is not, who is passive, and who is aggressive. Also be aware of how opponents perceive you, the hands they think you play, and the hand history you have with them. What do they think you are doing?

Use that information to determine what style to play and what gear you should be in. See what fits that environment. When my opponents are passive, I'm going to play aggressively. When they are playing aggressively, I'm going to play tight. Basically, you do the opposite of what the table is doing because they are going to be doing what they think is right for how you are playing. Get the whole table doing what you want them to do and making mistakes against you. That's how you can accumulate chips in poker.

WORKING OFF YOUR IMAGE

It wasn't long after that sixes-full hand that Joe and I got involved in another hand together. We both still had the 6-2 hand fresh in our minds and I was going to use that situation to my advantage. He was rattled and confused, setting up perfect conditions for me to make all sorts of moves.

Joe raised from middle position to $1,200 and I considered my options when the action came to me. I was pretty sure I wasn't going to reraise and I wasn't going to fold because Joe raises a lot of hands. I had already made up my mind that I was going to call, but I didn't want to call right away. I wanted to do some things to throw him off. I cut out $1,200 from my stack, plus what a raise would be, like $5,000 more. I stared at Joe for a while and looked back at my chips. Finally, I grabbed the raise and the bet, put them both in my hands and then tossed in only the bet.

As I was pulling the $5,000 back into my stack, Joe says, "You wanted to raise me?" He said my call smelled like A-Q, which was kind of funny because I actually had K-Q.

The Flop
Everyone else folded, so Joe and I saw the flop heads-up. It came Q-7-3 rainbow.

Hand in Action

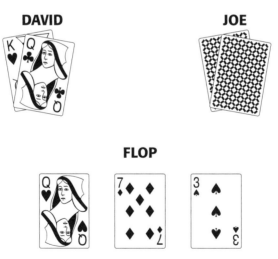

He bet $1,800 into me. I thought he might put me to the test and reraise me big if I raised it $8,000 more, even though he might only have pocket jacks. If so, he probably thought his jacks were the best hand and I was raising to represent A-Q.

I had to ask myself, "If I make it $8,000 here, am I prepared to call a big reraise if he reraises to $18,000? It's a scary situation. He might reraise thinking I don't have anything." But you've got to have guts to be successful in no-limit. I was prepared to get my chips in the middle if he moved in on me, because I really didn't think he had me beat. He probably thought I was just messing around. I decided to raise $5,000.

He called and I'm thinking, "Damn, he obviously doesn't believe I have a queen or else he has A-Q and he's really sick because he actually told me what his own hand is."

The Turn
The turn came an 8 and he checked. I played out some scenarios in my head. I could bet, but I'd have to bet big, because we had already put $8,000 each in the pot. I'd have to make it $15,000 to put pressure on him. I didn't want to risk getting raised out of the pot. If he moved in on me, did I really want to call $30,000, $40,000 or $45,000 on the turn with just K-Q? I didn't even have an A-Q! I'd rather see the river for free.

Maybe a king will dribble off, maybe a queen, so that I could get some money out of the hand. Plus, by checking the turn, I could keep the pot small. Then, if the river came a deuce and he bet $15,000, I'd only have to call $15,000 to see the showdown. But if I bet $15,000 on the turn and he raised me $45,000, I'd have to call another $45,000 just to *get* to the river. So I decided to play it safe and check, because I didn't have that strong a hand.

The added valued of the check in this situation is that it disguises my hand. It may appear to him that my raise on the flop was just a move and that I've given up with my bluff. Therefore, he may value bet a hand worse than queens, such as jacks or tens. Or if he checks, he may call with one of those hands, thinking that I'm bluffing.

The River
On the river came a 4. The final board is Q-7-3-8-4.

Hand in Action

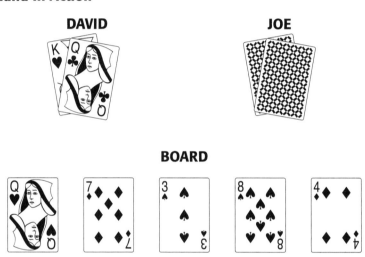

He checked again. I didn't think he had a 6-5—there was no way—and I was pretty sure all the other cards were irrelevant. It came down to whether he had A-Q or A-K. I knew he didn't have a set—he was not going to check a set in this spot—because it looked like I was going to check behind him. He must have a hand that he didn't want to put many chips in with, so I ruled out pocket aces and kings as well.

Now I had to think, "Does he have A-Q or not?" That's the only hand he could have to beat me. I could value bet him small, but I'd hate to bet $10,000 and have him call me with A-Q and lose another $10,000. I could make him lay down A-Q if he does have that, but I didn't want to risk $40,000, about the size of the pot, just to get him to lay down his queens. I decided that the best bet was to check. The pot was small enough, as we had only put in about $8,000 each.

"A-Q is good," he says, which means that K-Q is at least a tie. I turn up my K-Q and he shows me K-7 as he mucks. He had been dead to a 7.

Since he didn't know what to do after I raised him on the flop, I was able to get two free cards to see the showdown. He had to check to the river, because he didn't know what I had, and he was out of position.

It's one of those situations where he's thinking, "Is this guy raising me with a 6-2 again?" That's why he called my $5,000 raise on the flop. If any other player had raised him $5,000, I guarantee you he would have thrown his hand away. But because he'd seen me raise him small with bottom pair previously, I was able to extract an extra bet.

That was my thinking at the time. But on reflection, I probably should have bet the river, because, judging by the way he played his hand, there was no way that he could have me beat. Given my loose image, he probably would have called a value bet.

MAPPING OUT A PLAN

A lot of players watch the play only when they are involved in the hand. When they're not, they're looking at their I-pods or their buddies. Foolishly, they will not pay attention to the preflop if they're not in the pot. For example, one player will raise preflop, another will call, and the hand will go down to the river. If you ask them afterwards which one of these guys raised preflop, they won't know. How can you play the player and know the right moves to make when you don't know how that player plays? What moves he makes or doesn't make?

Watch all the hands go down from beginning to end. Remember what happened and the dynamics in play. You need to be able to think through a hand properly. Once you know the cards and have figured out how someone plays his hands, you can make the best plays against him when the two of you get involved in a pot.

Once you've mapped out your table and have pigeonholed your opponents according to how they play, you're ready to map out your plan. I sometimes divide my opponents into four types of players: Weak/Passive, Unbluffables, Players that Make a Lot of Moves, and Top Tier Pros. Here's how I would play against each type.

WEAK/PASSIVE PLAYERS

Attack the weak players and the passive players, the ones who don't have the guts to make moves. If I know a guy likes to limp and then often folds to a raise, I'm going to raise him frequently. I'm trying to keep him out of hands. When a player doesn't play back at you—he just gives up—he's the best kind of opponent you can have. This type of player is rare, but they are out there. You don't want to bluff guys in this category who like to pay off, because they will call you.

When you have a hand, just value bet them to death, pushing chips into the pot on every street and getting as much money as you can out of them. When they are betting into you and you have a big hand, you don't want to raise and scare them away. Just continue letting them do the betting for you. The pros call it "Walking the Dog." When a weak-passive player checks and you think you have the best hand, you want to bet just enough, an amount you think they will call, so that you can extract the most chips possible out of them.

UNBLUFFABLE PLAYERS

Don't tangle too much without strong hands against the unbluffables, guys that just call whenever they have some kind of hand. You are going to get hurt if you bluff at them too often. These players love K-Q and they aren't laying it down. Wait until you have a solid hand and punish these calling stations. When unbluffables put a chip in, they defend it. They don't necessarily raise you back, but when they do, they have a monster. *They have it.* They don't fold either. They love their pairs. If they hit top pair, they'll hang on. You want to see cards as cheaply as possible until you make something solid—then you can punish them.

PLAYERS THAT MAKE A LOT OF MOVES

And then there are the very active guys who are just all over the place. They're raising and reraising. They're making all sorts of moves. These are the players that you are going to try to trap and punish. Be careful about raising if they're sitting behind you, though, because they'll often pop you back. Ideally, you want to act after them. When you are in position, you can trap them with your big hands and take advantage of situations when they put too much money in with the worst of it, which they're prone to do.

TOP TIER PROS

Top tier players know all the styles and mix it up. They're the ones you can't predict. These players can raise a lot, they can call, they change their game enough so that you don't know what kind of hands they might have. You don't want to mix it up against these top pros very often. If you have a good hand, of course, you want to play it. But if you have a marginal hand, I suggest staying out of the pot. Just go ahead and let them have it. There is no reason to play against a top pro—unless you have the goods—when there are a lot of weak players at your table and you can get your money elsewhere.

It's important to set your ego aside. If you happen to sit at a table with nine good players, you have to do what you can, of course. Usually, however, there are weak spots at your table and those are the spots you want to attack.

BLUFFING CONCEPTS

A lot of people see star players on TV and they emulate them by raising every time. They push out big bluffs and follow that with more big bets, thinking that the pros get to these final tables by bluffing all the way through. People watching final tables on TV often don't realize that the pros don't raise every hand; they only raise when they think it's necessary, when they sense weakness, when they have a good read on the table, or when they believe they can get away with what they need to get away with to take down the pot.

There is a lot more to bluffing correctly and getting away with it than just pushing chips into the pot. You have to realize that what you see on TV is just a snapshot of highlights that don't represent what really occurs at the poker table—the nuts and bolts, grind-it-out poker that is interspersed with bluffs, value betting and all sorts of other moves. Bluffing is an art and a science. To be successful at pulling off bluffs, you have to make your moves in the right conditions and circumstances.

BLUFFING CONDITIONS

If you are going to mix it up, you'll be putting in your fair share of bluffs. The question is, what are the best conditions for your bluffs to be successful? We touched on some ideas earlier; let's explore this topic a little more.

MIXING IT UP

Three basic elements are essential to a successful bluff. As you'll see, they all interrelate with each other. Here they are:

1. Bet Sizing
2. Avoiding Patterns
3. Knowing Your Opponents

1. Bet Sizing

Proper bet sizing is critical to maximizing the amount of money you can extract from opponents when you have the best hand, and minimizing what you lose when you don't. It's a super critical component that pros deliberate over every time they make a bet. They're always asking themselves this unconscious question: What is the best bet I can make here to either induce my opponent deeper into the pot or get him out of it? In the first case, you want to make the bet as big as possible to extract the most chips while keeping him in the hand. And in the second case, you want to make it as small as possible to minimize your risk while getting him out of the hand. Either way, you must perform a fine balancing act to achieve your goal.

The second reason for bluffing—trying to get an opponent out of a pot—is the more common. It's risk versus reward. If you put too many chips into the pot on a bluff, you risk losing too much unnecessarily. That's a bad short-term result. If you put too few chips in, you may get a caller or induce a reraise and have to muck your cards. It's not easy to know the right amount to bet when bluffing, but if you pay attention to your opponents and the dynamics of how they feel about you, you'll get a feel for what's best in each situation.

In addition to the two key factors of bet sizing mentioned above—betting too little to achieve the result or risking too much—there is a third element you must be aware of: You don't want your bet size to telegraph whether you're bluffing or not. It comes down to the main point I've been stressing throughout this section: You must mix up your play to keep opponents off balance, which leads into the next element essential to a successful bluff.

2. Avoiding Patterns/Predictability

Avoid falling into a bluffing routine where you do the same thing every time you bluff. If you do that, it won't be long before your motives are transparent. If you've exposed your game by playing into a pattern, your bluffs will appear to your opponents as bluffs, and they will be able to capitalize on this by taking your chips in situations where you're hoping to take theirs. They'll get to know you, which is what you don't want to happen.

You don't want to bluff—or not bluff—with too much frequency, because if you're doing one or the other too much, your opponents will realize it. You want to show the nuts as often as you're caught bluffing, so that your opponents won't know whether you have it or don't have it.

That's why it's so important to stay unpredictable. On the other side of the coin, you want to get to know what your opponents are doing. That's the third prerequisite of pulling off bluffs and taking your opponents' chips.

3. Knowing Your Opponents

The third condition that is essential for a successful bluff, and one that is equally, if not more important than the others, is knowing your opponents. In the 6-2 hand I described earlier, I happened to know the first guy was betting with a weak hand and was not going to call my raise because he had a pattern. I *knew* how he played. So I started raising him every time he bet into me. If I raised preflop and he called me, he'd bet out on the flop to determine the value of his hand. That was his calling card. But if I raised him, he'd muck.

Had the opener in that three-way hand mixed it up and sometimes raised with the top set, or sometimes checked and called, I really wouldn't have known what to make of his play. And I couldn't have gotten away with my own aggressive moves. I was able to win that pot because I was able to gauge what my opponents' patterns were and what they would do. If I didn't know anything about those guys, I probably wouldn't have raised it $3,000, and would have given it up.

BLUFFING PRINCIPLES

1. Don't risk too much on a bluff

Just make small bluffs and do it against players who are predictable. You can figure out what predictable players are going to do most of the time. Granted, no one is going to do the same thing every single time and you can be wrong about what you assume they have, but you want to put your bluffs on the table in situations where you have a fair range of what kind of hand your opponents have and what their reaction to your bet or raise is going to be. If you think your opponent has nothing and you are bluffing too, you don't want to risk too much to get him to fold. However, there are exceptions. If you are fairly confident about your opponent's hand, you can put down a big bluff to make him lay down his cards.

2. Make small concise bluffs that have a high winning percentage

I pick my spots carefully, but try not to risk too many chips in case I am wrong. This leads to the next principle.

3. Don't bluff off all your money

As I discussed earlier, one of the problems people pick up from watching TV is the idea that the whole game is about bluffing. Viewers think the key to poker is bluffing and start bluffing everybody every time they play poker. But bluffs only work until the *last* time you try one.

One play I don't like is making a big bluff against an opponent that you suspect has a big hand, but is the kind of player that might lay it down when a mountain of chips are pushed out there. You have to stay away from those plays. They're dangerous, and while it's a lot of fun and profitable when they work, it's disastrous when they don't.

CHECK-RAISE BLUFFS

A lot of players like to use check-raise bluffing as a weapon to take pots away from opponents. When it works, it's great. You feel like the master of the situation as you rake in your opponents' chips with a ballsy bluff. But that's only when it works. When it doesn't, you pay a steep price, one that you can avoid with an even better play.

Often, a better move than check-raising against a predictable player is to lead into him with a big bet instead. Your bet is less than what the check-raise would be, and you find out the same information—if you know he is not the kind of player who is going to make a move or just call you with air. When you find it out in just one bet, it's a lot cheaper. That's something Daniel taught me. It was a mistake I was making a lot—check-raise bluffing. By leading out with the bluff, you risk less and enjoy the same percentage of success.

That's one of the reasons I don't like check-raising a player on the flop. You risk double your chips—your opponent's bet plus your raised amount—to find out if he's serious about continuing to play with you. If you get reraised or he moves in on you, you've lost a lot of chips.

Of course, you want to pick flops that are most conducive to success. If I am against a predictable player and I know that he is coming in with the goods, I'm not going to mess with him if the flop comes with a king, queen or jack. It often hits his hand and he's not afraid to follow through. And I avoid dumping chips into his pot. That's why, as I keep stressing throughout this chapter, you have to know who your opponent is, what kinds of hands he plays, what he's likely to do, and what he thinks you're doing.

PLAYING AGAINST PREDICTABLE PLAYERS

If an opponent raises and you know that he's the type of player that only comes in with solid hands, you usually should be in position with hands that are not easily dominated. Say that you're against a player that always raises with premium hands such as aces, kings, big slick, and perhaps A-Q. You don't want to call his raises with A-J or A-10 because it's easy to get trapped. You are better off with cards such as 7♣ 6♣ or 4♥ 5♦, hands with which you can gauge where you're at if you hit the flop.

If you can put your opponent on a range of hands, then you know he always has a big pair or A-K when he's raising up front. You'll be in position to steal pots from him simply because you know how he's playing. You know if he checks the flop, he probably has A-K and missed and you can fire at it. You can make calls when you know that your flush draw is good. These are the kinds of opponents you want to play against because you can figure out what they have.

You can call with weak hands if you know that you can take a pot away from a player. Now, if a predictable player is behind you, it's a little harder to play, but the fact that you know the range of hands he plays makes it a lot easier. If you know he's the kind of player that fires on the flop every time he has a hand, then you can use it to your advantage and can check your big hand. If you don't hit, you can check with confidence knowing that if he bets, he has you beat.

If an unpredictable player has position, you're at a disadvantage. You don't know what he'll do; sometimes he is going to check behind you and sometimes he is going to bet—you never know where you are.

If you get a really good feeling that a flop hit an opponent and he'll always follow through, you may want to check if you're up front. If he always makes a continuation bet, and follows through when you check on the flop, you have an edge because you know how he plays. I'll often check-raise players like this as long as the board is not too scary. For example, if the flop is raggedy, and you check and he fires, you might check-raise to take the pot away from him.

PLAYING AGAINST UNPREDICTABLE PLAYERS

Unpredictable players are a lot harder to play against, which is exactly why it's a bonus to be one. Against unpredictable players, you really have to play straightforward poker. You can't try to mix it up with them because most of the time, no one hits and they will try to win those pots by outplaying you. Unpredictable players can fire with the nuts or raise you with nothing.

And that's why position is so important if you're playing against a tough player that mixes it up. All great players understand the value of position. When you're against an unpredictable player *and* out of position, you're in a vulnerable situation.

PROTECTING HANDS

You don't want to be out of position against a tough, unpredictable player. It's risky and generally too costly to find out what your opponent has when you have to act first on three subsequent streets. If he has position, you have no clue where he is or what he is going to do. You've either got to show your weakness first, or tip off your hand by checking or betting first. If you don't hit and don't make a move, he is going to fire out some chips and you are not going to know where you are.

You want to be in position so that you can gauge what an unpredictable player is doing and make better decisions. Let's say that you are dealt a pair of queens and a player who is always mixing it up raises in front of you before the flop. He raises with 9-8 and the flop comes 8-9-2. In this situation, your queens are dead meat. This shows the danger of just calling preflop against this type of player. Take the lead. If your opponent makes it $150, raise it four to five times that amount. Make it $700 or $800 to shut him down. Don't allow a tricky opponent to get in cheap with these kinds of funky hands that can snap off your good hands.

Let's look at another situation. A tricky player comes in preflop for three times the big blind and you pick up a pair of queens in position. Against a Daniel-style player who might be raising with a variety of hands, you need to take control of the hand by raising. If you just call, you won't know where you are. Your opponent could be the kind of player who might have 9-8 or two aces. Unless you get this information up front—and you will get it by making the pot expensive to play—you won't know how to proceed after the flop. Your opponent might flop some kind of crazy hand and bust you, as in that 9-8 versus two queens example. This kind of disaster happens all the time to players who allow opponents to sneak in with garbage.

I recommend playing your good hands strongly in position against unpredictable players. You need to protect them. Say the blinds are $25/$50 and a tough player makes it $150. If you make it $700, that's enough of a raise that there is no value in your opponent calling with a hand such as 8-9, 5-6, or a pair of threes. If he has a real hand, say aces or kings, he is going to reraise, and you can evaluate where you're at in the hand. You can lay your cards down. Granted, a few players have the balls or the guts to re-reraise you with 8-9 and make you lay down your queens, but most good players won't do that. They figure that if you are raising that much in position, you've got the goods and are willing to go with it all the way. They're usually going to lay it down and you are going to pick up the money.

BEING THE AGGRESSIVE PLAYER

One of my favorite plays in a big tournament is to keep raising hand after hand. In one tournament, I raised twelve straight hands and no one reraised me. I think that's the strangest thing. Most of the time my opponents will just fold, but sometimes a player gets frustrated and makes the biggest mistake he can make. He'll just call. I love when a player just calls! The best defense against me is to reraise, because then you make it hard for me to call, unless of course, I actually have the cards to play along. But when an opponent just calls against a raise, he has no clue where I am. I could have aces, I could have pocket eights, I could have *anything*.

When the flop comes, most of the time it won't hit either of us. If I've been raising and he has just been calling, I'm generally going to fire another pot-size bet. If he hasn't improved, he'll be gone, leaving all the chips behind for me.

For example, let's say that I raise with 5-2 against an opponent who picks up two jacks. He's frustrated that I'm raising every hand, but instead of pushing me off the pot, he just calls. Then

I get a 2-2-7 flop, fire out again, and my opponent decides to take a stand and move in on me.

Hand in Action

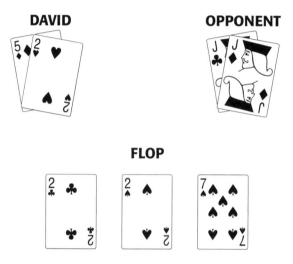

DAVID   OPPONENT

FLOP

What he doesn't realize is that instead of raising me preflop and forcing me to fold my 5-2, he's allowed me to see the flop for nothing extra. I'll bet $1,000 and the jacks will move in for $20,000 out of frustration. He figures I can't have anything. But now I've seen three cards, and if I've connected in some kind of hard way—which I did in this example—I'm going to bust him. That happens more often than you might think. I'm getting a windfall of chips, and he's broke and going home. The huge mistake here is that he opened the window by just checking preflop and giving me the chance to hit something he couldn't even guess at.

Several years ago at the $25,000 World Poker Tour championship, I was at a table where I was raising every hand and controlling the table. I had accumulated a big stack. About six people limped in on a hand and it came around to me in the small blind. I looked down at a Q-10. It was not a good hand, but with everybody limping, I saw no strength out there. I did a little Hollywooding, and then raised about the size of the pot.

A pro that I've often played with, one of the limpers, starts looking at me. He knows that I'm capable of raising with anything to steal and grab some chips. I'm thinking, "Oh God, don't reraise me, because if you do, I gotta fold." And he says, "Call!" It was music to my ears. I'd rather everyone folds, but when someone just calls, it's second best—it's more money in my pot. I get to see the flop for nothing extra and with a bonus—I get a chance at busting him if I flop good and he gets tricky. If neither of us hits, I am probably going to win the pot because I'll bet it and he'll likely fold. I'm hoping that the flop has the right texture. If so, I can jam the pot and get him to lay his hand down.

The flop came Q-Q-7, an amazing flop for me. I decide to fire out for $20,000, because I think he's going to make a mistake and just call. If he's got a strong hand, he'll move in on me and try to force me out. I thought about getting tricky and check-raising, but if I check-raise, he's probably going to lay down a lot of hands figuring I've got something scary. There is also the danger that he might check behind me and get a free card. I figure that he called me with something preflop. Hopefully, he has a hand that he's comfortable with and will move in on me.

Sure enough, he immediately moved in on me with some absurd amount of chips. I thought that he had a hand, like a big pair. If he had a queen, he would have done some thinking about how to extract the most from me. If he had a big hand, he wouldn't want to scare me off, he would just call and try to sucker me in. So when he moved all in like that, I immediately figured he had aces or kings, because the board was Q-Q-7. If he had A-Q or something like that, I think he would have contemplated sucking me in a little bit, or he could have a hand like Q-J, but I didn't think he would go all-in with that. He didn't know what I had. The way I had been playing, he could picture me with any hand. But for him to move all in, I figured he wanted me to go away; he didn't have a hand that wanted a call.

I had a big stack three times his chips, so I figured that if I was wrong and he had sucked me in, I'd still be in good shape. "I call," I said.

"You got the queen?" he asks.

"Hell, yeah, I've got the queen. Why else would I put all this money in?"

He turned over two jacks, the turn and river came blank-blank and he was busted.

Post-Mortem

When my opponent moved in on me, his raise was about seven times my bet. That was a big mistake. If he had raised me three or four times my bet, he at least would have left himself the option of laying down his hand if I moved in for the rest of his chips. The problem was that he gave me a big overlay.

Sure, most of the time I'm not going to have a piece of that flop, but a lot of times I might not even fire out at that flop against a player of his caliber. I might check, try to get out cheap. I could also, as I did, fire out and try to trap him. I have so many different moves, he really didn't know what to do. Out of the frustration of not knowing where I was in the hand or what to do, he just decided to move all his money in and hope for the best.

If he had reraised me preflop about four times my bet, I'm going to have to throw my hand away unless I have aces, kings, or maybe queens. And if I have one of those hands, he's going to find out right there that he is beat. But if he just calls me and I have one of those big pairs, and the flop comes 2-7-3, he's going to find out his mistake for all his chips and go broke if he moves in on me. He can find out preflop for a lot less, and make me lay down my Q-10.

However, once the flop came, he had already trapped himself and had no options. His preflop mistake didn't allow him to have a good play, a correct play, after the flop. He had already pretty much committed himself. He was going to put all his money in on the flop unless there was an ultra scary board such as A-K-Q. That's why his preflop call was a mistake.

When players just call like that preflop—as opposed to raising—they allow this kind of situation to occur. He could have flat-called me or he could have folded on the flop, but it's hard to fold his jacks if he just called me preflop. Because he flat-called me preflop, his only option on the flop was to either move in or raise me. For example, if he had eight units and I bet one, he then raises me to four. If I move in, it's hard for him to fold since half his chips are already in the pot.

Because he could not accurately predict what I had, he didn't know what to do against me. If I'm the kind of player that always pumps it up out of the small blind when someone limps in, he knows that most of the time I'll have a hand that he can get me to fold if he raises me. Or if I'm the kind of player that never plays a hand—I'm just a rock who sits there and sits there and sits there and finally I raise—he can lay down his jacks because he knows I'm coming in with the goods. Because I mix it up so much and am unpredictable, it's like, "Does he have it? Does he not have it? What am I going to do? I don't know, I'll just call."

One of the great advantages about mixing up your play is that your opponents will make mistakes against you. They'll let you take control of a hand. In this example, I was able to induce an opponent to make a big mistake in a tournament because he couldn't figure out what kind of hand I had.

TOURNAMENT CONCEPTS

In a tournament, you can only do so many things and make so many moves. At the end of the day, you only get a certain number of big hands. You're only going to get aces or kings a few times. The bottom line is that you can't rely on cards to get to the final table, you have to use your wits to get chips and go deep. Of course, luck plays an element, but to give yourself the best chance of winning, you must be aware of opportunities and take advantage of them.

Here are a few ideas to improve your chances for tournament success.

STUDY YOUR OPPONENTS

How do you decide what style to play when you sit down at the start of a tournament? First, get to know your players. The first thing you do is look around and evaluate each person. If you've played with someone before and have a history with him, you want to think back about hands you've played. Is he tight or aggressive? Does he mix it up? Is he weak? Is he a trapper? I go over the history of how these opponents have played with me before and get familiar with them again.

Most of the time, you won't know how your opponents play. They'll be new players you've never sat down with before. So your top priority in the first few rounds of a tournament is to survey the other players at your table. You want to know how they are playing, who is active and who is playing a lot of pots.

Find out which players are raising or reraising, and which ones are calling.

Pay attention to where the action is coming from, who's stealing the blinds, and who's defending them. If there are players who don't look interested in saving their blinds, you can attack those spots. Find out which players are limping and calling raises, and which ones are limping and folding to raises. Develop a sense of who is limping weak and where you can raise and pick up a pot. And definitely pay attention to the kinds of hands players are showing down. Are they aggressive or conservative in their betting? Are they limping, raising, folding, reraising, checking it down, check-raising a lot, or checking their big hands and betting their weak hands?

Keep an eye out for players who call overbets and don't understand the values of their hands. They present great profit centers because they are willing to put a lot of money in when often, their best strategy is to check or fold, or even raise. Don't bluff this type of player, just value bet him to death. Wait for your good hands and punish him. A lot of players will call with K-Q and if they hit a queen, they aren't going anywhere. They don't care what else comes; they are not giving up their hand. For example, if you get A-K and he has K-Q, you can make him pay full price if the flop comes something like 10-K-4.

To sum up, your first order of business is to learn how your opponents play. Then formulate your game plan. Knowing your opponents is the basic foundation for making the right moves.

OPENING GAME PLAN

You shouldn't start off playing too aggressively right off the bat. First get a feel for how the table is playing, see what everybody has, and if anyone is going to try to mix it up. I'll play straightforward poker for a few orbits just to see what people are doing. I don't get out of line right away because I first want to feel out the table, see what kind of dynamics are in play. I look for situations where I might flop a set and get my money in, or make some big hand and double up off somebody early. I'm looking to win a few big pots to build momentum.

Once I get it rolling, I can start playing my game. I'll make some crazy call with an ace-high and everybody will say, "Wow, how do you do that?" Once you strike fear in your opponents, they don't feel comfortable playing with you. Then I'll turn it up a little bit. I can make a big bluff and show 7-high, and everybody will laugh, because I might have bluffed a guy out of a big pot. After a few moves like that, opponents won't want to play pots with me. They'll feel outclassed. You can't push around the pros, but players that you don't know—and you'll see a lot of them in tournaments—start backing down to raises. You beat them into submission.

A lot of players try to get too creative, too fancy, and make too many moves right out of the gate. If you do that early in a tournament, you're probably going to go broke. It's better to play straightforward poker in the beginning against weak players, and wait until they make mistakes by putting their money in badly.

Once you have a deep stack, and your opponent has a deep stack, you can start to get creative and throw your little touches in there, mix it up, and try to get them to make more mistakes. A lot of players take it too far, however; they get creative at the wrong time. For example, someone who never plays a hand raises. Player B then reraises him. This guy has never raised a hand—what is Player B doing? It's clear that the raiser is going with his cards. Don't make those kinds of errors.

Of course, you can't always play in fifth gear. There are times to tone it down. You want to make your moves sparingly and be wise about them. Plan things out, pick your spots, and know when it's a good time to do something.

STACK SIZE DICTATES PLAY

In tournaments, the plays you make—and how you perceive the plays your opponents make—are greatly dictated by stack size.

I think the best stacks to play are the deep stacks or the short stacks. With a deep stack, you've got room to do all kinds of things. If a move doesn't work, you still have chips. It's not that you need an above-average stack to make moves and be unpredictable; you just want to have a big stack in relation to the blinds. Then you have plenty of room to make moves. For example, if the blinds are $100/$200, you can make moves if your stack is about $10,000 or more. Even though the average stack may be $20,000, or whatever, is irrelevant. Everything is in relation to the size of the pot and the size of the current bet.

With a short stack, it is different. If you are going to sit there and wait for aces and kings, your stack is going to dwindle away and you eventually will have no chips. Let's say you have a small stack, only ten times the big blind. As a little stack, you don't have much margin for error or room to make moves. You can't just splash chips out there; a bad move or two, and you'll be gone. You cannot afford to waste chips when you don't have a lot of them. As a result, you have to play in a fairly predictable pattern. Opponents will be able to put you on a somewhat straightforward range of hands.

But then again, if you have ten times the big blind, you can still be unpredictable and make an all-in move, which is very hard to defend against. Your bets are probably going to be bigger than the standard raise. You could have aces, you could have A-Q, you could have A-9—it's hard for opponents to figure out what you have when you make a desperate, short-stack move-in.

The middle stacks are the hardest to play. You can't really get too fancy or you'll become a short stack. You don't have much room. You'd like to get some momentum going, win a few pots with straightforward play, and build up your chips to have a big enough base to mix it up and play a big-stack game.

SMALL BLUFFS AND BIG POTS

I'll make small bluffs and small bets, but when I put a big percentage of my stack in, I pretty much have the goods. In tournaments, I'll create this image while playing small pots. I might bet a small amount with something like 7 high or jack high and someone will call me. And of course, I have nothing.

I show this crap with small bets and people think that when I make a big bet, the same thing must be happening. Man, are they in for a surprise! For example, I might flop a straight and raise an opponent six times his bet. He'll look at me and think about all the hands I've showed, how aggressively I've played. Surely I wouldn't move all in with a straight right there. And he'll end up calling with one pair.

This example underscores the point that the key at winning tournament poker is helping your opponents make mistakes against you. And that's why changing gears and mixing it up is critical. When your opponents cannot accurately guess where you are, or what you have, they make mistakes, and you win their chips.

THE MISTAKE FACTOR

You'd like to play perfect poker, but no one can. In some ways, doing well in tournaments is about how many mistakes you make and how costly they are. Beginners might play well for a while, but sooner or later, they nail themselves with a huge mistake and are gone. That's all it takes in no-limit hold'em,

> **THE KEY AT WINNING TOURNAMENT POKER IS HELPING YOUR OPPONENTS MAKE MISTAKES AGAINST YOU. AND THAT'S WHY CHANGING GEARS AND MIXING IT UP IS CRITICAL.**

just one bad play. Your goal is to make the least number of mistakes, and at the same time, entice your opponents to make mistakes against you. That's why I think Michael "The Grinder" Mizrachi is one of the best tournament players in the world. That guy always has a big stack and is always getting people to put their whole stacks in against him with just one pair. They never believe he has a hand.

The key to winning tournaments is getting players to make mistakes against you and minimizing the mistakes you make against them.

PLAYING THE ALPHA MALE

If I have the chips and the right table—that is, my opponents allow me to push them around—I try to become the alpha male. Obviously, if I'm at a table with all professionals, that's not going to happen. But if I get the right table, which happens often, I will try to take control of every hand, be the captain. I'll raise most of the hands, and reraise opponents as well. I'll tell the players when they need to fold, "Hey, you need to lay the hand down, you're not going to raise me, buddy. You think about it." I'm doing what I can to control them, sort of like pulling strings on puppets. And it works against some players.

Let me give you an example. Several years ago in the World Series main event, a new lady came to my table with a pretty big stack. She was wearing sunglasses and kept eyeing me. She was upset that she had come to this jungle where I was the alpha male. I was raising three times the big blind no matter what I had— my opponents were so submissive, I didn't even bother to look at my hand. I would raise and raise and raise and everybody would fold. Finally, she had had enough. I raised pretty big on one hand, I think I made it $2,500. In position, she made it $5,000, the minimum reraise.

It comes back to me and I'm trying to figure out my best move. I don't have any history with her or know how she's playing. She knows I'm playing a lot of hands. But she only raised me $2,500 more, which made it seem like she wasn't representing a very big hand. It seemed more like a tester, like she wanted to see if I would submit, if I would back down. I think I had something like 6-5, my standard junk hand. I decided to call, see the flop, and lead into her if I liked it. I didn't want to reraise her, risk a big bluff in this spot, because I wasn't 100 percent sure that her hand was mediocre.

The flop came K-Q-2. I studied her for a second; she didn't seem confident. Preflop, I think she wanted to see if I had a hand, but she didn't have the guts to raise me a real amount, like $8,000, to really see. I fired out a pot-sized bet, about $10,000. For her to call, she'd have to have aces or a king in her hand, perhaps a queen. But even with a queen she would probably have had to fold. She really had to be confident in her hand and her read to make the call. She was thinking and thinking and looking at me, shaking her head. Now I knew she was going to muck. And she did. I turned up the 6-5, collected the chips, and the whole table was shocked.

A few hands later, I went back to raising. I had raised about nine hands in a row when I got into another pot with her. Everyone folded and the play came to the same woman I had played earlier. She looked at me and started counting out chips. I realized she was thinking of reraising me. So I said, "Baby, you remember the last time you tried this, it didn't work out for you? You don't want any more of this now, do you?"

Finally, she just called. This was beautiful, because if she had raised me, I'd have had to muck. I was praying for the right flop, because now I had a free shot at busting her with my J-5 suited. I put her on a hand like A-Q, A-K. If I hit the flop hard, I was going to get a lot of her chips.

The flop came A-A-K, the worst flop possible for my hand. She immediately fired off a big bet. Since she had thought about reraising preflop, I figured she probably had a legitimate hand. Even if she was bluffing, I knew she didn't have worse than my jack high, so it didn't make sense for me to try to outplay her. I mucked my hand. She showed an ace before tossing the cards back to the dealer.

It looked like I lost the hand, but what really happened is, in a sense, I won. Because she didn't reraise, I got a free shot at seeing the flop. There's a lot of value in that. That's one of the situations where you really have to know your table. They saw me show her the 6 high earlier and now they saw me muck a hand against her.

After the hand I started playing super-tight, straightforward poker because my opponents were seething. They were waiting for a chance to get me. It was time to change gears to confuse them; if I had kept doing what I was doing, they would have started reraising me.

When you are in situations where you can no longer get away with the alpha-male-keep-raising-mode, you have to switch gears. After you get some momentum rolling—maybe you wake up with a big hand or flop big—you can quit playing passively and put your game back into gear five. Once they get tired of it and start fighting back, then you tone it down again.

It's a constant ebb and flow.

ALPHA MALE VERSUS ALPHA MALE

If another alpha male is at the table, it becomes difficult to play that aggressive style. You have to adapt. I was playing at a WPT event in Reno and was totally running over my table. I had beaten everyone into submission. I was up to about $60,000 in chips—we had started with $10,000—and things had gotten to the point where I was never getting raised. I was completely in control. Every pot I wanted, I took. But then I busted someone and a player came in to fill the empty seat—Phil Ivey with about $80,000 in chips.

The very first hand Ivey sees, he raises. I have K-5 suited, which I was going to raise with, but now I can't and fold. Everybody folds. He raises the next hand. A few people call, he bets the flop, they fold. The next hand he raises the pot again, and I realize that I'm not going to be able to do what I've been doing before. He's taken control. I can no longer be the alpha male.

In situations like this, you have to adapt your game and go to a different style. Here are some things you can do if an alpha male starts taking over your game.

DEFENDING AGAINST AN ALPHA MALE

Against an alpha male, try to use his aggression and play off it. You know what he is doing. You actually can get him to make a mistake and put his money in where it is bad. If you reraise him big in the right situations, you'll make him lay down those junk hands, making it tough for him to play.

If you get a hand such as jacks or queens, make sure to reraise him enough to protect against his seeing the flop. If you don't have a hand, you should probably dump it. You have to let an alpha male have the pot unless you're ready to commit a lot of chips to the hand. It is a mistake to keep raising another alpha male with junk hands because it will get you into trouble. You can sometimes flat call him when you have a hand, but you must be disciplined enough to not lose all your money on a flop. And be prepared: You're taking the risk of being outflopped. For example, suppose you flat-call an alpha male with kings, and the flop comes 7-7-3. If you put all the money in and he shows you A-7, you will want to shoot yourself.

Of course, it's awesome to just flat-call him with those same kings, get a K-7-7 flop, and have him go off with an A-7 for all his chips. But that's not going to happen very often.

Suppose you have a pocket pair such as sevens. Treat that hand just like tens or jacks. If you reraise, make it big enough that he won't call to see a flop unless he has a hand. You can do that a few times, but if you start reraising him all the time, eventually you are going to get third-raised by him and not be able to call.

In a nutshell, my strategy against another alpha male is to play straightforward poker in position, protect my big hands, and try to trap him with my little hands. But at the same time, when you're playing against an alpha male, you need to mix it up and change gears so that your play is not an open book.

If you don't have experience playing against that type of player, it's generally best to just raise it big, three to four times his bet, if you want to take him off his hand. If the blinds are $500/$1,000 and he makes it $3,000, make it $10,000 or even $12,000. You don't want to give him a good price to snap you off with some junk hand. And you want to make sure that your stack is big enough so that you can fold to a third raise if necessary. Understand that if he makes a third raise, he probably has it. He's not going to think that you have the guts to reraise him with nothing. If you reraise him he's going to know that you probably have a hand, so if he puts in a third raise, he has one too.

Suppose you don't have a big stack for the stage of the tournament you're playing, you have around $25,000. Do you still want to commit yourself by raising him to $12,000, knowing that you can't logically lay down your hand for the $13,000 you have left? Understand that if he moves in on you, you are probably committed to the hand. So, before you raise, ask yourself, "Is this a hand I really want to go with?" If not, consider just calling and seeing how you feel after looking at the flop.

CHANGING GEARS

Mixing it up means that you can play like an animal, but also change gears and play relaxed, straightforward poker. That's why image is so important. What do your opponents think of you? Are they getting tired of the raising? Who is at the table? Is there a new table captain? Did some top pro show up with a lot of chips and now he's raising every hand? You must adapt to whatever situation presents itself to take full advantage of opportunities that come your way.

That's the beauty of mixing it up. When you change gears, opponents will take a while to catch up to this fact. Then when you change again, they're behind the curve. If an opponent thinks you play one way, when in fact you've changed to another speed, it leads to mistakes that you can capitalize on. That's why you constantly want to think about your image.

One fundamental mistake you want to avoid is not *always* being out of line or making sketchy plays. In the past, I was constantly in gear four or five, trying to outplay everybody else, being tricky, dancing around, making moves, putting down bluffs. I never would lay down my hand to the reraise. I felt a need to always be the alpha male and control the table. It usually would work for a while, but inevitably, I'd get into trouble by being unwilling to slow down.

That type of aggressiveness can get you pretty far—until the one time that you are wrong. And then, boom, you're out and it's over. I'd find myself thinking that an opponent had something such as K-J and he was going to have to fold against my re-reraise. He'd end up calling me with two kings or two aces, and all of a sudden, I'd be busted.

Ivey once sat me down and gave me some good advice. "Listen David," he said, "you have to realize that 99 percent of the players are not going to reraise you with nothing. A top pro might, but the average player doesn't have the balls to do that." He pointed out that if you look at Random Joe over there and you've raised seven hands in a row and Random Joe finally raises you back, it may not be because he's just tired of it and is finally making a move. He's reraising you because he has finally found something, which means that you should muck unless you have the goods. Ivey said, "Let him have the pot and move on. You know what you do the very next hand? You go back to raising."

That advice really helped my game. At some point, opponents are going to play back at you. But the math still works out. If you are raising every hand but you lose one out of four of them, you are still making money. And one time they will get tired of your raising and make that move when you have aces or kings, and you will bust that player.

The key is that you sometimes have to pull back to gear two or three. *Slow down.* I realized that I could still play my aggressive game and bully opponents, but I didn't have to raise every hand. I could mix up my play, and mix up my image, but by staying in the alpha male role, I had become predictable. After I'd been pushing hard and raising every hand, eventually an opponent would play back at me with a real hand and take me down. Then my image would become weaker and I became more vulnerable, so my opponents started taking shots at me.

Sometimes you can feel the tension building as opponents become tired of a guy who's been playing table captain. They feel that they have to stop him. Unless the players are total sheep, they are eventually going to prevent you from raising. If they start playing back, you can flip a switch on them and pull back to first gear. That's when I'll play my hands in a straightforward manner and wait patiently for good cards. A lot of times my opponents won't realize that I've slowed down; all they remember is my raising and taking down pots with a 6-5, 7-2, 10-4 and other junk. They don't realize that, for the past half hour, for two orbits around the table, I've been folding every hand. They still think I'm in fifth gear. Then if I pick up two aces, they get into trouble with their pocket eights. When the flop comes 7 high, I bet, they move in, and boom! They're busted.

ANATOMY OF A HAND 3

Here is one last example illustrating how valuable it is to keep your opponents off balance by mixing up your play. I was playing at the Borgata in one of the WPT events several years ago. I had survived to see the second day of action. I think there were 101 players who made Day Two and I was in 99th place with about $18,000 in chips.

On this particular hand, Carlos Mortensen raised on the button, making the standard raise. The small blind folded. I had the 5-2 of clubs and called, deciding that I wanted to see a flop. It came 8-8-3 with one club.

Hand in Action

DAVID   **CARLOS**

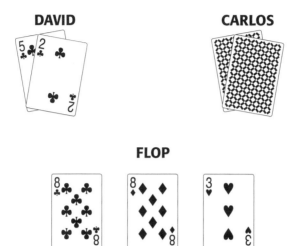

FLOP

I check and Carlos fires out his normal continuation bet, close to half the pot. I need chips here and I can't keep waiting for them to come to me. I thought that, a high percentage of the time, a player like Carlos wouldn't have enough of a hand to call, so I say to myself, "You have to show some guts. You have an opportunity to raise here and take down the pot, but this is going to be hard to do because you don't have a hand." I knew that if Carlos called, I would be in bad shape.

I count out what I have and what he has. I see that he's not priced in; he can make a laydown. So I just move in. I'm thinking, "Please don't call," because if he calls me, I'm dead in the water and my tournament is over.

Then he turns and stares at me. "I know you're bluffing," he says. I am just sitting there not saying a word. And he says, "But I was bluffing too. And you might be bluffing with a better hand." As he folds, he shows me 10 high and says, "You might have jack high and be bluffing and I still lose."

I show him the 5-2 and he goes nuts. He's still sick about it! From then on to the end of the day I was chip leader, ending up with about $600,000 after five levels or so.

I was able to gain the advantage in that situation because I mixed up my play, did something that my opponent didn't expect. Carlos didn't realize that I had it in me to stick all my chips in with nothing. I picked a good spot against the right opponent. I knew my player. I knew that Carlos was likely to have any hand; when he raised preflop, he followed through every time. I wasn't 100 percent sure he didn't have a hand— he could have had two nines, two aces or an A-8—but I knew that most of the time, he wasn't going to have a piece of that flop, and would have to fold. He didn't think I was capable of making a move, so he pretty much had to put me on a hand better than 10 high.

I wouldn't make that move against him now because he might call me with anything, but back then he didn't know me. I wound up coming in second place to Daniel and winning $580,000 in that tournament. I could have folded that hand against Carlos and still won some hands after this critical play. Who knows? However, that hand gave me chips, confidence, and the feeling that I could win. And it really cemented into my head the importance of mixing up your play and staying unpredictable.

PLAYING JUNK HANDS

When you're playing junk, you could bluff a guy off the pot without hitting anything if the right cards come. If I limp under the gun and call a raise, my opponent is going to wonder what I have. If the right flop comes, I can outplay him. A lot of top players do things that don't seem to make sense, but they actually do make sense. There is logic behind the play, though it might not immediately be apparent.

Playing junk hands can work out great because the raiser really doesn't know what you have. Do you have aces, or do you have nothing? That's why mixing it up is such a powerful strategy. Would you really call or reraise with a crappy hand, a 5-3, 8-4, or anything? Probably not. That's why your opponent would discount the hand you actually have. But you only want to make these moves when you know your opponent and how you're going to proceed. Otherwise you'd be wasting chips, getting yourself into trouble.

Some top professionals only play the nuts, and are rarely going to play junk hands. And there are others—pros like Daniel, Grinder, Tuan Le, and myself—who do things that don't make sense to the common poker player. You've got to take it beyond what's out there sometimes. Everyone's getting good—they're reading books, playing online, learning, and figuring out how to play poker—so you really have to do something different. Every now and then, not all the time, make random calculated moves just to trick opponents, simply to throw them off. Do something that's really unconventional.

For example, if I've been raising hand after hand and all of a sudden I limp under the gun, people tend to get confused and think that I must have aces or some other big hand. You can really throw opponents for a loop with a play like that.

If you make a crazy move and do something unpredictable, be sure to have a plan for how you are going to attack, what you are going to do. Are you going to bluff with a 5-2? Are you ready to make a move on the flop? If your opponent has a strong hand, will he get rid of it for a big enough bet? If he has a weak hand, how do you play? You need to have a good read on the table; that's the basis of your plan going into the hand. It all comes back to being aware of how your opponents play.

BETTER QUALITY JUNK?

Are some junk hands better than others? It depends on the situation. I like having hands such as 7-3 or 5-2, this kind of junk, because they are not easily dominated. They're also hard to get trapped with. Every now and then somebody will have an A-5, you'll have a 5-2 and it will come 5-5-8 and you'll get broke. It happens. But most of the time, you'll be up against premium cards and players won't put you on that kind of stuff. If it comes 3-3-7 and your opponent has two nines, he's ready to gamble. With your 3-4, you can get a lot of his money.

I'm more likely to play junk hands that can make straights rather than those that can't. A hand such as 7-4 is better than 7-3 because it's easier to make a straight. But in general, if I'm in position, I can play any two cards. When you get down to it, the hand is almost irrelevant. You're playing poker—the cards are just the backup. Whether you actually have that 7-4 or a 9-4 or some other junk, you can outplay your opponents on the flop if you sense weakness in them—especially if they are the kinds of players who check and fold a lot. The bonus comes when you catch a big flop and break someone.

On the other hand, if you have a hand such as A-J, you can get dominated and be in big trouble. If the flop comes A-A-2 and you have A-J—especially if the pot was raised preflop—your opponents could have an A-Q or A-K. It's rare that they are going to have A-9 or A-10 in a raised pot. Playing your A-J type hand will be very hard without trapping yourself and losing a lot of chips. Even though they are not strong,

> **WHEN YOU GET DOWN TO IT, THE HAND IS ALMOST IRRELEVANT. YOU'RE PLAYING POKER—THE CARDS ARE JUST THE BACKUP.**

the junk hands are way less risky to play, especially if you are in position, have good post-flop skills, and are a good reader, because you know how to play after the flop. You're going to need all these skills before you start playing junk successfully.

I'd much rather play 6-4 than K-2. It's hard to know where you're at if you are up against a K-J or a K-Q and you flop two kings or something like K-J-2. In these situations, you can get trapped and lose all your money. But if you get the K-6-4 flop, you can be pretty sure that nobody has a K-6 or K-4 and you'll usually get most of the money.

When amateur players get in there with 7-3, they are going to get beaten a lot of times because they don't know how to play junk. They flop one pair and get committed to it, or they get trapped by someone who hit the flop better than they did. Predictable players are going to have A-K, A-Q, K-Q, those kinds of hands. You are able to put them on premium hands and figure out whether you are beat, and get the most money out of them when you have a junk hand that connects with the flop.

MAKING MOVES

You can make moves if you stay alert to situations that arise, and have a handle on the types of players you are up against. These are a few of my favorites.

TAKING OUT LIMPERS

In a tournament, it's important to evaluate how players are playing when they're short-stacked in one of the blind positions. If the players who limped in aren't very active or aggressive—you know, weak players that play passively—I'm probably going to take a shot at the blinds if I'm in the cutoff seat or on the button. In situations where a bunch of people limp in and you raise late, you can pick up a lot of chips. The problem is that the pros know that move. And if they're at the table, they are going to know that I can make that move as well, and they are going to defend.

It's rare that someone who limps after a group of limpers will have aces or kings. Most of the time when a player limps in that situation, he has a pocket pair or two connectors. The players who are crazy enough to mix it up from the small blind also know that you know that, and that you are capable of raising from late position.

But if it's players I don't know who are fairly tight, I'm probably going to make that move with an average stack because it's a good spot. If the first guy who limped in under the gun doesn't reraise with a big hand, almost everybody else has a hand that is hard to call a raise with, and will probably lay them down. You are going to pick up a lot of money, four or five callers' money, plus the antes and the blinds. I'll probably make that move with an average stack if my opponents are the right kinds of players. Most of the time they are, though I prefer to do it with a big stack.

A BIG BOLD MOVE

Sometimes when you make the taking-out-the-limpers move, a player will know what you are up to and try to re-steal the pot from you. Let's say that after a few limpers, you also limp with pocket eights. From the blinds, I make a big raise to steal the pot. You realize what I'm doing, and after the first limpers fold, you reraise to take it away from me because you don't figure that I have a real hand. If the stacks are deep enough, I can take it up another level and make another big raise to represent a real hand. I know that you most likely didn't limp with aces or kings, so I'm making it very hard for you to call.

You have to be careful making moves this deep and complex. First, the stacks have to be big enough that the player who made the reraise against you can fold for a third raise. You don't want to try it on a person that has put most of his chips in the pot, because he will be priced in; that is, he will be forced to call. Second, you must be aware of what type of player made the move, and how you think he will react to a third raise. Is it a player who is tight enough that he could fold a medium pair, but not so tight that he would only reraise you with a big pair? Or is he a loose, tricky player that most likely is making a move? Also be careful not to make this move too often. You can usually do it only once. After that, players will start limping with big hands after a few limpers have entered the pot, counting on you to make this move when you are in the blinds.

THE RERAISE

A reraise is the hardest move to make in no-limit poker. It usually takes a hand. Most players can't put the second raise in without a hand. They don't have the guts to do that with garbage. That's what the true top players do; they sense weakness and attack it. Notice who is reraising at the table because those are the players you really want to be worried about. Players that reraise a lot in the beginning are the players that could reraise you. If you are planning to raise a lot of hands, you don't want to get reraised very often. You want to get called or have your opponents fold.

PLAYING IN THE DARK

I know many players that will raise without looking at their cards because they sense that a player is weak, but I think it's a mistake. Looking is free, so why not do it? Some guys won't look because they don't want to glance down, see a 7-2, and change their mind or give anything away with their body language. I think players who do that kind of stuff in the dark are just action junkies. They like the fact that they can squeeze and find a straight or find pocket aces. If I think my opponents are weak, I don't care what I see, I'm going to reraise them. I'm not going to get scared. Just the same, I like to look, because you never know, you might look at the situation and say, wait a minute, I'm not going to raise this guy, I'm just going to call and let him bleed off his money.

A FEW LESSONS FROM THE TOP PROS

As poker players, we're always evolving, learning new moves and perfecting old ones, picking up bits and pieces from the best in the game. Here are some lessons I've picked up along the way that have made me a better player.

PHIL IVEY'S BIG LESSON

The most important thing Phil Ivey told me is that when you are the alpha male splashing chips around, raising like crazy and getting tricky, you should back down when you get reraised by an average player. He doesn't have the guts to push back at you with nothing, so just fold the hand if you have to and go back to what you were doing. If your opponent is going to keep reraising you, now you know *he's* making moves, and you can let him have it. On the other hand, a top player has the guts to reraise with garbage, and in that situation, you have to go with your read. Sometimes the best plan when you have a pro at your table is to wait for a real hand and set up a trap.

DANIEL NEGREANU'S BIG LESSON

Daniel really told me about keeping pots small, losing the least in the spots where you have a marginal hand. I used to check-raise bluff a lot, which is a huge error. I would call before the flop out of position, check the flop, and after an opponent had bet, I would raise back big. A lot of times my opponent would fold and I'd win the money. But I lost so much more when he actually had a hand and either called my raise or raised me back. I had to fold and leave all the money in the pot. I'd lose their bet plus my raise, which was basically four times the bet amount since I like to raise three times their bet. For example, if they bet $1,000, I'd make it $4,000. So I lost $4,000 where I could have found out the same information by firing out just $1,000.

If they raised me in that situation, they pretty much had it because, as Phil said, they don't really have the guts to raise without a hand unless they are top tier players. If they just call, you're able to see the turn for only $1,000 and you're still in control of the hand—as opposed to being out $4,000 and not having any chance at the pot.

With this $1,000 "small-ball" play, you are the one driving and can evaluate on the turn what you want to do. That's the big lesson I learned from Daniel, keeping pots small. Why risk $4,000 when you only need to risk $1,000?

GRINDER'S BIG LESSON

One of the things that I learned from Grinder is how to get opponents to make mistakes. I would raise too much in too many hands and, consequently, wouldn't see many flops. On the other hand, Grinder raises a lot smaller, does a lot of limping and calling, and tries to see flops with inexperienced players in the hope of flopping a big hand and getting them to make a mistake on the flop. While I used to raise with a 7-4, for example, and everybody would fold, he might limp with a 7-4 or raise small with his 7-4. He might even call a raise when it's not a big percentage of his stack and give the flop a chance to hit him hard. This type of play gives his opponents the chance to make mistakes and give up their money. That's why Grinder gets so many chips. He sees a lot of flops with players who aren't as good as him, and he's better at playing after the flop than them. He might call them with 7-4, the flop will come 7-4-2, and he'll induce a guy with aces or kings to lose all his chips. Suddenly, he has a big stack.

Or Grinder might have an A-6 against a 7-6 and flop three sixes. While earlier in my career, I would have raised with the A-6, the 7-6 would never have seen the flop, and I'd never have had the chance to cold deck somebody and get all their chips. He allows the cold deck to happen more often than not by allowing players to see flops and playing poker with them. When you are raising so many hands so big like I was, you never get to see a flop with players who have weak hands because you raise them right out of the pot.

You do have to be careful, though; sometimes you end up on the wrong side of the cold deck. You need to have a strong read on your opponent and figure out when you could be on the wrong side. Then try to keep the pot small if you think you are.

Grinder's lesson reinforces the concepts I have stressed earlier— mixing up your play so that opponents cannot read you, and giving them the opportunity to put their chips in bad.

CONCLUSION

Staying unpredictable and allowing other players to make mistakes is where a lot of profit awaits you in any poker game. When you are predictable, you leave yourself open to being bullied out of pots. You give sharp players a chance to get away from your big hands with minimal damage to their stacks. Knowing what kind of hand you have and what you are going to do, your opponents will use that information to your disadvantage.

If you want to take your game to the next level, mix up your play. And then, who knows? We may be sitting across from one another at a final table with a million dollars on the line!

SMALL BALL

DANIEL NEGREANU

Daniel Negreanu is one of the best and arguably the most charismatic player in the world of poker. Best known for his unorthodox and aggressive style of play, Daniel's track record in tournament poker competition is overwhelming. At the age of 23, he won his first World Series of Poker title, which earned him the nickname, "Kid Poker."

In 2004, he appeared at eleven final tables, scored two World Poker Tour victories, and won his third WSOP bracelet, earning more than $4 million for his efforts. Daniel capped off the year by being named ESPN Player of the Year, *Card Player* magazine Player of the Year, and 2004-2005 WPT Player of the Year.

Negreanu exemplifies the confidence of the new generation of poker players who cut their gaming teeth on the Internet and video games, and are committed to poker as a sport. The young superstar appears regularly on the Fox Sports network, ESPN, and GSN. In addition, Daniel headlines the video game "Stacked," and the always popular website www.fullcontactpoker.com. He is also sponsored by PokerStars, where you will find him playing online.

Daniel is involved in the creation of a new poker training site called PokerVT.com, which is a web-based virtual training system that simulates one-on-one poker instruction from Daniel and a team of poker experts. The training curriculum features Daniel's in-depth video-based analysis of actual live hands that were played and a collection of training modules that reveal the secrets of the online pros.

As Daniel himself might say, "But wait, fans, that's not all!" He writes a nationally syndicated newspaper column, "Playing Poker with Daniel Negreanu," and a column for *Card Player* magazine. Doyle Brunson selected him to write the triple draw chapter for *Super System 2*, the celebrated sequel to *Super System*. Simply put, Daniel's success in poker is enormous, his talent unrivaled, and his personality unforgettable.

Negreanu's topic for this book is small ball, a revolutionary approach to winning at no-limit hold'em. The centerpiece of the book, his chapter will help you learn how to steadily increase your stack in no-limit hold'em tournaments without taking significant risks, just like some of the pros you see on TV. Many of the most successful tournament pros use the strategies Daniel gives you in this section.

"When you watch a player who is using a small-ball strategy," the author says, "you will notice that he appears to be in control of the table, yet at the same time, seems to be playing with reckless abandon, giving little thought to the strength of his starting hand. You will soon understand the method to that madness… that this liberal strategy is firmly founded in sound mathematics and logic."

The ultimate goal of this chapter is twofold. First, to show you that the key to success in no-limit hold'em is playing your opponent's hand rather than focusing on your own hand. And second, to teach you how to achieve extraordinary success at poker by doing exactly that.

SMALL BALL

Daniel Negreanu

SMALL BALL PHILOSOPHY

I'm really hoping that this chapter will help you learn how to steadily increase your stack in no-limit hold'em tournaments without taking significant risks, just like some of the pros you see on TV. This style of poker is one that many of the world's most successful tournament competitors use, including players like myself, Phil Ivey, Alan Goering, Erick Lindgren, Ted Forrest, Phil Hellmuth, Michael "The Grinder" Mizrachi and countless others.

After you've read through the small-ball material, you'll have a much better understanding as to why this strategy works, how to play it yourself, and how to defend against other players who are using a similar strategy.

We will start from the very beginning—from the struggle for the antes all the way to the river where you'll need to decide how much to bet or whether to check a marginal hand on the last card. Along the way, I'll be providing you with in-depth examples of how small ball works. When you watch a player at a table who is using a small-ball strategy, you will notice that he appears to be in control of the table, yet at the same time, seems to be playing with reckless abandon, giving little thought to the strength of his starting hand.

You will soon understand the method to that madness. You will learn that, in fact, this liberal strategy is firmly founded in sound mathematics and logic. Ultimately, this chapter will teach you that the key to success in no-limit hold'em is playing your opponent's hand rather than focusing on the strength of your own hand.

BLINDS AND ANTES

When you strip the game of tournament poker down to its core, it is a battle for the blinds and antes. The size of the blinds and antes dictates how many hands you should play and even how much you should invest in a hand. Let's look at an extreme example:

Let's say that you are playing in a no-limit tournament that has no blinds and no antes. In this situation, why would you ever play a hand unless it was precisely A-A? You could simply wait for aces and hope that someone else will play with you. However, if the others have any understanding of poker at all, they will be doing the exact same thing. The only time there would ever be a flop is when two players are dealt aces in the same hand!

Let's look at the other side of that extreme example. Let's say that you are playing in a one table, 10-handed tournament that starts you off with $2,000 in chips, blinds of $500/$1,000 with a $1,000 ante. Is there any hand you could justify folding in this situation? Of course not! Half of your money goes toward the ante, so if you fold, you'll be all in on the very next hand for the ante alone. Chances are that everyone else will probably play their hands when you fold. That would leave you heads-up with $1,000 in chips versus the opponent who won the last pot, who would have $19,000 in chips.

Neither of those two blind-and-ante structures makes for a very interesting poker game. In a typical televised tournament, you start with $10,000 in chips and the blinds start at $25/$50 with no ante. They then escalate as follows depending on the structure set up by the tournament director:

Blinds	Ante
$25/$50	None
$50/$100	None
$100/$200	None
$100/$200	$25
$150/$300	$25
$200/$400	$50
$300/$600	$75
$400/$800	$100
$500/$1,000	$100
$600/$1,200	$200
$800/$1,600	$200
$1,000/$2,000	$300
$1,200/$2,400	$400
$1,500/$3,000	$500
$2,000/$4,000	$500
$3,000/$6,000	$1,000
$4,000/$8,000	$1,000
$5,000/$10,000	$1,000
$6,000/$12,000	$2,000
$8,000/$16,000	$2,000
$10,000/$20,000	$3,000

The blinds and antes continue increasing until one player is left with all of the chips. Each level lasts anywhere from one hour to two hours, depending on the buy-in for the tournament.

Smaller buy-in tournaments ranging from $100 to $300 generally have twenty- and thirty-minute levels, which makes for a much quicker finish than the big buy-in tournaments. Some of them last for two to four days, or in the main event of the World Series of Poker, for nearly two weeks until a champion is crowned.

To maintain your starting stack, you'll need to win at least one set of blinds and antes per round. Since the blinds and antes continue to increase throughout the tournament, though, that simply isn't good enough to survive. Eventually a $10,000 stack will be in jeopardy, so you'll actually have to do better than breaking even. You'll have to fight a little harder to win more than your fair share of blinds and antes.

Premium hands coming to you when large pots are at stake are few and far between. Tournaments are won in the trenches by aggressively going after lots of little pots. The trick, of course, is learning how to do that without becoming reckless. Read through this entire chapter and you'll be one step closer to becoming a tournament winner.

STARTING HANDS

One thing you'll notice right away that separates this book from some of the others that you may have read, is that we'll be spending very little time talking about starting hand requirements. The theory behind small ball dictates that you'll be focusing more on what your opponent *doesn't* have than the strength of the cards you *do* have.

Here are some basic starting-hand guidelines that you should consider before playing a pot.

BIG PAIRS

A-A, K-K, Q-Q, J-J

Obviously, you'll be playing these hands in any position. The A-A and K-K are good enough to play for all your chips. There may be situations that come up where you could justify folding K-K, but it's not a good habit to get into. Having K-K when another player at the table has A-A is a rare occurrence. Even if you are unlucky enough to run into that trap, the K-K will still win the pot almost 20 percent of the time.

You should never feel ashamed of going broke with K-K before the flop. Now, folding K-K before the flop when no one had the A-A is a statistical nightmare! I've folded K-K before the flop exactly one time in my career. The situation was perfect and my opponent just had to have A-A. I threw my K-K into the muck face up, and my opponent turned up... Q-Q! Yikes! I'll never do that again. As you'll understand later in the chapter, when you are playing a fast-paced style of poker, your opponents will give you more action then they would if you were playing conservatively.

The good news is that you're more likely to get your A-A and K-K paid off. The bad news is that it'll be more difficult for you to play hands like Q-Q and J-J. Why? Because your opponents might try to take more shots at you because of your liberal style; therefore, it won't be as easy for you to fold hands like Q-Q and J-J when an opponent raises you. Frankly, you really don't want to play many big pots with Q-Q or J-J because more often than not, you are either way behind or only slightly ahead.

In fact, it's not a bad idea to play these hands a little bit more carefully preflop. You don't have to reraise with these hands, especially against a player who raised from early position. This will add yet another layer of deception to your game because it will let the rest of the table know that, just because you didn't reraise, doesn't mean you have a weak hand. That will help you a lot when you start calling raises with hands such as 5-6 suited.

MIDDLE PAIRS

10-10, 9-9, 8-8, 7-7

Too often I hear people say that middle pairs are the most difficult hand to play. That's only true if you overvalue them and play them as though they are premium hands, which they're not. They are good hands, but that's mostly because of their *implied* value rather than their preflop strength. (More about implied odds later.)

If you are the first one into the pot with any of these hands, you should make a standard "small-ball raise" (for more on that, read the "Betting" section). Your goal with one of these hands is to win a big pot by flopping a set. If you play a big pot with one of these hands and don't flop a set, chances are you'll be in big trouble.

That doesn't mean you should just fold if you don't flop a set, mind you, but if the action gets too hot and heavy, you need to muck that hand in a hurry.

SMALL PAIRS

6-6, 5-5, 4-4, 3-3, 2-2

Small pairs should be played similarly to the middle pairs. Once again, your goal is to flop a set. What you don't want to do with middle and small pairs is reraise your opponents before the flop.

I've heard several TV commentators make that mistake time and time again, saying things like, "This is a raise or fold situation." In the long run, reraising with middle and small pairs will just get you into trouble. When your opponent has a bigger pair, you'll be in a heap of trouble, and even when he doesn't, you may find yourself in a coin-flip situation against a hand like A-K. Sure, you'd be a favorite, but that's not how we want to get our chips in tournament poker.

Now, some players will reraise with small pairs before the flop and they'll do it successfully because it suits their style. But that's not what small-ball players do.

A-K AND A-Q

These hands really aren't that good at all in deep-stack tournaments. They might be a sight for sore eyes in a low buy-in, fast-paced tournament, but in the elite televised tournaments, these hands are often big trouble.

A-K is obviously substantially better than A-Q, but you still don't want to get all your money in before the flop with A-K. More often than not, you'll be on the wrong end of a coin toss; that is, if your opponent doesn't have A-A or K-K, which he will have often enough for it to be a legitimate concern.

A-K is certainly a hand you'd want to raise with before the flop, but it's the type of hand that doesn't play very well after the flop. Suppose the flop comes A-9-6 and you bet your A-K. Frankly, you don't even want a caller! Anyone who puts in any action after that flop could easily have A-9, A-6, 9-9 or 6-6, which would have you dead on arrival. A-K unsuited is a hand that will win you small pots, but is generally a dog if there is any significant action.

A-Q is just much worse in every way. Not only are you certainly dead if you play a big pot before the flop, but there is even more to worry about after the flop. If you play A-Q and the flop comes A-9-6, you'll have the same worries you'd have with

A-K—except that with the A-Q, you'll have to worry about A-K as well!

ACES AND PAINTS

A-J, A-10, K-Q, K-J, K-10, Q-J, Q-10, J-10

Now, here is something that may surprise you: In deep-stack tournaments, these hands are significantly better when they are suited. So much so, that it often makes the difference between calling or folding.

A starting hand such as K-10 offsuit, for example, is a hand that will end up making top-pair hands rather than made hands (straights and flushes). That's not a good thing in deep-stack tournaments because it doesn't go with our game plan. One-pair hands will rarely win you big pots, but if you play them wrong, they will often cost you big ones.

The other problem with a lot of these bastard stepchild-type hands is that they play second fiddle to all the premium hands and will do very poorly against them, costing you a lot of money. One in particular is known as the "rookie" hand because it looks tempting, but it's often nothing but trouble. K-J has probably mowed down more hometown heroes than any other hand.

The flop will come down K-5-4 and the rookie will never lay it down. Anytime he's up against a pro who is staying till the river, he'll be looking up at either a set, a K-Q, A-K, or A-A. Having said all that, it's more than okay to raise with any of these hands if you are the first player to enter the pot. In fact, you should do that and proceed cautiously afterwards, looking to win a small pot.

However, if someone raises ahead of you, then folding K-Q, A-J, and the rest of these hands will most likely be the best play—unless you are suited. The value of your hand rises immensely if it is suited. The extra outs that suited cards might give you will often allow you to win pots in several ways: either by making the flush, giving you a chance to semi-bluff, or even flopping a flush draw and catching a pair at the river to win.

If you play a K-Q suited against a raise, you are not going to be playing the hand based on the merits of flopping top pair. If you make top pair, that's fine, but you'll look to play a small pot. Your real goal is to make a straight or a flush, and then play a big pot.

ACE-RAG SUITED

A♥ 6♥, A♣ 4♣, A♦ 3♦, A♠ 7♠

The only real value in these hands is their flush potential and their potential to make two pair. Flopping a pair of aces is a good thing, too, but you don't want to commit yourself to a hand with one pair and a lousy kicker. If you are the first one in, this is a fine hand to attack the blinds. However, if you get any resistance (someone reraises you before the flop), calling the reraise with a hand like A♥6♥ is suicide.

Ace-rag suited hands, in particular, are much better off being played from late position. That way, you can control the pot size and possibly earn free cards in the hope that you complete a flush.

KING-RAG SUITED AND QUEEN-RAG SUITED

K♦ 5♦, Q♠ 7♠, K♣ 3♣, Q♥ 6♥

These aren't hands that are generally part of the portfolio. In fact, you shouldn't be raising with them outside of very special circumstances. They are hands that you can limp into multiway pots with, but they aren't the right kinds of hands to be raising with.

SMALL BALL

These types of hands scream of being second-best in many ways. You'll often flop top pair with a junk kicker, or worse, make a flush and lose a huge pot to the nut flush. King-suited hands are especially difficult to play, because a king-high flush is a hand that is extremely difficult to get away from.

The types of hands that do best with the small-ball approach are those hands that will be easy to get away from and aren't going to make a lot of strong, yet second-best hands in large pots.

SUITED CONNECTORS

5♣ 6♣, 6♠ 7♠, 6♥ 8♥, 4♣ 6♣, 4♦ 7♦, 5♦ 8♦

The small suited connectors are absolutely ideal for the small-ball approach. Since the goal with small ball is to make straights and flushes against top-pair hands, these hands give you straight potential and flush potential, plus two pair and trips.

Against particularly weak players, you could break them with 6-4 on a 4-4-10 flop if they have an overpair. The key to the success of small ball, and in particular these types of hands, is that your opponents won't be able to put you on a hand, and will often overplay an overpair when they are virtually drawing dead. Think of it in terms of fishing. You are putting a little itty bitty worm on the end of a pole and looking for a big fish to bite. All you are risking is that worm, but the payoff could be enormous.

The other benefit to playing these types of hands is that they are generally easy to get away from. If you don't hit the flop, you might decide to take one stab at it, but that's about it.

Wait, there's more! Once people start to figure out that you like to play the little cards, you can use that to your advantage in a different way.

Hand in Action

For example, let's say that I called a tight player's raise with the J♠ 10♠ and the flop comes 5♥ 6♠ 7♥.

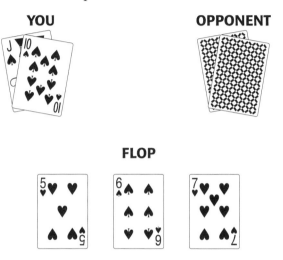

If I have position on this player, I could win the pot in one of two ways:

1. He has a hand like A-K and I can steal it on the flop.
2. He bets an overpair on the flop and I call him in the hope that another straight card comes on the turn. If a 4 comes on the turn and I bet, it would be an extremely difficult call for a player with A-A to make, especially since he knows that I'm willing to call raises with a hand such as 6-8.

The real homerun, though, comes when you hit a hidden straight against an opponent who can't get away from his hand. Say a hand goes something like this: A tight player raises in first position with K-K and I call with the 5♠ 7♠. The flop comes Q♠ 4♠ 8♦.

YOU

TIGHT OPPONENT

FLOP

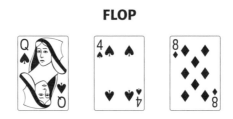

The tight player bets and I call with my flush draw and inside straight draw. If the turn card comes a 6, he won't know what hit him. I might just get his whole stack. I'd certainly get him to put all of his chips in if he had Q-Q, that much is for sure.

TRASH HANDS

Q-3, J-2, 9-4, 8-2

Trash hands are hands with no real inherent value, which should only be played when you are playing the *situation* rather than the cards. Examples of trash hands include 10-2, J-3, 7-2, 8-3, Q-2 and 10-6. Hopefully you'll be playing enough hands so that you won't even need to look twice at a trash hand. Since we aren't playing our hands—remember we are playing what our opponents *don't* have—there are definitely some situations where playing one of these hands might make some sense.

However, trash hands should only be played in situations where you are trying to win the pot with a reraise before the flop. Or when you are up against extremely tight players in the blinds who'll fold preflop a high percentage of the time or fold on the flop to a small bet if they miss.

Reraising before the flop with a middle pair isn't exactly the type of hand we'd want to do that with, but a hand like Q-3, 9-4, or even A-6 just might be. When you are making one of these plays, though, you must have the discipline to take your one shot before the flop without getting careless after the flop.

If you reraise a late position player with Q-2 offsuit and the flop comes with a queen, don't let yourself get carried away. Look to play a small pot and lose the minimum if you are beat.

BETTING

INTRODUCTION

The secret behind playing small ball isn't so much in the hands you choose to play, rather it's the amounts you choose to bet with the various hands you'll end up playing. In this section, you will learn how to bet less in order to win more. You will learn how you can get away with playing more hands before the flop without bleeding your stack.

We will also cover preflop bet sizes in different scenarios—when to call, reraise, limp, and fold when the heat is on.

PREFLOP RAISING

Popular theory is that a standard-sized preflop raise should be three times the size of the big blind. So, with the blinds at $400/$800 and a $100 ante, that would mean you'd be risking $2,400 to win $2,100 at a typical nine-handed table. That's a decent return on your investment if no one calls the raise. If you did that two hands in a row, and on hand number one everybody folded, but on hand number two someone went all in and forced you off the hand, your net loss would only be $300.

That's not a terribly poor result, but look what happens when we lower the size of the raise to two-and-a-half times the blind. Now, you'd be risking $2,000 in order to win $2,100.

If we simplify the game to the point where all you do during a tournament is raise to two-and-a-half times the blind and then just fold if anyone calls, it is possible to build your stack, provided that all of your opponents fold 50 percent or more before the flop. Think about it. On hand number one, you make it $2,000 and everyone folds—you pick up the $2,100 pot. On hand number two, you go for another steal attempt, only this time, the player on your left reraises you $10,000 more. If you raised with trash and fold, you'll lose back $2,000.

Obviously, the more aggressive you become preflop, it will lower the percentage of the time that everyone folds preflop. If people view you as a loose player they will likely defend their blinds with more marginal hands than if they think you're a tight player. That's not bad for you either. More often than not, you'll be in position against your opponent and will have one more opportunity to earn this pot after the flop, but we'll get into more of that in the next section.

RAISE MORE VERSUS TOUGH PLAYERS

Since your opponents will call a raise of two-and-a-half times the big blind more often than they would call a larger raise, you can actually choose what price you want to lay certain opponents based on the amount you raise. I highly discourage you from varying your raise sizes based on your hand strength, but I am all for changing your bet size based on your opponent's level of skill.

Let's say you're at a pretty tight, easy table, but there is one other player at the table who is a strong player. Now, if you are going to raise his big blind, he is going to defend it a high percentage of the time and force you to play a pot with him after the flop. Why would you want to play a pot against the other tough player? If you want him out of the hand, you can do that by raising as much as four or even five times the blind when he's on it. Others at the table may be confused by this bet, but there is no reason to explain why you just happen to be raising more on this particular hand.

This play will also help define a tougher opponent's hand since your larger raise will help you narrow it down if he plays with you. If you raise a tough player's blind just two-and-a-half times the blind, it will be extremely difficult for you to gauge the strength of his hand. While that's a legitimate concern against a tough player, you'd gladly make the smaller raise against lesser players because the mistakes they make post-flop should outweigh what you give up by not defining their hand.

MORE ACTION FOR LESS MONEY

The biggest benefit of playing this aggressive yet small betting style is that you'll get more action on your strong hands while risking fewer chips. For example, let's say you finally pick up a premium hand like aces. If you've just raised three hands out of the last four, your opponents will suspect that you're raising with trash hands in an attempt to just steal the blinds. If a player behind you picks up a hand like 7-7, he may decide to reraise you before the flop, figuring he has the best hand and can get you to lay down your hand.

If you reraise him again before the flop, he may be confused by your "wild image" and make the call. If he sees you raising all these hands, he might not be able to distinguish the difference between your raising preflop and *reraising* preflop. The reraise steal after a raise isn't a play that works all that well if your image is wild. For the most part, if you are going to raise a reraise, you should have the goods. That play just doesn't fit well with small-ball poker, which is what you want to play.

However, it's not a play that you'd abandon entirely, especially if your opponents are on to the fact that a reraise from you generally means that you actually have a very strong hand.

I can still remember the first time I saw this method of madness put to good use watching old-timer O'Neil Longston playing in a no-limit hold'em tournament years ago. With the blinds at $50/$100, O'Neil was raising virtually every hand, but each one of those raises was the bare minimum. He'd make it $200 to go, and if someone reraised him, he folded nearly every time.

Then he raised it again to $200 and a young player made it $1,200 to go with 9-9. When the action came back to O'Neil, he announced, "All in," and raised the young kid $8,000 more. The kid called rather quickly, only to see O'Neil's kings.

As he was leaving the room, the young player made the following comment, "Unbelievable! How unlucky was that? The guy raises every hand, but the one time I have a hand, he wakes up with pocket kings." Ahh, but you see, the one clue that this young player missed out on was that while O'Neil was raising virtually every hand, this was the first time that he actually reraised. There is a significant difference between being the first player raising a pot and being the player that comes over the top of an opponent.

CALLING RATHER THAN RERAISING

Too often I hear television commentators say things like, "This is a raise or fold situation," when, in fact, this is the exact type of situation where a player should call! If you are one of the better players at the table, you want to make most of your difficult decisions after the flop, not before it. It's a safer way to protect your stack and you'll likely make better decisions after the flop than your opponent would.

I seldom reraise before the flop no matter what my hand is. By not reraising, I'm able to disguise the strength of my hand preflop and also am able to trap unsuspecting opponents who interpret my smooth call as a sign of weakness. I've busted lots of players by not reraising before the flop with A-A. Of course, you run the risk of being outdrawn on the flop, but the rewards far outweigh the risk.

An example: A player from early position raises and you think he may have A-K, A-Q, or a big pair (J-J, Q-Q, K-K, A-A). You look down at 7-7 on the button. Again, I've heard many commentators say this is a raise or fold situation, and while folding is sometimes correct, it's rarely ever correct to reraise in this situation. For one, your opponent will call you only with a bigger pair, or when he is in a coin-flip situation with a hand like A-K.

As long as the stacks are deep enough, the best play here is to call. That way, you can play the hand in position after the flop, and if you are lucky enough to flop a set, you might just be able to get all of your opponent's chips. Also, if the flop comes ragged, say a 9-4-2 or 8-4-3, your pair just might be the best hand. You should be able to figure out when to continue after the flop based on your opponent's betting—but we'll get to that later.

If you reraise with the 7-7, you give your opponent a chance to shut you out of the pot. With a good "bust 'em" hand like pocket sevens, your goal is to get to the flop as cheaply as possible. If you reraise before the flop, your opponent may come back over the top of you, forcing you to lay down the hand. That's an extremely bad result because you may either:

1. Miss your chance to bust your opponent if he has A-A, or
2. You might allow the player to semi-bluff you off the hand if he in fact has A-K.

In my own journey to learning how to play this game, I can remember how much it annoyed me when the guy on my left would smooth call all of my raises. If he reraised me, that would make for an easy decision. However, if I had to describe the one type of player that I'd least like to face at a no-limit hold'em table, it's the player that just keeps calling my preflop raises in position. So I decided, "Why don't I become 'that guy'?"

That's where this pesky little strategy was born. Most players show their biggest weaknesses with their post-flop play. Lots of people have read books and have studied how to play the various preflop scenarios, but there are so many variables to playing after the flop that it's a much more difficult task to master.

So, if you are playing against players whose strengths are pre-flop rather than postflop, it would only make sense to see more flops with them by simply smooth-calling rather than reraising. This is especially important against players who overplay their hands preflop. For example, if you are up against a player who likes to reraise with hands like 9-9, A-K or A-Q, you should avoid reraising him before the flop with anything but the best of hands. Even with hands such as J-J, Q-Q, or A-K, it's often better to see a flop first than to reraise before the flop against such players. A good player doesn't want to race, but they do. By reraising with marginal hands before the flop, you'll be playing into their hands by neutralizing your postflop skills.

DEAD MONEY GRABS

In tournament poker, what I like to call "Dead Money Grabs," are slightly higher risk plays that also offer a high success rate. A dead money grab is one in which your sole goal is to win what's already in the middle with no intention of playing your hand post-flop. Since you have no intention of seeing another betting round, the value of your hand is basically unimportant. In fact, if you have a marginal to good hand, you might be better off not attempting a dead money grab at all, and instead, seeing the flop cheaply.

You wouldn't be a complete player if you stuck to one set of rules without ever varying from them. That's just not how poker works for successful players. The dead money grabs differ from many of the small-ball ideas in that you attempt to win chips preflop as opposed to postflop.

There are several ways to pick up dead money in a no-limit game. Following are a few tricks to get you started.

1. Pound the Limpers in Position

When you make the decision to rob the limpers, the most important limper to focus on is the first limper. Basically, the play works something like this: With the blinds at $100/$200 and a $25 ante, the first player limps in under the gun. Then, let's say two more players limp in after him as does the player on the button. From the small blind, you look down at a 9-3 offsuit.

YOU

If you read the first limper as playing a weak hand, this might be the perfect opportunity to take this pot down. With $1,325 in the pot, a rather large raise will win you the pot a very high percentage of the time provided that:

a. The big blind doesn't wake up with a hand
b. The first limper wasn't setting a trap
c. None of the limpers is severely short-stacked, or
d. The table is very loose and has been calling large bets with weak hands.

If you are going to try this play, you'll have to raise more than $1,000. A $1,000 raise with so much money already in the pot will invite opponents with hands like 7-7 or 8-8 to try to flop a set. A better amount would actually exceed $2,000.

Let's say you decided on a $2,600 raise. What you are basically doing is laying 2 to 1 odds that everyone will fold before the flop. That's not a bad price at all and, at most tables, your win rate will be much higher than 66 percent with this play. Once you've made this play a couple times, however, it starts to lose its effectiveness since people will eventually catch on. That could hurt you, but it could also really help you if you later find a hand like A-A or K-K in a similar situation and no one believes you. Still, it's not a play you want to overuse.

Also, it's extremely important to note that you shouldn't risk a high percentage of your chips on a play like this. If you invest too high a percentage of your chips, you may find yourself pot-committed with an absolutely trashy hand. For example, let's say you have a total of $5,000 and try a dead-money grab by making it $2,600. If you are being trapped, or if anyone plays back at you, you will be pot-committed even with a hand as bad as 9-6! Never put yourself in a position where you are pot-committed with a terrible hand.

2. Coming Over the Top

Just to keep your opponents honest and to let them know that every pot goes through you, sometimes you need to come over the top of them with a preflop reraise. Similar to pounding the limpers, there are some things to consider before coming over the top with a reraise:

a. **How many chips do you have?**

   If you are short-stacked, or a preflop reraise is too high a percentage of your stack, let it go. When you are coming over the top of an opponent with a trash hand, you are the one that's guessing. You don't want to be guessing when your tournament is on the line.

b. **How many chips does your opponent have?**

   For example, imagine that your opponent has raised from late position to $600. Take a look at his stack and see how many chips he has left. If he only has another $1,200, leave it alone unless you have a hand worth playing for $1,800. Generally speaking, if an opponent puts in over 25 percent of his chips on a raise, he'll call any reraise after that.

c. **How does your opponent perceive you?**

   If you've already come over the top of the same guy a couple of times, it's probably not a good idea to go to the well one more time unless you are sitting on a big hand. If he appears frustrated, or you think he might be on to what you are doing, stay out of his way for a little while until he calms down and your table image is restored. Nobody, and I mean nobody, likes it when someone continually reraises them before the flop. Eventually, some guys just snap!

d. **How much do I need to raise?**

   If you are going to make this play, you have to make sure that you don't price your opponent into the pot. Here is an extreme example: A player raises from late position to $600 and you reraise him to $1,200 with Q-2 offsuit from the big blind. That is a terrible play. Your opponent will call your raise with any two cards in that situation. Effectively, all you've done is make the pot bigger while playing rags out of position. Not good.

Every opponent is built differently and will react to various sizes of bets differently. It's your job to really pay attention and watch how your opponents react to getting reraised. For example, let's say that you saw Player X raise to $300 and when another player reraised him to $900, he called quickly. When it was time to see his hand, you noticed that he called the raise with a rather weak hand, Q-10. That one play should clue you into the fact that if you come over the top of Player X, you need to raise more than that. If you want to steal his $300, you probably must risk somewhere around $1,200 to $1,600.

Aside from it probably not being a good idea for you to come over the top of him, if you have no read on what your opponent's tendencies are when he gets reraised, you should generally make a substantial reraise, approximately four times larger than his initial raise.

If a player makes it $500 and you want to steal the pot away from him, it's best to make it about $2,500. By making a raise of that size or more, you will win the pot a higher percentage of the time while having a clearer picture as to the strength of your opponent's hand. If your opponent can call or even reraise that bet, it's very likely that you are dealing with a real hand. In other words, it might be time to abort mission and cut your losses.

There are many variations of a dead-money grab that can be useful plays, especially during the inevitable stretches during tournaments where you just can't seem to pick up a hand. You can't expect to win a big poker tournament by simply waiting for the best hands. You need to keep your focus sharp, be constantly aware of your table image, and always be looking to pick up pots before the flop that nobody seems to want.

PLAYING AGAINST A RERAISE

For the most part, if you are playing small ball, you'll be entering a lot of pots, and in the majority of those pots, you'll be coming in for two-and-a-half times the big blind. Obviously, you are going to run into various situations where you'll get reraised either by a premium hand, or even sometimes when people just get fed up with the fact that you won't stop raising their blind.

Generally speaking, when you get reraised, you should dump your hand unless the situation is just right. Several factors constitute the right kind of situation to take a flop, even after being reraised:

1. Your Hand's Strength

This should be pretty obvious, but if you have a premium hand like A-A or K-K, not only would you play against a raise, you should usually reraise before the flop.

2. The Reraise Was the Minimum

Suppose the blinds are $100/$200, you come in for $500, and an opponent reraises you to $800. There is simply no circumstance where it would be correct to fold, even if you were certain that your opponent had aces. In fact, if you knew your opponent had aces, it would be well worth calling an additional $300 to try to outflop him. The minimum raise has been more recently coined the "nuisance" raise, in that it accomplishes very little except adding a little more money to the pot. It's extremely rare to see an initial raiser fold for the minimum reraise before the flop.

3. You Have Position

Position is power. Therefore, if the reraiser has position on you, you should be less likely to call a raise unless you have a strong hand. However, if the player who reraised you is out of position, your marginal hand can become worthy of making a call. For example, let's say that you are on a semi-steal with the 8♥ 10♥. With the blinds at $100/$200, you raise to $500. If the big blind raises you $1,000 more, this isn't a bad opportunity to take a flop since you are in position. Had you been out of position, it would be difficult to justify calling the raise.

4. Stack Size

Aside from hand strength, stack size is, without a doubt, the most important factor when deciding to play against a raise. Bust 'em hands such as 6-6 or 7♥ 8♥ play better against a raise in deep-stack poker than they do when the stacks are smaller. For example, let's say it's the early stage of a tournament and you raise to $150 on the button with the 7♥ 8♥, leaving you with $9,850 in chips. The small blind decides to reraise you to a total of $500. He also started the hand with $10,000 in chips.

YOU　　　　　　　　**SMALL BLIND**

Not only do you have position, you also have the type of hand that could hit a home run with the right kind of flop. You should call with this hand and hope to win the pot by either:

　a.　Hitting your hand, or
　b.　Bluffing your opponent by using board cards that may scare your opponent away.

Now, imagine you have that same hand, the 7♥ 8♥, only this time the blinds are $1,500/$3,000. You are sitting on $88,000 and your opponent in the small blind has $112,000. On the button, you go for the steal and make it $8,000 to go. The small blind raises you to a total of $30,000. In this case there is no play left. There is no home run to hit. Calling here would commit too high a percentage of your chips to the pot with a bust 'em type hand. Generally speaking, you shouldn't jeopardize more than 10 percent of your stack on a bust 'em type hand.

If you are serious about trying to apply a small-ball style of poker you must get used to being involved in a lot of pots, in many of which you'll get reraised. It's very important to keep your composure if that happens more than you'd like. Don't get away from your strategy by making sloppy calls. If you are having trouble laying down hands like Q-J, K-10, or K-Q to a reraise, it might be time to take a walk! All of those hands do horribly against a preflop reraise. Avoid them like the plague.

CALLING ALL-IN BETS OR RAISES

Later on in a tournament, you'll start to see more and more players getting short-stacked, which means you'll be faced with a lot more all-in reraises and all-in bets. When that happens to you, you should adhere to the following thought process when deciding if you should call the bet:

1. What Range of Hands Does My Opponent Have?

When deciding that, you should factor in all the variables including your opponent's level of desperation. For example, if a player goes all in under the gun for $8,000 and the blinds are $1,500/$3,000 with an ante, you should drastically broaden his range of hands to include virtually any hand with an ace in it. If you have chips and a hand such as 7-7, it probably makes sense to call a desperate bet like that one.

Or, in other situations against tighter players, you can drastically narrow your opponent's range of hands based on his tendencies and the action in front of him. If a tight player goes all in, even after several other players have entered the pot, it would increase the likelihood that you are looking at a very strong hand.

2. What Price Am I Being Laid?

When faced with a bet, the first thing you should do is count what's already in the pot in comparison to the bet you are currently facing—otherwise known as calculating your pot odds. This practice should and will become common practice for you when you start to play in no-limit hold'em tournaments on a more regular basis.

Let's look at an example. With the blinds at $2,000/$4,000 and a $500 ante at a nine-player table, you come in for a raise to $10,000. The player on the button goes all in for a total of $34,000 and the action comes back to you. Counting your $10,000, the all-in player's $34,000, and the blinds and antes, there is $54,500 in the pot. The bet to you is $24,000 more, so the price you are being laid is $24,000 to win $54,500 ($24,000 divided by $54,500 equals 2.27 to 1 odds). You don't need to bring a calculator with you to figure this out; it's not as hard as it might seem. Here's how I like to do it:

The bet, $24,000, goes into $54,500 at least twice so I know I'm getting at least 2 to 1 odds. What's left over is "about" $6,000, which is about one-fourth of $24,000. That gets me to about 2.25 to 1, which is close enough. You don't need to worry about being accurate right down to the decimal point.

3. How Does My Hand Stack Up Against the Range of Hands I Suspect My Opponent Has?

Now that I know my pot odds, it's time to figure out how my hand stacks up against the range of hands my opponent might have. This can be a little more tricky and isn't quite an exact science, and you should definitely take your time if you need to work it out.

Let's look at an example of how I might think my way through such a decision. Okay, I have A-9, which I know for sure is the worst hand right now. I'm totally dead if my opponent has A-A, and am a little worse than a 2 to 1 underdog against any other hand. In fact, if he only has a pair of sevens or eights, I'm in a coin-flip situation. Even if my opponent has A-K, I'm not in terrible shape, only getting slightly the worst of it. So, I'll call.

Often, when you are calling an all-in bet, or any bet for that matter, you aren't calling simply because you think you have the best hand. You are calling because the odds the pot is laying you dictates that it would be a good investment.

Here's an extreme example to illustrate this concept. I tell you to pick a number from among 1, 2, or 3. Only one of those numbers wins for you, while if you guess wrong, I win. Your long-term win rate would be approximately 33 percent. Now, if we each put up $100, that would be a silly bet for you to make. What if I told you that I'd put up $400 to your $100? Now, despite the fact that you are an underdog to actually win the bet, the bet has great value for you. All you have to do to break even is be correct one out of four times, but your win rate would dictate that you'll do much better than that.

Compare that to a poker hand. I have the A♥ 9♥ and you have K♣ K♠.

SMALL BALL

DANIEL **OPPONENT**

There is $200 already in the pot and you go all in for your last $100. In this case, you could show me that you have me beat, but I would be a fool not to take that bet! I'd be risking $100 to win $300. I'd be getting 3 to 1 odds when my hand is only about a 2 to 1 underdog against yours.

PLAYING A SHORT STACK

Unfortunately, our small-ball strategy of liberally raising a lot of hands before the flop gets thrown out the window when the chips dwindle. For small ball to be effective, the preflop raise needs to represent a very small portion of your overall stack size. If you have $20,000 in chips and the blinds are $50/$100, raising to $250 represents a little more than 1 percent of your stack size. Now, if you had that same $20,000, but the blinds were $2,000/$4,000, a standard small-ball raise of $10,000 would represent 50 percent of your total stack. In that case, the play becomes obsolete.

However, you still have ways to play a short stack that will allow you to use your post-flop skills. You'll just have to be a little more creative and add limping to your repertoire. Let's look at an example where you might be able to make this play work for you.

Let's say you are the first one into the pot and look down at K♠J♠. Your stack size is $100,000 with $3,000/$6,000 blinds and a $1,000 ante. A standard small-ball raise would be $15,000, which is 15 percent of your stack and is more than you'd like to invest with a hand that you'd have to fold to a raise. K-J is not a hand you want to play for all your chips preflop, but it could become a strong hand after the flop.

By limping in, you increase your chances of getting to the flop. That is your goal on a short stack—get to as many flops as possible. Your opponents may misinterpret your limp as a trap and fear that you have a hand like A-A or K-K. Other players may raise anyway, but they likely would also have raised your $15,000 bet had you made a standard small-ball raise. If they do raise, you'll likely have to play like a little mouse and give up on the hand, saving $9,000 and leaving you with $94,000 to play with.

When things start to look really bleak, you'll also have to cut out limping from your portfolio as well. If your stack happens to dip below 10 bets, then you'll have virtually no choice but to play for all of your chips when you finally find the hand you've been waiting for.

Small ball is most effective when your chip stack is above average. It's a style that should help you to continue to build without taking too many major risks. Once you've lost the ability to play deep-stack poker, you'll need to get back to a more traditional approach: play conservatively, wait for the right hand and situation, and then hope for the best.

FLOP PLAY

INTRODUCTION

The key to the whole small-ball concept is being able to outplay your opponents after the flop. The best players in the world are those who make good decisions after those first three cards hit the board. If your goal is to become a great player, the most important skill you'll need to improve upon is your post-flop play. Preflop play is a lot more systematic. After the flop, so many different variables come into play that it makes for harder decisions.

In this section, we'll cover how small preflop raises will make it easier and less risky for you to steal pots after the flop. Also, we'll talk about how to play hands based on position, your opponent's tendencies, and the texture of your hand. This discussion will help you understand why the pros make the decisions they do. Once you understand that, you'll be able to make those types of decisions yourself by following a few of these simple rules.

SMALL PREFLOP RAISES CAN WIN YOU MORE MONEY AFTER THE FLOP

In the previous section, we talked about lowering your raises to two-and-a-half times the big blind; enough of a raise to get your opponents to fold the garbage hands, but almost forcing them to call with a wide variety of marginal hands.

A standard preflop raise is generally three to four times the big blind, but if you are planning on playing lots of pots and raising frequently, you'll do better in the long run when you lower the size of your raise. That way you'll risk fewer chips every time you raise and someone reraises you before the flop, while at the same time forcing the player in the big blind to either:

1. Fold a hand that he should have defended with; or
2. Force him to play a marginal hand out of position against you.

Let's take a look at how a typical hand may look. With the blinds at $100/$200 plus a $25 ante, you raise to $500 as the first player to enter the pot with the K♥ 10♠. All players fold to the big blind who looks down at the 9♦ 7♣.

YOU   **BIG BLIND**

To make the call, the big blind would need to put $300 more into the pot. With nine players at the table, he'd be getting over 3 to 1 odds ($300 to win $1,025 equals 3.4 to 1). Your K-10 rates to beat his 9-7 about 64 percent of the time, or close to 2 to 1.

If the big blind folds, that is an excellent result for you. You forced him into a mistake. You laid him 3.4 to 1 on a proposition where he was only a 2 to 1 underdog. Obviously, betting after the flop and his positional disadvantage have a major effect on the result. That's where the power of small ball really starts to come into play.

Here comes the flop: Q♣ 6♦ 4♠.

YOU   **OPPONENT**

FLOP

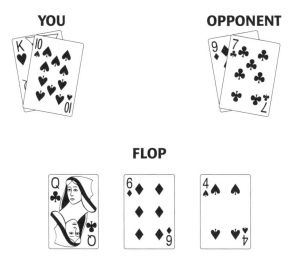

You still have your king-high and your opponent still has his 9-high. Since the big blind missed the flop completely, he will likely check to you. At this point, with $1,325 in the pot, it's yours for the taking.

So how much should you bet?

There's no reason to bet more than you need to. If your opponent will fold for $1,325, then he'd also fold for a $1,300 bet. You can take that a step further. Obviously, in this example, the 9-7 will fold to any bet, but generally speaking, a bet of anywhere from 50 to 80 percent of the pot will give you the desired result. In this case, a bet of $750 or $800 will get your opponent to lay down his hand and give you the pot.

At the same time, when you happen to run into an opponent who has a hand, you'll be saving a few bucks on your bluff. Suppose your opponent had A-Q and intended to check-raise you on the flop. By betting $750 instead of $1,325, you save $575 in chips. Those are chips you can use to attack the next blind.

Or, suppose you have a hand and flop a set against your opponent who has A-Q. You are still making a solid-looking bet and your opponent may check-raise you just the same. While it's true that you may make more in this specific situation by betting $1,325 rather than $750, it's important to note how rarely a situation like this will come up. More often than not, both you and your opponent will totally miss the flop. Besides, you can make up for the smaller flop bet on the turn or river. You could still potentially get all of your opponent's chips.

What you want to avoid doing is betting the $750 when you are bluffing, and then betting $1,325 when you actually have a strong hand. If you do that, it won't be long before your opponents are dialed-in to your betting pattern.

Let's flip the script and see what happens if you have the 9-7 and your opponent has the K-10 in the blind.

Hand in Action

You open the pot with 9-7 and your opponent defends his blind with K-10. Once again, the flop comes Q♣ 6♦ 4♠.

YOU

OPPONENT

FLOP

Your opponent misses the flop completely with the K-10 and checks to you. You bet out $750 to win $1,325 and your opponent folds.

Now, ask yourself this question: In this example, does it even matter what you have? I mean, if you had 7-2 offsuit in position and made this play, would it have mattered at all? No, it wouldn't. You'd still pick up the pot because you aren't playing your cards, you are simply betting on your opponent to miss the flop so that you can pick it up with a bet.

However, there is no reason to stretch your list of playable starting hands that far. You'd be much better off having a hand that actually has some potential after the flop. Even a hand like 6-4 offsuit has the potential to pay off big for you with the right flop.

From time to time, you are going to play against someone who wants to take the pot away from you with a bluff, and that's okay. Back to our example: Let's say that you have the K-10 and the blind has the 9-7 again. An aggressive player may check-raise your $750 bet with absolutely nothing. Obviously, you'll let him have the pot and move on to the next hand. It's no big deal—you have to train your mind to believe that. You need to have faith in the fact that if you keep plugging away, your stack will steadily increase rather than bleed away.

You'll go through stretches where you flop absolutely nothing and get raised time and time again. But hey, that's poker! You just need to keep your composure and eventually you'll start hitting some flops. If not, there's always the next tournament.

Having people make plays at you with nothing can actually pay off for you as well. I mean, every once in a while you'll actually have a hand when you bet the $750! The good news is that if your opponent check-raises you with nothing on the flop, you'll win some extra chips. After a bet of $750, you can expect your opponent to make it at least $2,250 or maybe even as much as $4,000. At that point, you'll have options. You can continue to slowplay your hand in the hope that your opponent will continue to bluff through the hand. Or you could just take it down right there with a reraise. Your decision should depend on several factors: the texture of the flop, your opponent's tendencies, as well as how many chips you have left.

Your bluffs will cost you $750, but when your opponent tries to bluff you back, it will cost him much more than that when he's wrong. This is a very aggressive style, but when executed properly, the losses are manageable. You aren't making any monster bluffs that risk your tournament life with this approach.

Instead, you will be chopping away at smaller pots looking to minimize damages until the right situation comes along where you finally flop a big hand and someone plays a pot with you.

As a general rule, you want to do the majority of your bluffing in the small pots while having the best of it in any of the big pots you play.

POSITION: THE BLACKJACK ANALOGY

For small ball to work best, position is extremely important. That's why, ideally, you want to play every pot you can heads-up against the big blind. When your opponent has to act first, you have the power to control the pot size and you can do it at little risk. If the player out of position wants to manipulate the pot size, he has to risk more chips and do a lot more guesswork.

To best illustrate the power of positional play in no-limit hold'em, let's look at how blackjack works. In blackjack, the dealer always gets to wait and see what you do before deciding what he'll have to do. For example, if you have 15 and catch a 9, the dealer wins. The dealer doesn't have to do anything—his hand is totally irrelevant.

As a blackjack player, you have no idea what the dealer actually has until you've already made your decision. Suppose you are dealt 16 and the dealer is showing a king. The book tells you that you should hit on 16 if the dealer has a face card. However, what if you knew that the dealer had a 6 in the hole? Well, according to the rules, you can stand on 16 but the dealer has to hit on 16. If you stand, you're a statistical favorite since you will win if the dealer catches a 6, 7, 8, 9, 10, jack, queen, or king. You will only lose if the dealer catches an ace, 2, 3, 4 or 5. You are about an 8 to 5 favorite to win the hand.

So how exactly does all of that apply to position at the poker table? Let's look at an example.

SMALL BALL

Hand in Action

You raise two-and-a-half times the blind with the 6♥ 7♦ from the button. The big blind defends with the 6♦ 7♥. The flop comes A♥ K♠ 9♣.

YOU   **BIG BLIND**

FLOP

Since you are in position and raised preflop, the big blind will likely check to you. Now, you go ahead and bet about 60 percent the size of the pot, and your opponent will likely throw his hand away. Of course, he may try to make a wild play at you, but that won't happen often enough to make your play lose money in the long run. Remember, sometimes you'll actually have a hand too!

While the big blind could win the pot by check-raising the flop, he may also be able to win the pot by simply leading out and betting the flop himself. In this case, you'd just fold your hand. Later on, I'll explain how even this defense against small ball is exploitable.

When you are playing no-limit hold'em in position against one opponent, it is akin to being the dealer in a one-on-one game of blackjack. The advantage lies in the fact that you get information from your opponents without their knowing the strength of your hand or even what you will do.

PLAYING DRAWING HANDS ON THE FLOP

There are a few times that you will veer from your strategy of betting 50 to 80 percent of the pot after the flop. When you actually flop a drawing hand is one of those times. Of course, it depends on the type of drawing hand you have, as well as the tendencies of your opponents.

If your opponents have been at your table for a while, they have seen you continuously raise before the flop and then bet virtually every flop in position. Therefore, they will be even more likely to go for a check-raise against you since they figure you'll bet most flops.

Hand in Action

One of the worst plays you can make in no-limit hold'em is to shut yourself off a draw by betting yourself off the hand. For example, let's say that you raised preflop with the 6♥ 4♥ and the big blind called you. Something about the way he called made you suspect that he had a very strong hand. Now, the flop comes K♥ 7♦ 3♠.

SMALL BALL

YOU

BIG BLIND

FLOP

This flop gives you a gutshot straight draw and a backdoor flush draw. Suppose your opponent has A-K or even K-K and is looking to set a trap for you. If you bet the flop, you'll have to fold if your opponent check-raises you, thus giving up the opportunity to fill your belly-buster straight draw.

However, if you give yourself a free card and check the flop, you could potentially win a monster pot if you hit the 5, or you could even pick up a backdoor flush draw.

The danger with checking this flop deals more with your overall table image. You don't want to make plays at the poker table that become too obvious to your opponents. If you check every time you have a drawing hand on the flop, but always bet with either garbage or good hands, it won't take a rocket scientist to figure out what you are up to.

More Considerations

There are very few absolutes when it comes to flop play. With all the added variables (stack size, position, player tendencies, flop texture, table image, and so on), you don't want to approach every situation the same way. You need to weigh several factors and make sure that in the end, the strategy that you are applying isn't easy to decipher. There are several ways to mix up your play on the flop, which I'll go into more detail on in another section. For now, understand that you shouldn't always check the flop when you have a draw, nor should you always bet the flop with top pair or even a garbage hand.

We've touched on a weak drawing hand (the inside straight, backdoor flush draw hand), but what happens when you flop a legitimate drawing hand such as a flush draw, open-ended straight draw, or even an open-ended straight-flush draw with overcards? You need to put a lot of thought into whether or not you should bet a drawing hand. By betting out of position, your semi-bluff could end up backfiring if you get raised, or even called.

Betting the draw makes the pot bigger, which in turn means that if your opponent raises, the raise will be bigger as well. In fact, his raise could end up being so big that it forces you off the hand. Or, if your opponent calls your bet on the flop and you miss your draw on the turn, you'll be forced to totally guess as to what you should do. Continue the bluff on the turn? Check and call? You'll be forced into a difficult decision. A check and call may reek of a drawing hand and let your opponent know exactly where you're at.

Your stack size should be one of the key factors in determining whether or not you bet the flop with the draw, regardless of whether you are in position. For example, if you are extremely short-stacked, you have a perfect opportunity to semi-bluff with an all-in bet. If your opponent folds, great; but even if he calls, you'll have a chance to win a good pot and double up.

Or let's say you are a big stack and your opponent has a big stack as well. In this case, it's probably safe to bet a drawing hand since you'll be able to call if your opponent raises. The times you might want to check a drawing hand on the flop are those situations when an opponent's raise on the flop might represent such a large portion of your stack that you would be forced to lay down the hand.

We are primarily talking about straightforward flush draws and straight draws. What if you have a monster draw? Let's say a straight and a flush draw, a pair and a flush draw, or even a flush draw with overcards? These are very strong hands. Usually, they end up being a statistical favorite after the flop. For example, let's give your opponent the A♣ A♠, while you have 6♥ 7♥ on a flop of 4♥ 5♥ 6♠. Despite the fact that at the moment your opponent has you beat, you have the better hand. Your hand will end up winning the pot almost twice as often as the A-A!

Favorites After the Flop
Let's look at the chart to see how hands match up after the flop.

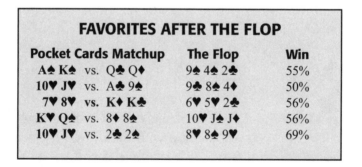

Pocket Cards Matchup	The Flop	Win
A♠ K♠ vs. Q♣ Q♦	9♠ 4♠ 2♣	55%
10♥ J♥ vs. A♣ 9♠	9♣ 8♠ 4♦	50%
7♥ 8♥ vs. K♦ K♣	6♥ 5♥ 2♣	56%
K♥ Q♠ vs. 8♦ 8♠	10♥ J♠ J♦	56%
10♥ J♥ vs. 2♣ 2♠	8♥ 8♠ 9♥	69%

As you can see, a monster draw is a powerful hand. You can play aggressively with a draw like this because, even in the worst cases, you can't be in terrible shape. By being aggressive, you give yourself several ways to win the pot:

1. Your opponent folds;
   or
2. You get your money all in on a coin-flip situation.

Let's look at some extreme scenarios where a monster draw could be in trouble.

FAVORITES AFTER THE FLOP: 2		
Pocket Cards Matchup	**The Flop**	**Win**
A♠ K♠ vs. 9♥ 9♦	9♠ 4♠ 2♣	25.5%
10♥ J♦ vs. 9♠ 9♦	9♣ 8♠ 4♦	25.5%
7♥ 8♥ vs. 6♦ 6♠	6♥ 5♥ 2♣	42%
K♥ Q♠ vs. A♦ 10♥	10♠ J♠ J♦	45%
10♥ J♥ vs. A♥ 3♥	8♥ 8♠ 9♥	45%

The beauty of these monster drawing hands is that even when you run into a strong, made hand, you still aren't dead in the water. Even in the most extreme cases, you'll still win the pot over 25 percent of the time. That's not great, but it's far from being dead.

Deciding whether to bet a drawing hand in tournament poker should also heavily depend on what stage of the tournament you are in. This is an extension of stack size, but in general, it's much safer to get drawing hands earlier in a tournament as opposed to later in a tournament when the blinds are high. At that stage of the tournament, you want to give yourself every opportunity to win the money in the middle. Besides, just because you missed your draw and didn't pick up the pot on the flop doesn't mean that you can't try to take it down on the turn with a bet—but more on that in the section devoted to playing the turn.

PLAYING MARGINAL HANDS AFTER THE FLOP

While you always want to think aggressively when playing no-limit hold'em, it's often correct to play passively with marginal hands in marginal situations, especially when there isn't much danger of being outdrawn by your opponent. Let's look at an example.

Hand in Action

You raise with pocket queens and a player behind you calls on the button. The flop comes A♦ 6♠ 6♥.

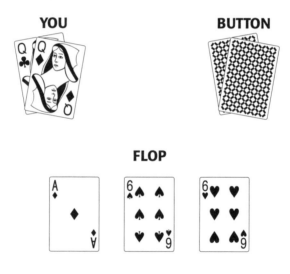

This is one of those situations where if you have the best hand on the flop, it's highly likely that you'll win the pot, while if you don't have the best hand, you'll have little chance of winning it. There is just no good reason to play a big pot in this situation. And since no draw is present on the board, you take little risk in giving your opponent a free card. If you are in the lead, the best your opponent could have with a hand such as K-J is precisely three outs in the deck to outdraw you if a king hits the turn or the river.

Getting Information

Some will say that by betting the flop you'll find out where you're at in the hand. Will you really? So, if your opponent raises, that would mean what? Well, most likely that he has an ace, or maybe, just maybe, he doesn't think you have an ace and is trying to steal the pot from you. What if your opponent just calls? Does that mean that he has the ace or a six? Once again, that depends on your opponent's tendencies.

The point is, if you check you'll also get information, but it may cost you less money. If you check to a player that never bluffs and he bets, you can safely fold your Q-Q at no cost, saving that bet on the flop. If you are up against a looser, more aggressive player, it may be wiser to check and call a smallish bet on the flop and see if he follows through with the hand. While that play may seem weak, it's strangely deceptive. When you check and call on the flop, your opponent will know you have something. If he has nothing, he'll likely give up after firing a bullet at the pot.

By check-calling the flop, your opponent may even fear that you have A-K, A-A, or even a six in *your* hand. If he has a hand such as A-10, he may never make another bet at the pot all the way through to the river showdown. By playing the hand this way you actually make it *less* likely that your opponent will bluff you, at the same time risking less money.

Replaying the Situation

Let's go back and see what happens if you bet the flop. Say you made it $500 before the flop and one player called. With the blinds and antes, there is $1,525 in the pot. If you bet out $800 on the A-6-6 flop and your opponent makes it $2,500, what are you going to do? I'm guessing you'll probably have to lay it down since it's very likely that your opponent has an ace.

SMALL BALL

What if your opponent suspects that? From his perspective, he's looking at your $800 bet and figuring that if you have the ace you might check, but if he raises he'll find out for sure. He could smooth call the $800 on the flop and try to steal the pot on the turn (if he doesn't have the ace), or he could risk $2,500 to win $2,325 figuring that you either don't have the ace or won't call the raise.

If you check the flop, you take that play away from your opponent. If you don't bet, he *can't* raise you off the hand! If you check-call $1,000, you'll put your opponent in a quandary on the turn wondering if he should continue to bet the hand through. For this play to be effective, you'll need to make sure that you play Q-Q, as well as A-K, the same way on the flop. In fact, if a player calls your raise behind you and the flop comes A-6-6, you should check a very high percentage of the time with any hand. Again, that may seem weak, but in the long run it's a more cautious way of making sure that you don't get bluffed off the best hand.

> **POSITION IS POWER. WHEN WE HAVE POSITION, WE NEED TO USE IT—**
>
> **BUT WHEN WE DON'T HAVE IT, WE NEED TO RESPECT IT.**

To play hands this way, you'll have to make sure that you have a good read on your opponents. Who likes to represent the ace a lot? Who will fire one bullet and give up on the turn? Would that player try to bluff-raise you on a flop that contains an ace? The more you know about an opponent's tendencies in these types of situations, the better.

In this example, we were out of position and played meekly, which could almost be the motto for small ball. Position is power. When we have position, we need to use it—but when we don't have it, we need to respect it.

Hand in Action

Let's look at an example of how we might play a marginal hand in position. You've raised preflop with A-10 in late position and the small blind called. The flop comes J♣ 10♠ 4♦ giving you second pair with a good kicker.

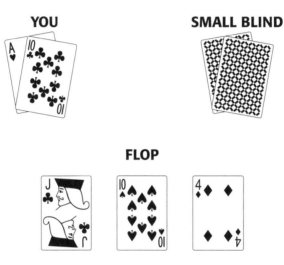

YOU   **SMALL BLIND**

FLOP

There are several ways to play this hand and as always, several factors influence whether you lean one way or the other. If either you or your opponent is on a short stack, get your money in the middle. It's that simple. When you are on a short stack, you need to take a few risks and this is the kind of situation where it would make sense to go all in. However, if the stacks are deeper, you need to pay close attention to your opponent and see if you can pick up any physical tells as to whether he likes the flop or not.

If your opponent leads out at the flop, the standard play is to call the bet and see what develops on the turn, provided that his bet wasn't too big. More likely though, your opponent will check the flop regardless of what he has. At that point, you need to ask yourself some questions. What range of hands will this player call you with from the small blind? Is he the type of guy that would call you with hands such as 6♥ 7♥? Or is he the type that likes to only play big cards and pairs?

If you decide that your opponent could have anything from 6♥ 7♥, 8♦ 8♠ and J♦ K♠, to A♥ Q♦, checking is the right play. By checking, you show some weakness. If your opponent is an aggressive player, he may see that as an opportunity to steal the pot from you on the turn if a blank hits. Also, if he indeed has pocket eights, he may feel as though he has the best hand.

Against K-J, we are in a little bit of trouble, but by checking we can minimize the damage. Other hands such as A-Q, K-Q and A-K are the ones that we'd be giving a free card to, but is that really so bad? None of those hands would likely fold on the flop anyway, so why not just see what hits the turn first before committing to the pot? If the turn comes with a 9, a queen or a king, you might be able to get away from the hand cheaply if the action gets too hot and heavy.

While the queen would give you a straight draw, it's probably the worst card you could see hit the turn since it hits every one of the hands you just gave the free draw to (A-Q, K-Q and A-K). The ace, while making you two pair, is also a card you should proceed with cautiously. You'd be dead against an A-J or K-Q, but it could also be a great card for you if your opponent called your raise with A-9 or worse. Still, you should be careful with aces and tens in this situation. You only want "some" action, not too much!

LOSING THE MINIMUM

One of the real keys to applying small ball effectively is the ability to get away from situations where it looks like you are in danger. By playing so many hands and playing them aggressively, you are going to find yourself getting raised quite often. If that gets under your skin a little bit, it could cause you to veer from the central concept that makes small ball effective.

While you want to be the aggressor at the table, you should be extremely cautious about continuing with the hand when someone plays back at you—unless your hand is very strong, or you strongly suspect that your opponent is bluffing you.

We talked about folding to reraises before the flop. The same applies to raises after the flop. Let's look at an example.

Hand in Action

You raise before the flop with 8-8 and only the big blind calls the raise. The flop comes J♥ 6♦ 4♣.

YOU   **BIG BLIND**

FLOP

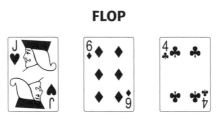

Your opponent checks, you bet about 65 percent of the pot, and your opponent check-raises you. This is a tricky situation. The main reason this is a more difficult decision than it might otherwise appear is that your opponent is more likely to raise you with weaker hands if you have been playing lots of hands and betting the flop consistently.

SMALL BALL

Depending on your opponent, he could have any of the following hands in this situation:

1. Top pair or better
2. A flush and/or straight draw
3. A pair lower than 8-8
4. Ace high
5. Absolutely nothing

How you proceed is obviously very read dependant, but I would strongly advise you to lean towards folding. Yes, while it's true that your opponents are more likely to be making plays against you, you don't want to play the guessing game in marginal situations for large percentages of your chips.

Also, the 8-8 just doesn't play very well after the flop. In fact, in this situation you'd be much better off with a hand such as K-6. It is almost as good as 8-8, but with the K-6, you'd have five outs to improve your hand rather than just two.

SMALL BALL THINKING

You are going to get bluffed from time to time. If you don't, you simply aren't playing all that well! The goal with the small ball approach is to look for high-percentage opportunities to play big pots, and avoid playing big pots that require a lot of guesswork. While this approach might seem easily exploitable, that's not the case. Players will often try to use a counterstrategy: They will try to force you to play big pots by overbetting the pot. With that strategy, though, your opponent is risking a higher percentage of his chips on his bluffs. And when you have a strong hand, he'll be giving you extra action with his overbets.

I can't stress enough how important it is to keep your composure when playing small ball. You'll go through streaks when you get raised time and time again—don't crack! Have faith in the system. A good opportunity will usually present itself. I've seen far too many good, young players go broke after being reraised and bullied a few hands in a row. Eventually, the youngster gets fed up with it all, makes a move at the wrong pot, and winds up heading for the exit sign.

Let me illustrate a situation where that could happen to you.

Hand in Action

With the blinds at $100/$200, you make it $500 to go with an A-J. The small blind reraises you to $2,000. This is the fourth hand in a row that you've been raised before the flop! Out of frustration, you make the call.

That's mistake number one. Generally, if you've been reraised three times in a row and then a player reraises you after that, he's even more likely to have a strong hand—not less likely, as you might think. Calling a reraise with A-J is already a bad play, but in this case, it's even worse.

So anyway, now you've made it to the flop, which comes J♥ Q♣ 4♥.

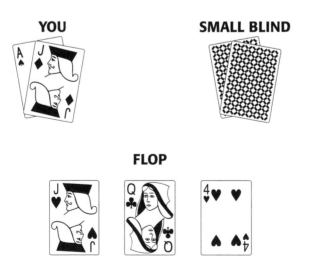

Your opponent hesitates and finally checks. You decide to bet $3,000 with your pair of jacks, and the raiser goes all in for $7,000 more. It's pretty clear that you should fold your hand, but if you allow your mind to play tricks on you, you may find yourself looking for any excuse to believe that your opponent is bluffing. So you make the call only to find that you're drawing dead when your opponent turns over Q-Q. Oops! An "oops" that could have been avoided if you had kept your composure either before the flop or after it.

Here is probably the best advice I could ever give you when it comes to no-limit hold'em tournament poker:

> **PEOPLE DON'T BLUFF NEARLY AS MUCH AS YOU THINK THEY DO. PROS WIN BECAUSE THEY PLAY BIG POTS WITH THE BEST HAND, NOT BECAUSE THEY USE SUPER-ADVANCED BLUFFING STRATEGIES. PROS WIN BECAUSE THEY DEPEND ON THE FACT THAT YOU JUST WON'T BELIEVE THEM.**

In order for a pro to cultivate that "wild" image, he may choose to play lots of hands, giving off the impression that he's doing a lot of wild bluffing. Watch a little closer. Sure, the pro may be raising tons of hands before the flop, but notice what happens when the big money goes in after the flop. Look at the types of hands a pro will turn over when everything is on the line. One thing you can be sure of is that you'll generally see a premium hand, not some random hand with no chance to improve.

Pros will bluff with drawing hands, but you'll rarely see a pro get all of his money in on a flop of A♥ K♦ 4♣ with a hand like 8-9 suited! Those types of plays are for the amateur player. If a pro gets his money all in on this type of a flop, expect to see him turn over at least aces and kings.

To become a top professional, there is one essential variable for success that can't really be taught—discipline. Discipline becomes even more important if you choose to apply the small-ball strategy. Playing small ball is a double-edged sword. You'll create more action for yourself and get your premium hands paid off more regularly, but at the same time, you will invite people to bluff you more often as well. As you improve as a player, you'll welcome those weak bluffs when you become more adept at sniffing them out. In the meantime, be content with letting the odd pot go to a bluffing opponent. If he keeps that up, you'll hopefully be able to trap him for a much bigger pot down the road.

KEEPING THE POT SMALL

Earlier I explained that you are often better off checking the flop with drawing hands so as to not bet yourself off the draw. Obviously, if you check the flop only when you have a drawing hand, your opponents will be able to figure you out very easily. Luckily, there are other situations where it might be a good idea to check the flop: when you flop a monster hand and want to trap your opponent; and when you have a piece of the flop, but not a big enough piece to feel great about your hand. Let's look at a few examples.

Hand in Action

You raise before the flop with the K♥ 9♥ and the big blind calls you. The flop comes 10♥ 9♠ 8♠, giving you middle pair.

SMALL BALL

YOU

BIG BLIND

FLOP

This is an extremely dangerous flop for your hand, which might lead you to believe that you should be aggressive and look to protect your hand with a big bet here. I don't think that's a very good idea. You could very easily be beaten on this flop. Even if you are ahead, there are drawing hands out there that wouldn't be afraid to play a big pot with you. If your opponent has a K-J, J-9, or any flush draw, he'll at least call a bet on the flop.

By checking the flop, you give yourself an opportunity to avoid losing any chips unnecessarily, while keeping the pot small so that you'll have a better chance of protecting your hand on the turn. For example, suppose the turn card is a 2♦ and your opponent checks again. You can make a decent sized bet to force your opponent into either taking a bad price by calling or letting go of his draw.

Hand in Action

Here's another situation. You raise preflop with Q-Q and the button calls you. The flop comes K♦ K♠ 4♣.

YOU

BUTTON

FLOP

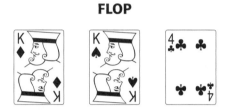

You have little reason to bet. If your opponent has a king, you're just dead meat. If not, the only hands you need to worry about are 4-4 and A-A. What's even more likely, though, is that your opponent has a maximum of three total outs against you. For example, if he has an A-J, you'll be giving him a free chance to outdraw you if you check the flop and he hits the ace. That's not such a big deal. Or, if your opponent has a hand such as 9-9, you might be giving him a free shot at one of the two remaining nines to beat you. Again, a very low percentage hit for him.

If the queens are good on the flop, they are probably strong enough that it's okay to play it weak since they'll likely be good by the river too. If you are beat, you want to cut your losses. The other key benefit of checking the flop is that you'll give your opponent an opportunity to either bluff off his money or protect what he believes to be the best hand.

If he has 9-9, he'll probably bet the flop to protect his hand and try to find out where he's at. No need for you to get frisky against a bet here—you should totally shut down and go into defense mode. I'm going to steal a quote from another top pro,

Layne Flack, who says, "Why do the pushin' when the donkey will do the pullin'?"

Hand in Action

The texture of the board says a lot about how you should play marginal hands after the flop. For example, suppose a weak player limps in from middle position and you raise him from the button with A♠ 8♠. He calls and the flop comes A♥ 6♦ 6♠.

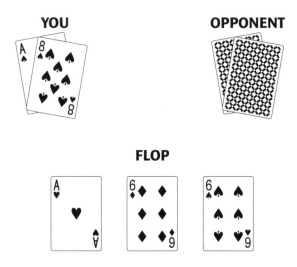

YOU   **OPPONENT**

FLOP

If the limper checks to you, what should you do? You have aces up on the flop, which look good. But what type of hands will your opponent call you with on a flop that has absolutely no possible draw?

There is an outside chance that he'll call you with a pocket pair if he is truly awful. But more likely than that, if he calls your bet on the flop, he'll have at least an ace as well. Your 8 kicker could be in trouble. And even if it isn't, chances are that by the river you'll be splitting the pot with your opponent. Any ace, 6, 9, 10, jack, queen or king would nullify your kicker.

Why not check this flop? The only real danger in checking is that your opponent might have a hand such as 3-3 and catch a 3 on the turn. You'd be losing a pot you would have won with a bet on the flop, but that's simply not going to happen often enough to make you worry about it.

If you check the flop, you may induce a bluff from your opponent. Let's say the turn card is a 9, for example, and your opponent has 7-7. He may put you on a pair of queens or kings and try to represent the ace on the turn with a bet. If he does that, once again, there is no reason to raise him. He just might have you beat, and if not, your risk in giving him a free card is likely minimal.

The key reason you are able to check a flop with a marginal hand is that a bet likely won't change the outcome of who wins the hand. In the first example, any player with a drawing hand will likely call a bet anyway. In the other examples, there are very few cards that could outdraw you on the turn or the river. Now let's look at one more example.

Hand in Action

Before the flop, a tight player raises from under the gun and you call from the button with 10-10. The flop comes 8♥ 4♥ 3♣.

SMALL BALL

YOU

OPPONENT

FLOP

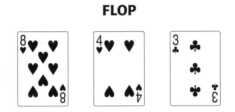

The tight player checks to you. In this situation, you should bet for several reasons:

1. You have position and a bet will help define your opponent's hand
2. Your opponent likely has A-K and if you check, you'll give him a free chance at catching any one of six cards (three aces and three kings) to beat you.
3. A flush draw is present. If your opponent has the A♥ Q♦ and you check the flop, he not only can catch an ace or a queen to beat you, but also might pick up a flush draw on the turn if another heart hits the board.

If a tight player check-raises you on the flop, it's a pretty safe bet that your tens are no good. Even if he just checks and calls a bet on the flop, you should proceed with caution. He could have aces and is waiting to trap you on the turn. With 10-10, you basically want to make your case for the pot right on the flop. But if there is too much resistance, you need to seriously think about letting the hand go. If your opponent is brave enough to check-raise you on the flop with the A♥ K♥, so be it. By the way, even with that hand, he'd still be the favorite—two overcards and a flush draw is a 55 percent favorite to your pocket tens.

MIXING UP YOUR PLAY ON THE FLOP

Here are some simple guidelines on how to mix up your flop play when using the small-ball approach.

When To Bet

1. **When you miss the flop entirely, but also have position, you should still bet the flop if you think your opponent also missed it.** Be wary of flops that contain two or more cards above 8. Flops like J-9-7, A-Q-9 and J-10-4 hit a lot of hands that many opponents will call with.

2. **You should bet the flop with good hands that also need protection.** If the flop comes J-8-4 and you have K-J, you should bet the flop a high percentage of the time.

3. **You should bet monster drawing hands.** You want to either steal the pot on the flop, or build a bigger pot for when you hit your hand.

4. **When you pick up a tell.** Anytime you pick up a tell and feel as though your opponent is going to fold, even if you have a marginal hand, you should bet. For example, if the flop comes J-6-4 and you have 4-5, you should bet that flop if it looks like your opponent is legitimately uninterested in the hand.

When To Check

1. **When you have a drawing hand and want to catch your card cheaply.** If you bet the flop, your opponent may raise you, thus forcing

you to lay down a drawing hand that potentially could have won you a big pot.

2. **You should often check on flops that pose little danger of outdrawing your hand.** If you have A-A and the flop comes 2-2-9, there is little danger in giving away one free card. If your opponent has a hand like K-Q, you might win more money from him if he catches a pair on the turn. The risk of checking in this situation is minimal.

3. **If you have a marginal hand on a dangerous board.** In these situations, it's often better to check the flop and see what develops on the turn before committing any more chips to the pot. You can even do this with strong hands. For example, if you have 9-9 on a flop of 9♥ 10♥ J♠, checking wouldn't be a bad idea at all. If the turn card is a 7, 8, queen, king, or a heart, you could limit a loss that may have been inevitable.

4. **When you suspect an opponent has caught big on the flop.** When you pick up a tell on your opponent that leads you to believe that he's hit a big piece of the flop and you have nothing, checking is in order. Pay close attention to your opponent's behavior and you can save some bets in situations that might otherwise have been automatic betting situations.

HIT OR MISS FLOPS

Flops such as K-K-4, A-6-6, Q-Q-2, and 2-2-3 are what I like to call hit or miss flops. If you started with the best hand, it will remain the best hand after flops like these a high percentage of the time. Your opponents will either hit those flops big, or they will miss completely. By playing your marginal hands cautiously after these types of flops, you'll be able to minimize your losses without taking a major risk of losing the entire pot.

HIT OR MISS FLOPS

Flop types your opponents will either hit big or miss completely

K-K-4
A-6-6
Q-Q-2
2-2-3

MANIPULATING THE POT SIZE

Keeping the pot small by checking the flop is one way you can manipulate the size of the pot. Other times you'll actually want to play a bigger pot when you hit a hand, and there are ways to do that as well. This concept is even more important in a game like pot-limit hold'em, but if you are playing small-ball poker, your approach to the game is similar to playing pot-limit hold'em since you rarely bet more than the amount that's already in the pot.

In the last section, we touched on keeping the pots small with marginal hands. However, when you have a monster hand and think your opponent does too, sometimes it makes sense to build a sizeable pot on the flop.

Before I continue, it's extremely important to remember that you shouldn't follow any of the strategies in this chapter to the tee. You want to use these tools as general rules, but anytime you always do the same thing in the same situation, you run the risk of giving away too much information. For example, I'm giving away a lot of information in this chapter about my own play. Players who are very perceptive should be able to better understand how I approach various situations, and be able to use that knowledge against me—provided I don't mix up my play.

As I write this, I think to myself, "Wow, if I played against a guy who played exactly like this, it would be very easy to figure him out." If you follow the "rules," a raise on the flop would set off alarm bells in your opponent's head. Remember, we've already made it quite clear that we want to play small pots, so if we raise on the flop, it must mean that we have a monster hand. That should be true most of the time, but if it's true *all* the time, you'll just never get paid off.

You need to raise the flop from time to time as a pure bluff in situations where you just *feel* that your opponent is weak and believe you can take the pot away from him.

Hand in Action
For example, let's say that a player raised to $600 under the gun before the flop. You call from middle position with 6♥ 7♥. The flop comes A♦ J♠ 4♣.

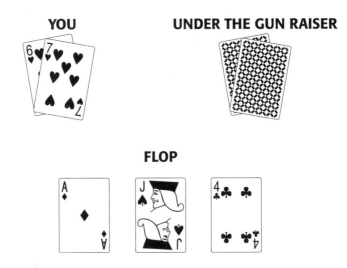

YOU

UNDER THE GUN RAISER

FLOP

Your opponent makes a weak-looking bet of $850 on the flop. Trust your instincts. If you don't think he has an ace, you should go after this pot on the flop with a raise. If you have, say, $28,000 in chips at that point, risking $3,000 to win about $2,500 isn't so bad—if your instincts are sharp, that is.

The reason I bring up this bluff is that it's an integral part of being able to manipulate the pot size when you actually have a big hand and want to get paid handsomely. If you never bluff-raise the flop, you'll be giving away far too much information about the value of your good hands when you raise on the flop.

Now that we have that concept out of the way, let's look at ways to favorably manipulate the pot size in order to bust your opponent.

Hand in Action

With the blinds at $100/$200 and a $25 ante, you call a preflop raise of $600 from an under-the-gun raiser. You are in position with 3-3 in a three-way pot. All three of you have over $30,000 in chips. The flop comes 8♠ 7♠ 3♦.

SMALL BALL

YOU

UNDER THE GUN RAISER

MIDDLE POSITION

FLOP

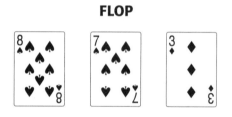

This isn't the type of hand you want to slowplay in this situation because a lot of cards could come on the turn to kill your action. The 6♠, 9♠, or 10♠ will complete several different draws, and an opponent with an overpair is likely to shut down.

Let's say the initial raiser bets out $1,500 and the middle position player calls. This is the perfect opportunity to build the pot. If you make it $5,000 to go, for example, the initial raiser may decide to reraise in order to shutout a possible drawing hand in the middle. If he has A-A, he may be hoping that you have 9-9, 10-10, or J-J and can get the hand heads-up with you.

Suppose he does indeed have A-A and makes it $15,000 to go. The middle player folds. Now you can stick in the rest of your chips. At this point, the player with A-A is all but committed, and he could rationalize that you could have K-K, Q-Q, or a hand such as the 9♠ 10♠.

Hand in Action

Here is another example. Before the flop, everyone folds to the small blind, who raises just a little bit. You are in the big blind with J-8 offsuit and call with position. The flop comes J♠ 8♦ 4♠ and your opponent bets out at you.

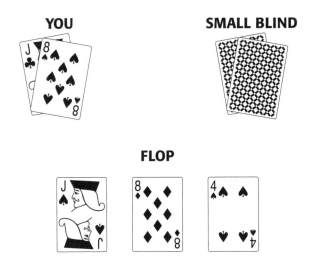

YOU   SMALL BLIND

FLOP

Your dilemma is to either smooth call the bet or raise the pot, hoping that your opponent has something like A-J, Q-Q, K-K, or even A-A.

There is an obvious problem with calling here. With a few straight draws on board and a flush draw present, there are too many cards that might hit the turn and scare your opponent into shutting down one of those premium hands. Any spade, 5, 6, 7, 8, 9, 10, jack, queen, king or ace could potentially be an action killer for you.

SMALL BALL

Hand in Action

Let's look at it from your opponent's perspective for a second. You are sitting there with A-J in the small blind and the big blind just called you. The turn card comes the Q♥.

YOU **BIG BLIND**

BOARD

What would you do in that spot? It's a terrible card for your hand. So terrible, it all but forces you to check the turn. You don't want your opponent to get away that easily from a trap that you have set up on the flop. By raising this hand on the flop, while you took the bluff away from your opponent, you also gave him a chance to bury himself if he decided to reraise you there.

As I mentioned earlier, it's very important to mix up your play a little bit to make this play effective. Sometimes, you must raise that flop with a hand like A-7 or even 3-4. You don't need to overdo it, or even risk too many chips, but I can't emphasize enough how important it is to avoid predictable patterns.

Let's look at one more situation.

Hand in Action

Before the flop, a player raises from early position and you call from the big blind with the J♦ 9♥. Miraculously, the flop comes perfect: J♥ J♠ 9♠.

YOU   **PREFLOP RAISER**

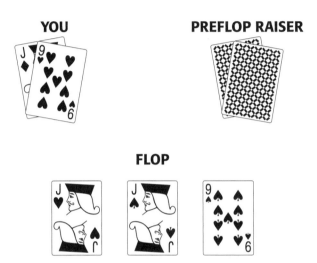

FLOP

You check to your opponent who bets out half the pot. Against a rookie player, you could smooth call and realistically expect him to bet the turn again without trips. However, most experienced players will be very wary of your call on such a board and will check the turn, even with A-A.

Therefore, since the jig will be up after you smooth call on the flop, why even bother? Why not check-raise the flop and hope that either:

1. Your opponent is trapped with A-J
2. He doesn't believe you and makes a re-steal attempt
3. He puts you on a drawing hand and tries to protect his overpair (A-A, K-K or Q-Q) against it

If number one is true and you don't check-raise the flop, you run the risk of minimizing your win. For example, if a spade hits the turn—or an 8, 10, or a queen—your opponent may fear that a drawing hand has gotten there and he'll shut down. Not only will he fear drawing hands, but aside from J-9 and 9-9, he'll also have to fear that you hit your kicker on the turn. If you check-raise the hand on the flop, there probably is no escape for him.

If you play the hand aggressively on the flop, you trap him when he also has a monster hand and you give him some rope to hang himself if he decides to bluff you. In fact, by playing the hand in a straightforward manner, it actually becomes deceptive.

Number two could come into play as well if you have been pounding on this particular opponent. If you've beaten him several hands in a row, he may get so frustrated with you that he tries to push back—and at the worst time possible for his own welfare.

If number three is true, your opponent may not want to guess on the turn and, instead, will try to find out immediately whether you have the jack. That's okay, since a reraise would have to be pretty sizeable, meaning that you'd get some more money out of him; and also avoid a disaster if he hits a two-outer (one of the two cards left in the deck that are the same rank as his overpair) on the turn or river by going all in.

CHECKING BIG HANDS ON THE FLOP

Another trick you should add to your repertoire is checking big hands on the flop to let your opponent catch up. We've already added some texture to our game by checking marginal hands and some draws, plus checking when we sense strength on dangerous boards. We also need to check some big hands as well.

Following is a situation that illustrates the concept.

Hand in Action
You raise before the flop with A♥ K♥ and the flop comes K♣ 10♥ 8♥.

YOU		OPPONENT

FLOP

This appears to be a dangerous board. If you check the flop, your opponent may misinterpret the meaning of that check for weakness. Or he may believe that you are on a draw—which you are, but with a strong hand as well. Checking this flop could allow you to hit a monster hand at the same time as your opponent, only you'll end up with the nut hand. If your opponent has a J-9 offsuit, for example, the 7♥ on the turn could crush him. Even though you checked the flop, it would still be hard for him to get away from his straight.

Hand in Action
Let's look at an even better example: You raise with A♠ A♦ preflop and the flop comes A♥ 6♦ 6♠.

SMALL BALL

YOU

OPPONENT

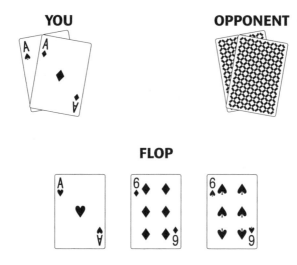

FLOP

If your opponent has a 6 in this hand, you'll probably win a big pot no matter how you proceed. If he has a hand like 9-9, though, the only way you'll be able to trap is to let him see a free card on the turn. If it's a 9, that's your home run ball right there!

Hand in Action

One more example. You raise with A♥ A♠ before the flop and the flop comes 9♥ 6♥ 3♥.

YOU

OPPONENT

FLOP

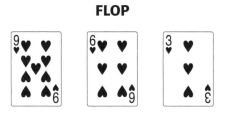

This flop is totally safe for you to check. Your check could trick your opponent into believing that you are either simply on a flush draw, have flopped nothing, or have a hand such as the A♠ K♠. Since you checked the flop, your opponent may try to make an aggressive bet on the turn if a heart doesn't hit; or he may bluff if a heart comes. He may not believe you'd check the flop with the nut flush draw and/or a pair.

The best result you can accomplish with a check on the flop is to allow a hand such as Q♥ J♦ to catch up a little bit. A heart might trap your opponent for a little bet, but a queen or a jack on the turn would likely induce him to protect his pair with a bet. Even if he has the Q♠ J♠, a hand that has your opponent virtually drawing dead, hitting a pair on the turn could trap him into losing bets he would not have lost had you bet the flop.

CALLING ON THE FLOP WITH NOTHING EXCEPT THE INTENTION OF STEALING THE POT LATER

In most heads-up situations, neither you nor your opponent will hit the flop with a very strong hand. The player who is able to get the best of the situations where neither of you have much of anything after the flop is usually the player that will come out ahead in the long run.

There are several ways to approach these types of situations, but there is one particular way of stealing pots from your opponents

SMALL BALL

that is low risk, has a high success rate, and fits the mold of the small-ball approach. When you are in position against just one opponent, your hand is often unimportant; instead, what's most important is the strength of your opponent's hand.

Let's look at a couple of situations to understand this concept more clearly.

Hand in Action 1
With the blinds at $100/$200 and a $25 ante, a player raises to $600 from late position before the flop. You call him from the button with the 10♥ J♥, and the blinds fold. The flop comes A♣ 9♥ 2♠.

YOU

OPPONENT

FLOP

Your opponent bets $800, about half the pot. Normally in this situation, folding would be your best option since you've completely missed the flop and your opponent could easily have an ace. Or maybe not. Suppose your opponent has any of the following hands: 7-7, K-Q, 10-10, or 9-10. He may very well bet any one of these hands after the flop, but if you call or raise him, he will likely fold as he can only beat a bluff.

If you decide to make a play at the pot, smooth calling is actually a slightly better play than raising on the flop, especially since that's what you would normally do anyway if you had a hand such as A-J or A-Q. The other reason that smooth calling is a better play in this specific situation is because you actually have a hand that could turn into a monster draw with the turn of a card. An 8 or a queen would give you an open-ended straight draw, and a heart would give you a backdoor flush draw.

Let's say that you make the call on the flop. By the turn, you should have a much better idea as to the strength of your opponent's hand. If he bets, you should probably just give it up—unless you've improved your hand by catching a queen, 8, or a heart, and his bet is not too big. If you happen to hit a straight or a flush on the river, and your opponent has a set of aces, for example, the payoff could be huge. He'll have a difficult time putting you on a straight when the board comes A-9-2 rainbow!

But what happens if your opponent checks on the turn, appearing to put up the white flag? With about $3,000 in the pot, you could bet about $1,500 and probably pick up the pot. Not always, of course, because a tricky player may decide to either check-raise you on the turn, or possibly even be happy to check and call with a better hand than yours. The point is that this play doesn't need to work even half the time to make it profitable since you are keeping your bets small, thus giving yourself a good price on the bluff attempt.

In this case, you'd be risking $1,500 on the turn to win $3,325 ($300 in blinds and $225 in antes). That's better than the 2 to 1 odds that your opponent will fold. Of course, if you factor in the $800 call on the flop, that lessens your odds to something like $2,300 to win $3,325. However, that's not entirely true when your opponent actually bets the turn. If he checks and you pick up a draw on the turn, you could potentially win more without having to invest anything on the turn. If you hit a backdoor draw, you have the potential to win even more.

Hand in Action 2

In this hand, you have a two-way play on the flop. With the blinds at $25/$50, your opponent makes it $150 to go from early position preflop. Everyone folds around to you on the button. You call the raise with the 6♥ 4♥, and the blinds fold. The flop comes K♥ 7♠ 3♦.

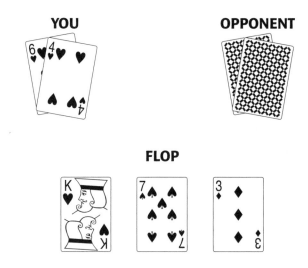

YOU   **OPPONENT**

FLOP

With $375 in the pot, your opponent bets out $300. All you have is an inside straight draw, and you aren't really sure what your opponent has at this point. In one sense, you hope that he has A-A or even K-K, but if he has a hand like A-Q, that's not bad either.

Calling on the flop with this gutshot straight draw will actually give you two ways to win the pot. The most obvious way is to nail the straight on the turn, but the other way is to take control of the hand with a bet on the turn.

If your opponent has A-A, K-K, or even A-K, a 5 on the turn will look like a completely innocent card. In fact, if your opponent has K-K, he will think he has the absolute nuts. Based on that alone, it's often worth calling to hit the straight, because the potential payoff is huge.

That situation isn't going to happen very often, but that's okay because you can always fall back on Plan B. If your opponent raised with A-Q, Q-Q, J-J, A-J, or several other hands, he may be afraid of your call on the flop, thinking that you must have a king. If he checks the turn, you can often pick up the pot with a bet of, say, $600. Betting $600 to win $975 in this spot is pretty good, with the added bonus of still having an out if your opponent calls.

Things change dramatically when you are out of position since you lose control of the betting and don't get enough information about your opponent's hand on the turn to make this play profitable in the long run. In position, you get the benefit of seeing your opponent either check or bet before you have to act. Out of position, this calling-with-nothing-on-the-flop play doesn't work nearly as well.

Let's look at an example.

Hand in Action

The flop comes K♥ 7♠ 8♥ and you are out of position with J-9. You check the flop, your opponent bets, and you call. The turn is a 4♣.

SMALL BALL

YOU

OPPONENT

BOARD

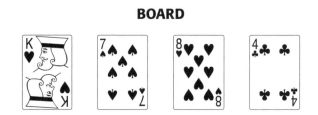

You check again. This time, your opponent also checks. Had the positions been reversed, you could have bet on the turn card in the hope of stealing the pot.

You do get one more chance to steal this pot on the river, but by then the play is much less effective. Based on the way you have played your hand, if you bet the river card, your opponent will call you with a wide variety of hands. You showed no real aggression until the river, plus several draws are on the board that you may have missed. For example, if your opponent has Q-Q, he will call your bet on the river a high percentage of the time. In fact, he may call you with as little as ace high!

The power of position allows you to take control of a hand like this and keep the heat on your opponent, who can't be sure that he won't be facing yet another large bet on the river. With marginal hands out of position, you may be able to force an opponent off a hand if you play your cards right.

The key to this play working for you is that your play has to be *believable*—as in, you would play a strong hand the same way as you are playing this hand. With a small-ball approach to the game, you'll routinely be smooth calling with top pair, middle pair, sets, gutshots, overpairs, and all sorts of hands. Playing this way will make it easy to sell the idea that your call on the flop does not necessarily signify weakness at all, which will allow you to exploit your opponents even if they suspect what you are doing!

Seriously, the beauty of this approach to playing the flop is that, even if your opponents know that you like to smooth call with all sorts of hands, they don't know when you have a strong hand and when you are calling with nothing. Their defense against this sort of play is minimal since you are forcing them to play the guessing game.

WAITING UNTIL THE TURN FOR MORE INFORMATION

Another bone of contention I have with certain authors is the theory that you should play your hands aggressively on the flop so as to better define your hand, and at the same time, gain more information from your opponents. This theory is actually very effective in limit hold'em, but it doesn't translate well to no-limit tournaments.

The main reason it doesn't work as well in no-limit is simple: It's too expensive. In limit hold'em, a raise represents just one extra unit, but in no-limit hold'em, if you raise someone on the flop to "find out where you're at," it can cost you a pretty penny.

Hand in Action
With the blinds at $50/$100 a player from early position makes it $300 to go before the flop. You call with the A♥ J♥. The big blind calls, so three of you see the flop. It comes A♦ 8♠ 3♥.

SMALL BALL

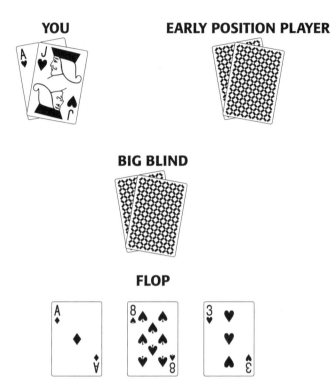

YOU

EARLY POSITION PLAYER

BIG BLIND

FLOP

The big blind checks and the preflop raiser bets out $800. If you were to raise him here, a standard raise would cost you about $2,400 in chips. So, let's say you do put in a raise, the big blind folds, and now the first raiser calls the bet.

Exactly what information have you gained? What if the under-the-gun player reraises you? In this case, it would seem as though you've gained some valuable information and your A-J is likely behind. You could fold and take your $2,400 loss.

Let's look at the benefits of just calling on the flop. You'll see that, instead of $2,400, you can get the same information with an $800 call on the flop, plus a chance to reevaluate on the turn. Okay, so you just call on the flop and the big blind folds. The turn card is a queen and your opponent bets $1,600. You still aren't sure if your A-J is the best hand, but the fact that your opponent bet again should direct you towards thinking that you are beaten. Since you are unsure, though, you call the $1,600.

At this point, it has cost you the exact same amount of chips that you spent when you raised on the flop instead of just calling. The only difference is that playing this way, you've made it all the way to the river. To help you figure out the best course of action on the river you have the following information: Your opponent raised preflop and followed through with a continuation bet on the flop. You called the bet, a queen hit the turn, yet your opponent wasn't afraid and bet again. You called that bet as well. Therefore, if your opponent makes a big bet at the river, he has to know that you have a strong hand and are not on a draw.

That's a lot of information. Your opponent could still bluff you on the river, but the same could be said about his flop reraise. He may be coming over the top of you on the flop with a weaker ace or just as a bluff.

There is one other key benefit to smooth calling on the flop in this situation rather than raising—you allow yourself a chance to suck out! If your opponent has A-K, bets the $800, you make it $2,400, and now he reraises you off the hand, you've just lost $2,400 with no chance to get lucky. However, if you just call the flop, you could get really lucky and spike a jack on the turn or river. Or, you could even make a backdoor flush with the hand and possibly win a big pot.

The only thing that's better about raising on the flop is that you protect your hand from being outdrawn when you are ahead, and you also get information about your opponent's hand quicker. However, getting outdrawn with A-J on an A-8-3 rainbow flop should be the least of your concerns. If you are in the lead, you will be substantially in the lead. A worse ace can

SMALL BALL

only hit one of three kickers, and a pocket pair can only hit one of two cards. The biggest threat is a total of five outs if your opponent has a hand such as 8-9. That's hardly something to be overly concerned about. As for the other benefit, who cares when you find out your opponent has you beat? If it costs you no more to see the river, but it takes longer to come to the conclusion that your opponent has you beat, how could that hurt you in the least?

The next example combines several small-ball concepts.

Hand in Action

The blinds are $200/$400 with a $50 ante when a player from middle position raises to $1,200 preflop. You are sitting right behind him with Q-Q and smooth call the raise. The big blind also calls, building the pot to $4,250. You are sitting on $85,000 in chips, the big blind has about $22,000 in chips, and the preflop raiser has about $71,000. The flop comes J♣ 4♠ 5♦.

YOU

RAISER

BIG BLIND

FLOP

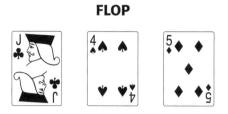

The big blind checks and the preflop raiser bets $3,000. You could make a case for raising to knock out the big blind, but that's a risky play in this situation. Here's why: Suppose you make it $12,000 "to find out where you're at" and the big blind folds. The preflop raiser then decides to go all in. You don't know much about this player, so you are in no-man's land as to what you should do. You are behind against A-A, K-K, and any set, but you can beat top pair.

The real problem lies in the fact that if your opponent has an A-J, he may genuinely believe that he has the best hand and is pushing with it. Because you smooth called before the flop, playing careful small-ball poker, he might think that you have a jack with a worse kicker. The safe play for you to make here would be to fold your queens, forfeiting the $12,000 you put in on the flop, plus the $1,200 you called before the flop. All the while, you could easily be folding the best hand.

Once again, let's see what changes when you just call on the flop. If you smooth call on the flop, your opponent may put you on one of the following hands: a jack with a mediocre kicker, a pocket pair like nines or tens, or possibly a set of fours, fives, or jacks.

If the turn comes a blank, your opponent will likely give up on the hand if he can't beat a pair of jacks, though he might continue to bet with a pair of jacks or better. You have a strong overpair, but your opponent could easily be holding a bigger pair, or possibly even a set.

If your opponent bets the turn, I would suggest smooth calling once again unless the turn card is an ace. In that case, you will have to do your best to get a read on him. If you can't come up with anything, you should still call the turn provided the bet isn't too big.

APPEARING TO PLAY WEAK POKER

Anytime you choose to play what appears to be weak poker, you're probably giving up something. That's true, but there are also several things you gain. Let's look at both sides of the coin.

What You Give Up

Free cards. By not playing aggressively on the flop or the turn, you give your opponent a free shot to outdraw you. But how risky is that really? If your opponent has a pocket pair smaller than yours and you allow him to see the turn *and* the river, he will win the pot just 8.38 percent of the time. If your opponent has an A-J, he has a total of five outs against you. If he sees the turn and the river, he'll win the pot just 20 percent of the time. That's really not that scary, especially considering the fact that if he does outdraw your pocket pair, you'll get to see it.

Either an ace or a jack on the turn would be a scare card to your hand. The biggest draw he could legitimately have would be A-K. With an A-K, if he goes to the river, he will outdraw you 23.54 percent of the time. It's a risk, but I wouldn't call it the end of the world when you factor in the benefits of being cautious.

What You Gain

You trap an opponent with top pair into continuing to bet thinking he has the best hand. You show weakness, which he may pick up on, and decide to push through the hand with something like 9-9. Lastly, by cautiously playing a hand such as queens against a flop like J♣ 4♠ 5♦, as in the example above, you make it highly unlikely that you'll be bluffed off of the best hand.

Over the years, there has been so much emphasis on being aggressive that the idea of being passive is often seen as weak or poor play. Aggressive players may even mock a player who proceeds cautiously, not understanding that there is a time to be aggressive, and there is a time to be careful and protect your stack.

Aggressive players will often amass large stacks of chips by playing wildly aggressive after the flop. If they continue to play recklessly, it's only a matter of time before they will run into a trap that they can't escape.

Playing small-bet poker as a style will keep you involved in lots of pots, but the main objective is to win the pots you are supposed to win without taking any unnecessarily large risks. A small-ball player isn't trying to get all in before the flop with pocket queens, or get all in on the flop with top pair or an overpair. In fact, a small-ball player doesn't ever want to be all in at any point in the tournament—unless he has the absolute nuts, of course!

Playing cautiously after the flop will help you avoid getting involved in large pots in marginal situations. Yes, you'll lose some extra pots when your opponents outdraw you, but you will more than make up for that with the money you save by avoiding playing big pots that you'll lose, and with the money you earn by letting your opponent bet the hand for you.

> **PLAYING SMALL-BET POKER AS A STYLE WILL KEEP YOU INVOLVED IN LOTS OF POTS, BUT THE MAIN OBJECTIVE IS TO WIN THE POTS YOU ARE SUPPOSED TO WIN WITHOUT TAKING ANY UNNECESSARILY LARGE RISKS**

TURN PLAY

Without a doubt, the most difficult and important decision you'll have to make in a typical hold'em hand will come on the turn. That's when you need to collect all the information you've processed up to that point and decide whether it makes sense for you to continue to the end of the hand.

More specifically, the turn is the most crucial street in small ball because you are nearing big-pot territory after the preflop and postflop action.

WINNING POTS WITH POSITION

The majority of your stack-building during a tournament will come when you are playing hands in position. Out of position, it is hard to get maximum value for your winning hands unless you have a very strong hand. Further, it is difficult to successfully execute bluffs.

The real beauty of small ball is best illustrated by turn-play in position. You can keep the pot small with your betting, and force your opponent to take large risks if he decides to get aggressive. Let me share an example with you that really helps tell the story.

Hand in Action

In this hand, I'm not even going to tell you what you have just yet. With the blinds at $50/$100, a player from late position makes it $300 to go. You call on the button and take the flop heads-up. The flop comes A♠ 8♦ 4♣. Your opponent hangs on to the lead by betting $600 on the flop. You call.

The turn card is the 5♠.

YOU   **LATE POSITION**

BOARD

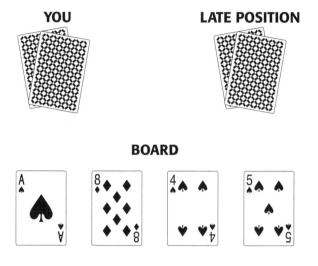

Whatever your opponent has, he is not going to love that card—unless he has the absolute nuts of course. The 5♠ hits a 2-3 straight, a 6-7 straight, and also makes a flush possible. If you were in your opponent's shoes with a hand like A♥ K♥, how much would you really love your hand on the turn? Sure, you have aces with a king kicker, but if you play a big pot in this situation, how in the world could you ever be in good shape?

Many players might check the A-K in that spot, and if you are a small-ball player, you should too. If you bet the turn and get raised, your opponent could easily be semi-bluff-raising you with the A♦ Q♠, for example. Since it would be difficult to call a raise with the A-K when you're out of position, checking is the cautious play.

Okay, so we still don't even know what we have yet—and I'm still not going to tell you! With $1,950 in the pot, you should bet about $1,200 with virtually any hand. If you have the flush, you are betting it for value; if you have 8♣ 9♣, you are betting it as a bluff; and if you have an ace you'll be betting it to:

SMALL BALL

1. Protect your hand, and
2. Help define your opponent's hand.

Here's where the beautiful part comes into play. Even if your opponent knows that you'll often "float" the flop with a weak hand, because he is out of position and his weapons are limited, raising would not usually be his best option. In fact, anything other than checking and calling would be a risky play. Folding may be a little too weak facing a $1,200 bet and check-raising is usually very costly when a player is beat.

While you actually prefer your opponents to check and call rather than check and raise so that you can control the pot size, even when they check-raise, in the long run it's beneficial to you as a small-ball player.

If your opponent check-raises you with his A-K, he'll probably risk anywhere from $4,200 to $6,000, or possibly even his whole stack. That puts him in a vulnerable position and allows you to play a big pot on your terms. If you are bluffing, oh well, you let him have the $1,200 bet. It's not the end of the world and won't put a huge dent in your stack. However, when you do have the goods, your opponent has already laid a big bet out there for you to capitalize on. In fact, with his check-raise, he may have committed himself to a pot where, in many instances, he will be drawing completely dead.

Let's look at another example, only this time I'm going to tell you what you have!

Hand in Action

With $100/$200 blinds, you raise preflop from late position to $500 with 10♥ J♥. The big blind, a rather conservative player who rarely reraises unless he has a premium hand, reraises the bet to $1,500. It's $1,000 more to you, and both you and your opponent are sitting on about $30,000 in chips. You call.

The flop comes 6♣ 7♥ 8♣, giving you nothing but a gutshot straight draw and a backdoor flush draw.

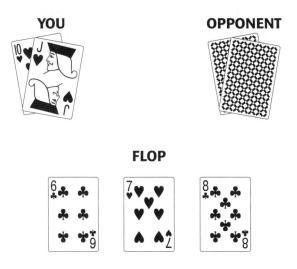

YOU   **OPPONENT**

FLOP

Your opponent bets $2,000 into the $3,100 pot.

Despite having only a measly gutshot straight draw, this is an excellent flop for you given the fact that your opponent's hand is pretty transparent (A-A, K-K, Q-Q, or A-K), while your hand is well-disguised. Lots of different cards could roll off on the turn that will help you take this pot away from your opponent. If a 4, 5, 8, 10, or any club hits the turn, your opponent is certainly going to worry about your hand being better than his. Add all of those draws to the fact that you also could easily have flopped a set, and this board is perfect for you to make a play at the pot. Also, if you happen to get really lucky and hit a 9 to make your straight, you can milk your opponent slowly, being careful not to scare him out of the pot.

Okay, so let's say the turn card is the 5♠.

SMALL BALL

YOU   **OPPONENT**

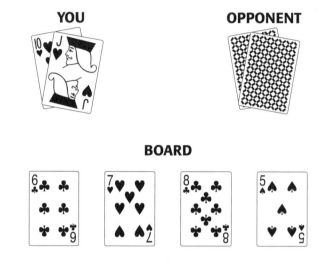

BOARD

Your opponent will likely check the turn. If he doesn't and bets, you should seriously consider making a raise. It doesn't have to be a big raise either. If your opponent bets $4,000, you could make it as little as $9,000 to go. Any raise will get you the desired information you are looking for, and by making a smallish raise, you might convince your opponent that you are inviting him to call.

If he checks, as he is more likely to do, then you can approach the situation one of two ways:

1. You can make another smallish bet on the turn. If he was just making a continuation bet on the flop with an A-K, he'll fold to a small bet on the turn. However, if he has A-A or K-K, he may decide to call a small turn bet and see what you do on the river. Making the small turn bet is actually the "greedy" way to play the hand, provided that you are committed to bluffing the hand on the river as well. By making a minimal turn bet, you increase the likelihood that your opponent will call the bet, which will give you more chips to steal on the

river! If your opponent calls your bet on the turn, you'll need to make a much larger bet on the river to take it down.

2. This option is actually a little safer since it will usually end the hand right then and there before anything crazy happens. If your opponent checks the turn, a bet of anywhere from 50 to 65 percent of the pot will allow you to take it down, even if he has A-A.

When making these types of plays, you must make sure that you are up against the right type of opponent—one who is on the conservative side and who is aware that you could have any sort of a hand in this situation. Strangely, small ball works even better when your opponents know that you'll sometimes raise with small cards. It actually opens up even more bluffing opportunities since you could feasibly hit any flop, whether it comes with high cards, middle cards, or even wheel cards. Every flop could look dangerous to your opponent.

The worst type of image you could have in a deep-stack, big buy-in tournament, is that of a player who only raises with pocket pairs and ace-paint. If your opponents know that you only raise from early position with those types of hands, they'll have too much information, and that will work against you when the flop comes small or is coordinated. When a flop comes 5-6-7, that sort of image will hurt you regardless of whether you have A-K or K-K.

THE JOHNNY CHAN PLAY

I can't think of anything better to call this play. Since Johnny Chan is the master of the check-call, and lead-the-turn play, I thought it would only be appropriate to credit him with this weapon.

SMALL BALL

When you are out of position on the turn, your ability to maneuver is limited. Chan developed a play years ago that would allow him to neutralize his opponent's positional advantage over him at minimal risk. Strangely, this is a play you should never consider making in limit hold'em, but in no-limit hold'em, it can be a very effective way of taking control of a hand while playing small-bet poker. Let's look at an example of how this play works.

Hand in Action
At a nine-handed table, with the blinds at $200/$400 and a $50 ante, a player raises to $1,200 from middle position before the flop. You—pretend you are Johnny Chan for this example—call from the big blind with 10-10. Both you and your opponent are sitting on more than $30,000 in chips. The flop comes Q♥ 4♠ 4♦.

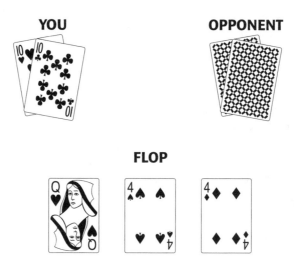

Not a great flop for your hand, but it's not exactly a terrible flop either.

You check and your opponent makes a continuation bet of $2,000. You have three options here, all of which you may use depending on your opponent.

1. If your opponent never bluffs, you can consider folding on the flop.
2. If your opponent usually plays pretty aggressively, you could check-raise the flop to around $5,500.
3. Or you could do what Johnny Chan or I might do: Just call the bet.

Let's say you've called and the turn card is a meaningless 7.

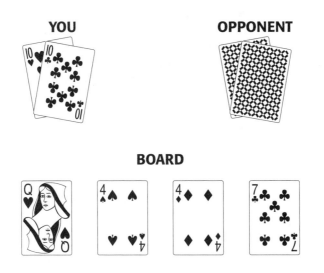

You could check it again and hope that your opponent gives up on the betting, or you could pull a Chan and take control of the hand by betting it yourself. If you bet $3,000 on the turn, your opponent will be forced to guess where you're at. Could you have the 4? Of course you could; you were in the big blind, after all. Could you have the queen? Why not?

If your opponent is sitting there with the best hand, there is a chance that he might not even raise you. With queens, kings or aces, he may fear that you have the 4 and just call your turn bet. If he does call, you have to assume that your tens are no good. So unless you catch a 10 on the river, you can safely muck your hand if he bets after the last card. If you do have the best hand, by betting the turn yourself, you avoid having to face a large bet on the turn, guessing whether your tens are good and your opponent is bluffing.

Your bet is a protection bet in many ways. It protects against overcards when you have the best hand, and it also protects you from facing a large bluff on the river. Your opponent could raise you on the turn as a bluff, but it's highly unlikely—only a handful of players are capable of that play.

There is an added bonus to playing your hand like this—you could bluff out the best hand. Let's say that instead of 10-10, you have 6-6. You make that same play and you'll have a good chance to take the pot away from an opponent with 7-7 through J-J. If he happens to call you on the turn, it will almost certainly be check-check on the river, so all it will cost you is the turn bet.

More Thoughts on the Johnny Chan Play

To keep opponents off your back, you'll also need to play very strong hands this way from time to time as well. You might be wondering why this play is sometimes better than just check-raising on the flop. While it costs you virtually the same amount, the information you receive won't be as telling. Your opponent is more likely to call a check-raise on the flop with a wider range of hands than if you check-call on the flop and lead on the turn.

Since your opponent is more likely to call the flop bet, that creates another problem for you on the turn. What do you know? With the pot being much bigger now, a standard bet is going to cost you about $10,000 in chips. Betting is very risky, since your opponent called the flop. More often than not, you'll be forced to check the turn and then be forced to guess on the river if your opponent bets.

Obviously, this play has pros and cons and should be used only occasionally. I've talked about the pros, which far outweigh the only real con—giving free cards. By letting your opponent see the turn card, he might outdraw you if he has an A-J or something similar. The good news is that his hand won't be hidden. If an ace hits the turn, you aren't committed to following through with the play and can abort mission. Besides, you won't be giving your opponent two free cards, since if the turn is a safe card, you'll be taking over the lead right there.

In limit hold'em, this play just doesn't make any sense. In limit, you would certainly go ahead and check-raise the flop if you planned to bet the turn. Check-raising isn't as risky since it only costs you one bet on the flop, and it doesn't affect the size of the turn bet. However, check-raising in no-limit hold'em makes the pot bigger, which also means that it will force you and your opponent to make larger bets. Since this is a marginal situation at best, that's the last thing you want to do, especially out of position.

By using the "Chan Play," you take control of the size of the pot on the turn by not allowing your opponent to decide how much goes in on the turn—unless, of course, he is prepared to raise you.

Any time you are using a play, it is important to make sure that you have the right opponent. Many top pros will see through this play, recognizing it as a weak leading-bet, and they *will* pounce on it as a bluff. These types of players are in the minority. Most average players would never try to take this pot away from you.

CHECK-RAISING THE TURN

One powerful weapon at your disposal on the turn is the check-raise. However, although you should often use it in limit hold'em, you should check-raise only occasionally in no-limit if you're a small-ball player. There are three main reasons for this:

1. The most obvious reason is that a check-raise makes the pot bigger, so you had better be sure that's something you want to happen before making this play.

2. If you're out of position and your opponent calls you on the turn, you'll be faced with a difficult decision on the river.

3. A check-raise might cost you pots that you could have won. That could happen one of two ways.

   a. You check-raise with a drawing hand and your opponent reraises, forcing you off the hand.

   b. He could reraise you as a bluff, representing a hand that he doesn't think you have.

The turn check-raise is a powerful weapon, but like all power tools, it should be handled with great care. The play also goes against many small ball concepts since it is designed to get more money in the pot which will forcer bigger bets on the river. This is good when you have the nuts or close to it, and it's also why I suggest that you have a monster hand when you check-raise the turn.

Check-Raising With Drawing Hands

One of the worst moves I see players make—those with some talent, but rough around the edges—is to check-raise the turn with a flush draw or a straight draw. Yuck! The reason I don't like this play very much is that you have an opponent who has bet the turn, which shows significant strength in most cases.

Far too often, he will at least call your check-raise, or worse, move all in on you. If he moves in, you will be forced to gamble for your whole tournament life on a draw with one card to come, or waste a bet with no chance to even see the river card. On the other hand, if you just call the bet, you'll have a chance to hit your draw and potentially get paid off on the river.

The only time when these plays have some merit is when the stacks are extremely deep, but even then, the check-raise with a drawing hand on the turn is a kamikaze-like gamble that doesn't fit into the small-ball strategy very well. If you consistently make this type of play, it will be difficult for you to have any sort of consistent results on the tournament circuit. You'll catch lightning in a bottle on the odd occasion, but more often than not, this type of play will cause you to hit the rail prematurely.

Check-Raising With the Nuts

Once your opponents catch on to the fact that you will often check-call out of position, that will make some of them more likely to fire a second bullet on the turn in the hopes of either:

1. Protecting their hands, or
2. Stealing the hand from you with nothing.

Against these types of players, check-raising on the turn with a set, a flush, or a straight will be a play that works well.

Here's an important thing to think about on the turn when you have the nuts: If you check-raise, make sure you don't take the "play" away from an opponent who may want to try a resteal, or even a reraise with a hand he thinks is the best hand. Let's see how this might play out.

SMALL BALL

Hand in Action

With the blinds at $25/$50 both you and your opponent are sitting on $10,000 in chips. You raise to $150 from early position with 9-9, and the opponent to your left makes it $400 to go. You suspect a strong hand, but decide to call anyway to try to flop a set. The flop comes perfect, 9♥ 4♦ 2♥. You check, and your opponent bets $600. You could play this hand several ways, but suppose you decide to represent a drawing hand and just call, in the hope that, in fact, the draw misses.

The turn card is perfect, the 7♦.

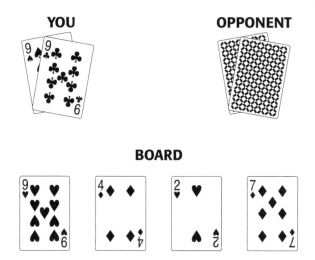

You check once again, and this time your opponent bets $1,800. With only $10,000 in chips, you could go all in now, but since you put your opponent on a strong hand preflop, likely A-A or K-K, you don't want to scare him off. Additionally, you want to represent a drawing hand so that your opponent shoves after you check-raise.

With $9,000 in chips after the preflop and postflop betting, I would suggest raising the bet to around $4,000, just $2,200 more. If your opponent has an overpair, he may decide to protect what he feels is the best hand, and shove it all in. Sweet! Had you moved all in yourself, he still may call, but the all-in bet may scare him off too.

This example shows how you might approach check-raising with the nuts when you put your opponent on a strong hand. But what about when you put your opponent on a bluff? Let's look at that.

Hand in Action

With the blinds at $100/$200 and $18,000 in chips sitting in front of you, you raise to $500 preflop with 4-4 and get one call on the button. The flop comes Q♥ Q♠ 4♥, giving you a full house. You check the flop and your opponent checks as well. The turn card is the 10♠.

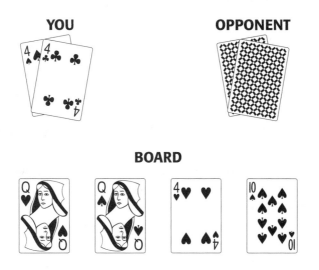

YOU   **OPPONENT**

BOARD

You decide to check again against an aggressive opponent who you don't think can sit on his hands for two streets in a row! As expected, your opponent fires out a bet for $1,000. You see that he only has about $7,000 left, so you don't want to discourage him from continuing to play by putting him all in.

Instead, you'd rather see him make a move on you for his last chips. It's a perfect opportunity to put in a check-raise.

Any amount from $2,000 to $2,500 is a good number of chips to raise. That way, if he thinks you're bluffing, he may decide to represent the queen (little does he know that's no good!) and shove it all in with anything from A-10 to a straight and/or flush draw.

Two different examples, but in both you allow your opponent to hang himself. The lesson here is that when you have the nuts, you always want to give your opponent a chance to hang himself by making a play at the pot. If your raise is too big, you take that play away from him.

Check-Raising as a Stone Bluff

Your bluff-raise is going to look just like your legitimate raises when you have the nuts. To effectively bluff the turn using a check-raise, you'll need to have a good read on your opponent. If you just sat down at a table and have no information on your opponents, you simply shouldn't bother with this play. However, once you've mapped out the table and know who the rocks are, and have spotted the bluffers and the weak players, you can use your reading skills to take some pots away from your opponents with absolutely nothing. Let's see how.

Hand in Action

With the blinds at $50/$100, an aggressive player raises preflop to $300 from late position. You are the only caller, coming in from the big blind with Q-J. The flop comes 9♠ 6♦ 4♣. You check and your opponent checks. The turn brings the A♦.

YOU   **OPPONENT**

BOARD

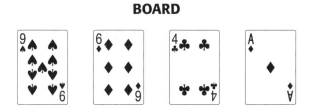

You check again. Now, your opponent bets out $350.

Based on your read of this particular opponent, if he had ace high on the flop, he would have bet to protect his hand. You also picked up a tell—based on his bet size and the way that he bet his chips—that he doesn't have the ace at all. There is no flush draw present, and if he had a straight draw on the flop, your read tells you that he probably would have bet on the flop. Your hand is irrelevant in this situation.

Including his $350 bet, there is $1,000 in the pot. By making it $1,000 to go, you are essentially making an even-money bet that your information was accurate: A $1,000 raise to win a $1,000 pot.

Your check-raise here should win you the pot more than half the time, and that's all you need for it to be a profitable play. Sometimes you'll be wrong and he'll have an ace, and sometimes he may even bluff you back, thinking that you don't have an ace. Or maybe he flopped a set and was setting a trap. All these outcomes are possible. But the good news is that the play didn't cost you very much and, even when you get caught, you can use that play to enhance your table image later in the game when you check-raise with the nuts.

The key to check-raising the turn for a profit is understanding your opponent's betting patterns and playing your hand in such a way that your opponent will believe your lie. Let's look at another example.

Hand in Action

With the blinds at $100/$200, a tight player raises preflop to $600 in first position, and you call from the big blind with 9♥ 7♥. Both you and your opponent have over $15,000 in chips. The J♣ 3♠ 4♣ flop completely misses you. You check and your opponent also checks behind you, which leads you to believe that he either flopped a set of jacks or has an A-K. Since there are two clubs on the flop, though, you lean more towards your opponent having an A-K.

The turn card brings the 5♦.

YOU   OPPONENT

BOARD

You could take a stab at the pot right here, or you could see what develops if you check. You check the turn and your opponent bets $1,000. If he has an A-K, he's probably thinking that his hand is still good, and he doesn't want a free card to come off. With his bet, there is $2,300 in the pot.

With a 3-4-5 on board, there are lots of hands you could represent: A-2, 6-7, 5-5, 4-5, and so on, or a hand as simple as J-10. To steal this pot, all you need to invest is somewhere in the neighborhood of $2,500 to win $2,400 in a spot where it doesn't look as though your opponent has much of a hand. At the same time, the board looks like it could easily have hit your hand. The fact that you actually have just 9 high and a gutshot straight draw is irrelevant since you know that your opponent is unlikely to call a check-raise with a hand such as ace high.

Contrary to popular belief, poker isn't all about bluffing, nor are elaborate yet risky all-in bluffs the way to consistently win on the poker circuit. When they work, you may look like a Mozart, but more often than not you'll end up looking foolish.

Bluffing is an art form. In a sense, it's believable story telling that doesn't require bets that are out of character for you. In fact, when you make outlandish bets that don't seem to fit in with your playing style, alarm bells go off in your opponent's head telling him that you are likely to be bluffing. When bluffing is effortless, you know you're doing it right!

Check-Raising to Find Out Where You're At

Once again, this isn't a play I'm too fond of, but it can be useful in certain situations against the right opponents. It's an extension of the Johnny Chan "check-call lead-the-turn" play. You use the check-raise to help define your opponent's hand, possibly bluff him off a better hand, and protect yourself from facing a large river bet. Let's see how it works.

SMALL BALL

Hand in Action

With the blinds at $25/$50, a player raises preflop to $150 from middle position. You call from the small blind with 9-9, and it's the two of you to the flop: Q♠ 7♦ 2♠. You check and your opponent bets $300. Unsure if your hand is good against an aggressive player who routinely bets the flop after raising, you decide to call to see what the next card brings. The turn is the 7♣.

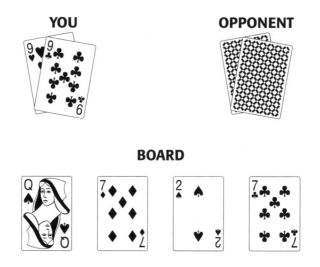

YOU   OPPONENT

BOARD

You could use the Chan play here, but you are worried that this particular player is capable of sniffing out the weak-lead play and will bluff-raise you. You check, and your opponent bets $600. Still unsure as to whether your hand is good, you could call and hope that the river bet is small, or you could check-raise the turn to define your opponent's hand.

That 7 should scare your opponent a little bit if he doesn't have it. You could easily have a hand like 7-8. With the flush draw present, your opponent may even bet a hand such as 4-4 to protect it against what he perceives to be a flush draw. Your biggest worry, though, is that if you call $600, your extremely aggressive opponent is capable of firing a third and large bullet at the pot on the river, which would put you in a difficult situation.

One defense against that is to check-raise the minimum on the turn. Anything from $1,200 to $1,500 should scare your opponent and he will almost never play back at you as a bluff. If he reraises you after you make this play, you should feel pretty safe that your 9-9 is definitely beat.

Again, the added bonus is that your opponent may let go of J-J or 10-10 to your raise. However, if your opponent calls the turn raise, you should check the river, unless you hit the 9, of course. Your opponent should be slightly worried that you are going for another check-raise on the river and will likely be happy to check down the best hand if he has you beaten. In essence, you'd be paying him off on the turn ($600) and river ($600 to $900 depending on how much you bet), but on your terms. You decided how much the river bet would be by check-raising the turn.

Of course, if your opponent calls the turn and then bets the river when you check, he has you beaten. It's plain and simple. The only hand he could have that he'd be bluffing with on the river is a missed flush draw. Even then, very few players will bluff at the river in this situation after you have check-raised the turn.

REPRESENTING HANDS ON THE TURN

When you flop a drawing hand, you should always think about ways you could win the pot if you don't happen to make your draw. If you are always banking on hitting the flush or straight without ever bluffing when you miss them, it'll be difficult for you to show a profit with drawing hands after the flop. Let's look at an example of how to use fake "extra outs" to help you win more pots.

SMALL BALL

Hand in Action

With nine players at the table and blinds of $400/$800 with a $100 ante, you call $2,400 from the button preflop with 5♥ 6♥ in a four-way action pot. The raiser is in first position, and there is a middle position caller, yourself, and the big blind. Every player in the pot is deep in chips with over $100,000. The flop comes 7♣ 8 ♥ 3♠ and the initial raiser bets $5,000 on the flop. Knowing this player, you know that he will make a continuation bet a high percentage of the time, even with an A-K on a flop like this.

The first player folds, you call, and the big blind folds. The turn is the J♣.

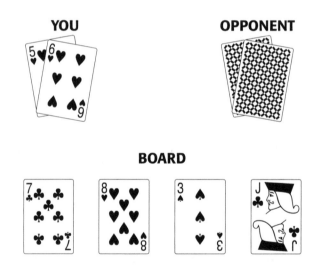

YOU	OPPONENT

BOARD

Your opponent checks. This is an excellent card for your hand. No, it didn't help you one bit, but your opponent has to think that if you didn't flop a set, there is a very good chance that you have 9-10 for a straight, or maybe even J-9 or J-10, which he still can't beat with a hand such as A-8, A-K, or K-7.

Although you still have a draw at your straight, it isn't a "good draw" anymore, as it's unlikely that you'll be able to hit a big payday. If a 9 hits, a four-card straight will be on board. Even if your opponent has a big hand, he's probably not going to call unless he has the straight. Besides, the 9 might be no good to you anyway as he also could make a straight with it if he has a 10 in his hand.

With $22,900 in the pot already, this would be a good situation for you to represent the straight and pick up the pot. A bet of anywhere from $10,000 to $12,000 should do the trick. Even if your opponent has A-A, he may consider folding on the turn! If not, you are still getting a good price for your steal attempt, risking $12,000 to win $22,900. Also, even if he calls you on the turn, you might be able to steal the pot with a bigger bet on the river. Remember though: Don't bluff at the river unless you are in the right situation against the right type of opponent.

Hand in Action

Let's look at a simpler example in a hand that's less stressful. With the blinds at $50/$100, you decide to limp in with the 9♥ 10♥ from early position. Another player limps in, and the button makes it $500 to go. You call, as does the other limper. The flop comes 7♣ 8♣ 4♠, giving you an open-ended straight draw and two overcards, although you are legitimately worried that the raiser has a pair of queens or better.

You check to the raiser, as does the limper. The preflop raiser bets $1,500. You are sitting on $37,000 and your opponent has $24,000 in front of him, so you call hoping to win a big pot. The other limper folds.

The turn card is the 5♣.

SMALL BALL

YOU

OPPONENT

BOARD

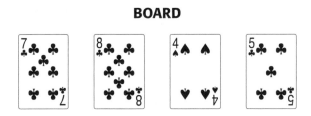

You just have to bet that card. You have nothing, and could even be drawing dead, but you have to take your chances on such a dangerous looking card. The way the hand has been played up to this point, your hitting that card is very believable, while it's unlikely that the preflop raiser liked the card. A bet of $4,000 represents about 60 percent of the pot, and is serious enough to make your opponent consider folding an overpair. The only real risk you face is that your opponent not only has an overpair, but he also has a club in his hand and has picked up a flush draw. Well, that and A♣ K♣, but let's hope he doesn't have that!

If your opponent doesn't have a club in his hand, he'd be making a very risky call on the turn in the hope that you have precisely the 9-10. After all, what could he beat other than that?

If he calls, you will face a dilemma on the river. Obviously, if the river card is a club, you must wave the white flag and give it up. If you make your straight, you can go for a value bet. If it's a blank, though, you'll have a tough decision to make as to whether or not you should bluff. Once again, you really must know your opponent to justify throwing any more money into this pot on the river. If you have no idea what this player would do with A-A on the river, you should probably conserve your chips and let him have the pot.

Finally let's look at one more example of a draw that misses, but one in which the turn card opens up a bluffing opportunity:

Hand in Action

The blinds are $300/$600 with a $75 ante when a tight middle position player makes it $1,800 to go preflop and gets called by the button. You're in the big blind and defend with A♦ 3♦. The flop comes 5♦ 6♠ 7♦.

You put the initial raiser on a premium hand, either an overpair, A-K, or A-Q. You decide to bet $2,500 on the flop to try to figure out where your opponent is at in the hand. The middle position player raises to $6,000, the button folds, and you call, leaving you with $54,000 in chips.

The turn card is the 9♥.

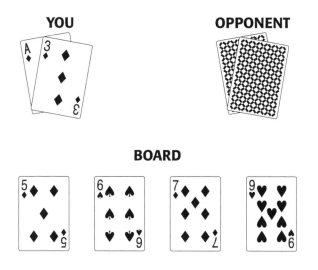

YOU   OPPONENT

BOARD

Since you don't think your opponent has an 8 in his hand, and there is no reason why you couldn't have an 8 in your hand based on the way the hand has been played, you should take the lead on the turn with a bet of anywhere from $9,000 to $12,000.

Unless your opponent had precisely 8-8, how can he raise you? He really shouldn't, but if he does go all in (highly unlikely), you'll be forced to fold. What is more likely, though, is that the bet will force your opponent to lay down A-A. If he calls, that's not the end of the world either since you have outs with your flush draw. If he calls, what you do on the river depends on many factors that I'll touch on in the next section.

CALLING WITH DRAWING HANDS ON THE TURN

Playing drawing hands on the turn can be tricky, but there is a basic set of rules you should follow with drawing hands on the turn. If you put some thought into your decision-making, drawing hands will often play themselves. Here's a quick set of tools that will help you make the right decisions.

The first thing to consider is the pot odds you are being laid. For example, if there is $3,000 in the pot and your opponent bets $1,000, your pot odds would be $1,000 to win $4,000, or 4 to 1—the $3,000 in the pot plus your opponent's bet, versus the $1,000 you need to call to see the river card.

Once you've figured out your pot odds, the next step is to determine the odds of catching the card you need.

Hand in Action
For example, let's say you have 4♥ 5♥ and the board reads K♥ 2♥ 9♠ 10♦.

YOU

OPPONENT

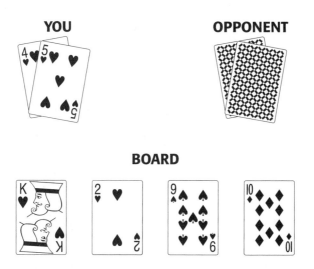

BOARD

In this case, you'd need to catch one of the nine remaining hearts in the deck out of 46 unseen cards. You already know your own two cards, plus the four board cards, leaving 46 cards that you haven't seen. Of those cards, nine are good ones, and 37 are bad. So, your odds of making the flush would be 37 divided by 9, which works out to 4.111 to 1.

On the surface, it seems like you are getting the right price to call with your flush draw, but there are other considerations to factor in. Could your opponent have a higher flush draw? If so, that could cost you a big bet on the river. If your opponent has a set, two of your outs are taken away, as the 9♥ and 10♥ will no longer help you.

You understand your pot odds, the odds of making your hand, and you're asking yourself if you're drawing at a winning hand or a second-best hand. But there is more to consider. The next step is to determine what the implied odds might be. Calculating implied odds is an inexact science since you can never be certain what your opponent will do on the river.

However, much like chess, it's important to think ahead and factor your river play into the equation.

Let's look at a more complex example to see this more clearly.

Hand in Action

You have the 4♥ 6♥ and the board reads K♥ 7♥ 3♠ Q♦. Both you and your opponent have $12,000 in chips. There is $800 in the pot and he bets $600.

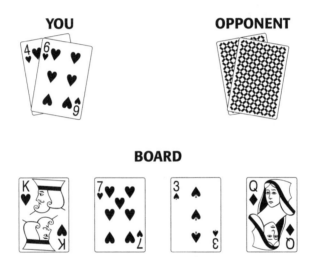

You go through your routine:

> **Pot Odds:** $600 to win $1,400, 2.333 to 1
> **Odds of Improving**: 9 hearts + 3 fives equals 12 cards out of 46 unseen cards—12 good ones and 34 bad ones equals 2.833 to 1

If there will be no additional betting on the river, you should fold your hand. The pot odds are smaller than the odds of your hand improving. Therefore, if your opponent is all in for $600, for example, you should muck your hand. However, when you factor in the implied odds of catching a 5 or a heart to swing things in your favor, this situation has the potential to pay off in a big way, especially if you hit the 5 since you would have a well-disguised hand.

There is some danger here that also needs to be considered: You might make a losing flush, but the addition of the gutshot straight will counteract that. In these types of situations, despite the fact that you obviously know your opponent has the best hand, it's still important to figure out what he might have. You should figure it out on the turn; it will help you with your little math problem, in that the strength of your opponent's hand will dictate how much you can win on the river.

For example, suppose you think your opponent is very strong and has a hand such as K-Q or K-K. In that case, you should be able to get paid off on a rather large bet on the river—and possibly end up with all of his chips—especially if you catch a 5. However, if you think your opponent has a marginal hand, your implied odds will be diminished since he would be less likely to call with a hand such as Q-10, for example.

So before making the call on the turn, you need to decide how much you will bet on the river if you hit your hand. Figure out what you will bet depending on what your opponent does. As an exercise, let's figure out a sum for all the possible outcomes in the following eight scenarios.

1. You hit a 5 and your opponent checks _____

2. You hit a 5 and your opponent bets $1,500 _____

3. You hit the A♥ and your opponent checks _____

4. You hit the A♥ and your opponent bets $1,000 _____

5. You hit the Q♥ and your opponent checks _____

6. You hit the Q♥ and you opponent bets $2,000 _____

7. You hit the 2♥ and your opponent checks _____

8. You hit the 2♥ and your opponent bets $600 _____

Even more scenarios are possible, but let's start with these. Fill in each one and then we'll discuss what it has done to your pot odds on the turn call. Again, here is how the situation looks:

YOU   **OPPONENT**

BOARD

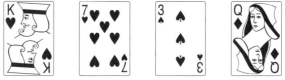

1. You Hit a 5 and Your Opponent Checks

If your opponent checks an innocent card like a 5, it's unlikely that he has a strong hand. This means that you won't be able to make a big bet since he'll be less likely to call. With $2,000 in the pot, a bet of about $900 sounds good. Those implied odds will change the original problem so that you are now getting a good price, 2.833 to 1 against to hit your hand, but $600 to win $2,300 (if he calls), which equals pot odds of 3.833 to 1. Even if your opponent folds on the river, you would still only be making a very minor mistake on the turn by calling as a 2.833 to 1 underdog, only getting 2.333 to 1 odds on your money.

2. You Hit a 5 and Your Opponent Bets $1,500

This is the ideal situation, the home run ball you've been waiting for. If your opponent bets the river, there is a good chance that he is prepared to call a big reraise, or maybe even go all in with a hand such as K-K. You could raise him anywhere from $2,000 to $4,000 more, depending on how strong you think his hand is. For example, suppose you raise him $3,500 more. Let's take a look at what that does to your turn problem. You were a 2.833 to 1 underdog to make your draw, and the pot odds you were being laid were 2.333 to 1. Assuming your opponent calls the river bet, that figure changes dramatically, from 2.333 to 1 to 9.667 to 1 ($5,800 divided by $600). That's a pretty sweet payday, and it could be even tastier if your opponent decides to go all in. Of course, if he folds for the $3,500 raise, that's not so bad either. Your investment still would be positive at $600 to win $2,900, or 4.833 to 1.

3. You Hit the A♥ and Your Opponent Checks

This isn't a great card for you if your opponent checks the river. It's unlikely that he'll be able to call a big bet, especially if he has a hand like K-J or Q-10. In fact, he might not call a bet of any size with such a scary river card. With $2,000 in the pot, you don't want to bet more than half of what's in there, unless you think that will cause your opponent to think you're bluffing. Your betting history with this opponent will play a big role in how much you should bet, but for this example we will use $800 as a general guideline. Your opponent will probably still fold, but you don't really want to bet any less than this amount, because it will hurt you in the long run to make such a drastically obvious change in your betting pattern when you want to be called.

I would guesstimate that your opponent will call the $800 approximately 25 percent of the time, depending on the player, of course. At that rate, three times you'll be getting slightly the worst of it on your turn call (2.333 to 1 on a 2.833 to 1 underdog), but one out of four times you'll get 3.667 to 1 odds on your turn call. That works out to $600 to win $1,600, or 2.667 to 1—only a marginally bad bet for you.

4. You Hit the A♥ and Your Opponent Bets $1,000

This can be a very tricky situation and how you respond to his bet is very read-dependant. Unless you have an excellent read on your opponent—you know that he is aggressive and would bet without a flush on the river—you should lean towards just calling the bet ($600 to win $2,400, or 4 to 1). Raising on the river with such a small flush is a dangerous proposition since it could not only cost you valuable chips, it could also allow your opponent to steal the pot from you. For example, let's say he has a hand such as Q♥ 10♠. If you raise on the river, your opponent may decide to reraise, knowing you can't have the nuts since he holds the key card, the Q♥. What would you do then? Now, I'm not ruling out raising on the river as an option, but if you are going to raise with your baby flush, you had better know a great deal about what your opponent is capable of doing. If you make the aggressive move, you could raise as little as the minimum, $1,000 up to maybe $2,000.

5. You Hit the Q♥ and Your Opponent Checks

If your opponent checks when the Q♥ hits, chances are that he doesn't like it. Either that, or he thinks you've made trips or a flush and he's looking to check-raise you with a full house!

For all of those reasons, it doesn't make sense to make a big bet in this situation. If your opponent check-raises you, you'll probably be forced to fold. Also, if you bet too much, your opponent may release a hand like K-10. Once again, I would suggest a bet of approximately $800.

6. You Hit the Q♥ and Your Opponent Bets $2,000

Consider folding. Seriously. If your opponent makes a pot-sized bet after the Q♥ hits, it's highly unlikely that he is value betting with a hand that you can beat. The size of his bet makes it look like he's hoping that you have a strong hand, figuring that you are forced to call. I'm assuming here that you have some kind of feel for how your opponent plays. But what if you don't? If you don't really know your opponent's tendencies, you should probably make the call, getting 2 to 1 odds on the river, hoping that your opponent made trip queens or is somehow running a bluff at you. There are lots of new young players in the game today that will make some wild bluffs in bizarre situations, so with a hand as strong as a flush, you'll have to keep them honest until you have more information about their game.

7. You Hit the 2♥ and Your Opponent Checks

Your opponent may be checking with a hand as strong as A-K here. He may be worried that you've made the flush, and is happy to check-call rather than being raised on the river and being put to a decision. In this case, look to get some value for your hand, betting anywhere from $1,200-$1,600. If you choose to bet $1,500 on the river and your opponent calls, your initial decision to call the $600 on the turn with your drawing hand will earn you $2,900 (4.833 to 1). Since you are only a 2.833 to 1 underdog to make your hand, betting $1,500 on the river will be a profitable play, provided your opponent calls the bet.

8. You Hit the 2♥ and Your Opponent Bets $600

A $600 bet into a pot with $2,000 in it on the river usually signifies a pretty weak hand. It's a defensive bet designed to keep you from betting more on the river. As always, you need to really understand your opponent in these types of situations in order to make the best play available. Folding is out of the question because you have much to gain with little relative risk. Calling is the safest play, but you should probably try to get some value out of this hand by putting in a raise. You want to make a raise that's not so big it scares your opponent off. At the same time, you don't want to put a huge dent in your stack in case the hand doesn't work out. Raising to $1,500 or $1,600 is reasonable.

Thinking Through the Turn

There is more to making a turn call than simply figuring out the current pot odds. Your perceived implied odds can turn what seems to be a longshot draw into a very profitable play under the right circumstances.

If there is one street in hold'em where you should take your time and think it through, it's the turn. Not only are you thinking about the bet you are currently facing, but you should also be one step ahead, planning what you'll do on the river.

CALLING WITH DRAWS AND FACTORING IN BLUFF OUTS

As you can see from the previous section, there are certain situations where it's highly likely that your opponent will fold to a bet on the river when you hit some of your drawing hands. Knowing this, you can take advantage of your opponent by sometimes calling with longshot draws with the intention of either:

1. Hitting a home run,
or

2. Bluffing your opponent when a more traditional draw hits the river. I call those "bluffing outs," cards that could hit the river that will scare your opponent into folding the best hand.

Using bluffing outs in your calculations on the turn is an advanced skill. Not only are you factoring in your pot odds, your odds of improving, your odds of drawing to the second-best hand, and your implied odds, you are also thinking about what cards could hit the river that will likely win you the pot by allowing you to bluff your opponent. Being able to read your opponent, understand his tendencies, and determine his likely hole cards are a big part of using bluff outs. Let's look at an example:

Hand in Action
With the blinds at $100/$200, a tight opponent raises to $600 from first position before the flop. You call the $600 with 3♣ 5♣ from middle position. Everyone else folds, so you will see the flop heads-up. Both you and your opponent have $45,000.

The flop comes 5♠ 6♣ 7♠, giving you bottom pair and a gutshot draw to the idiot end of the straight. You could easily have the best hand with a pair of fives, but if your opponent bets it hard on the flop and turn, he probably has a big overpair. On the flop, your opponent bets $1,000. Trying to catch a 3, 4, or a 5, you call the bet.

The turn card is the J♣.

SMALL BALL

YOU

OPPONENT

BOARD

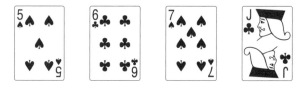

The J♣ gives you a backdoor flush draw as well. With $3,500 in the middle, your opponent overbets the pot by putting in $7,000. Now it's time to go through your routine:

> **Pot odds:** $7,000 to win $10,500 equals 1.5 to 1
> **Odds of improving your hand:** 3 threes, 2 fives, 3 fours, and 9 clubs equals 17 outs out of 46 unseen cards—17 good ones and 29 bad ones, 29 divided by 17 equals 1.705 to 1.

Despite the fact that you likely have a ton of outs against your opponent, you are still not getting the right price to call the bet, unless you factor in implied odds and bluff outs. There are loads of cards that could hit the river that miss your hand completely, but would look like they could easily have hit your hand. An 8 would put an open-ended four-card straight on board. Rivering a 9 would mean that if you had the four-card straight draw with an 8, you would have just completed that straight. On top of that, the flush draw on the flop is a hand you could easily represent if it hits the river.

I'M GOING TO REMIND YOU ONE MORE TIME TO STRESS THE IMPORTANCE OF THIS CONCEPT: IN ORDER TO MAKE PLAYS LIKE THE FOLLOWING, IT'S ESSENTIAL THAT YOU HAVE A VERY GOOD READ ON YOUR OPPONENT'S TENDENCIES. IF YOU DON'T, I WOULD ADVISE YOU TO AVOID THESE PLAYS ALTOGETHER.

With the type of draw you have, there are some cards that could hit on the river that would win you a really big pot. There are also a lot of cards that could hit that will scare your opponent into thinking that you've just hit one of your draws. If you only play suited connecters with the hope of making straights and flushes, you will become very easy to read. Sure, people will know that you play all kinds of goofy hands, but they will soon catch on to the fact that when the funky draws hit and you bet big, you've got it. Perceptive players will stop paying you off unless you mix up your play by making calculated bluffs as well.

Seven Scenarios

Let's take a look at how to proceed if you call the $7,000 bet and various cards hit on the river. Again, both you and your opponent have $45,000 each. Here are seven scenarios:

1. A club falls _____

2. You make a straight _____

3. You make trips _____

4. You make two pair _____

5. The river card is an 8 _____

6. The river card is a 9 _____

7. A spade falls _____

SMALL BALL

1. A Club Falls

Obviously, if a club hits, completing your flush, you are going to make a value bet in the hope that you get paid off. With $17,500 in the pot, a bet of anywhere from $9,000 to $12,000 will put pressure on your opponent, but not so much that he might look you up. After all, there was only one club on the flop, so it will be difficult for him to believe that you hit a backdoor flush.

2. You Make a Straight

If you hit the straight, it will be the dummy end with the 4, but since your opponent is a conservative player it's unlikely that he has the 8 in his hand. As far as a betting amount goes, you have a lot of options, but you have to understand that your opponent will be hard pressed to call anything. You could even try to milk him for as little as $5,000, but it's probably better to bet between $7,000 and $9,000. You don't want your value bets to stick out by making them so much smaller than your bluffs. You don't want to make your bluffs any smaller either, since that will make them less effective.

3. You Make Trips

Rivering a 5 is probably the absolutely best card you can catch because your opponent might think it was a good card for him if he has A-A. If you hit trips on the river and you put your opponent on an overpair, you should go for a good payday, betting between $12,000 to $15,000 on the river.

4. You Make Two Pair

Your opponent isn't going to be very afraid of a 3, but at the same time, he isn't going to bet that card either. If you bet the river, he's probably going to pay you off if he has an overpair. Once again, I suggest a bet between $9,000 and $12,000.

5. The River Card is an 8

If the river is an 8, you have a good opportunity to steal the pot from your opponent. You don't want your bet to look any different from a bet you'd make had you actually made the hand. If you bet $12,000 on the river, your opponent will be hard pressed to call. He might, but even if he calls you one half of the times you make this type of play, your river bluff will still be profitable as you are risking $12,000 to win $17,500.

6. The River Card is a 9

Same as above, when the river card is an 8.

7. A Spade Falls

This is the most common draw that you could be on after calling the flop bet, and it is probably the card that your opponent is most afraid of. You want to play it as if you were looking to get paid off handsomely, and should bet between $12,000 and $15,000. As is the case with all of these scenarios, the amount you ultimately choose should depend on your opponent and his perception of you, plus the past hands he has seen you play.

So, despite the fact that you really only have what looks like 17 outs, when you factor in the bluff outs, there are 28 cards that could help you win the pot. That's well over half the deck. Of course it's not that simple, as you will get yourself into trouble occasionally when you hit your hand and it's a loser; or when an opponent who doesn't believe you calls your bluff. Overall, though, adding these plays to your repertoire will help you out in the long run since your value bet-to-bluff ratio will be very high.

Bluffs are most effective when used sporadically and in situations where it seems "obvious" to your opponent that you must have the best hand.

PLAYING TOP PAIR AND OVERPAIRS ON THE TURN

When you play deep-stack poker, it's important to understand that one pair, regardless of how big it is, is rarely ever good enough to risk going broke with after the flop. You obviously wouldn't fold A-A or K-K before the flop. On the flop, it's usually correct to continue until the turn since the pot size is still manageable. On the turn, however, the bets generally get larger. And the turn is the street where you'll often have to make the critical decision as to whether you should continue to see the hand all the way to the river.

> WHEN YOU PLAY DEEP-STACK POKER, IT'S IMPORTANT TO UNDERSTAND THAT ONE PAIR, REGARDLESS OF HOW BIG IT IS, IS RARELY EVER GOOD ENOUGH TO RISK GOING BROKE WITH AFTER THE FLOP.

Overpairs and top-pair hands can be trap hands that cost many players their tournament lives when they overplay them. As a small-baller, these are the types of players that you'll thrive on when you fill a belly-buster straight or flop baby trips.

When you are the one with the overpair—yes, we play those hands too sometimes!—it's important to think in terms of avoiding traps that can get you broke. To do that, you are often going to sacrifice value and lose a few extra pots all in the name of protecting your stack.

PLAYING OVERPAIRS OUT OF POSITION

Let's look at a few examples of how to play an overpair in various situations.

Hand in Action 1

With the blinds at $50/$100, you make it $250 to go with A♣ A♠ before the flop. A player on the button calls you, as does the big blind. The flop comes J♦ 7♦ 8♠. The big blind checks and you bet $600. The button calls and the big blind folds.

The turn is the 6♥.

YOU

BUTTON

BOARD

This is a potentially dangerous situation for you since you have a strong hand that's difficult to get away from. You could easily be in big trouble. If you bet this hand on the turn, you run the risk of getting raised and making the pot bigger, while not knowing for sure if you are ahead or behind.

Before deciding whether to bet or check on the turn, the absolutely most important thing to consider is your opponent's playing style. You have to answer these five questions:

1. Does he call raises with hands like 9-10 suited?
2. Would he call you on the flop with K-J, or would he raise you?
3. If he had a set, would he smooth call you on the flop?
4. If I bet the turn and he raises, could he be bluffing?

5. If I check the turn, will he try to bluff at it or value bet the worst hand?

Against an unknown opponent, I would suggest betting somewhere in the neighborhood of $1,200 to $1,400 on the turn. If an unknown player raises you on the turn, you must think long and hard about a hand you can beat. The safe play is to fold and wait for a better situation when you have more information. An even safer play, though, is to check the turn against an unknown opponent. If he bets, you can call and see what develops on the river. This way, you accomplish these things:

1. You keep the pot small in a dangerous situation.
2. You lose the minimum amount when you are beat.
3. You induce the worst hand to value bet against you.
4. You avoid being bluffed by a hand such as A-J. If your opponent checks behind you, that's okay too. The weakness you showed on the turn may convince your opponent to call you on the river with a much weaker hand than he would have otherwise.

For example, if your opponent has 10-10, he may call the flop bet. Then on the turn, when it goes check-check, he'll likely think he has the best hand. Provided the river card isn't too scary, he'll have to pay you off on the river with his 10-10 in a situation where he may have folded to a bet on the turn. While checking the turn may seem weak, there are several benefits to the play—most importantly, keeping the pot small and protecting your stack.

Hand in Action 2

Let's look at a similar example to further illustrate this concept:

With the blinds at $600/$1,200 with a $200 ante, everyone folds to you in the small blind. You look down at K-K and make it $3,000 total. The big blind calls, so you'll see the flop heads-up. Both you and your opponent have $65,000 in chips. The flop comes 10♣ 4♠ 4♦. You bet $4,800 on the flop and your opponent calls. The turn card is the 7♦.

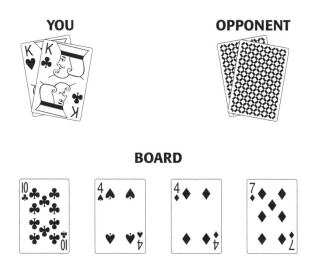

YOU   **OPPONENT**

BOARD

What would you do?

This is what I call a "hit or miss" type of flop. That is, your opponent either has you crushed and you have only two outs, or you have your opponent dead to two or three outs. There is no gray area here. Since this board has no draw to protect against, I would suggest checking the turn for several reasons:

1. If your opponent called on the flop with the intention of stealing the pot on the turn, let

him try! If you bet the turn yourself, you may discourage him from continuing with the bluff.

2. If your opponent has a 10 in his hand, he will surely bet to protect his hand. Therefore, whether you bet or not is irrelevant since it makes no difference who bets—money will go into the pot.

3. If your opponent has a 4, he will bet, but his intention will likely be to not scare you off. Therefore, he'll make small bets that allow you to lose the minimum when you are beaten.

The problem with being aggressive and out of position on the turn is that you'll put yourself in situations where you'll often be forced to guess. It's true, you'll also be guessing when you check the turn and your opponent bets; but the size of the bets will make it easier for you to call. However, if you bet the turn and get raised, you are in an impossible situation: You have to make a huge decision as to whether your opponent has a 4 or a 10. If at all possible, it's best to avoid putting yourself in these types of situations, even if that means that you will get outdrawn a small percentage of the time.

PLAYING OVERPAIRS IN POSITION

In the above examples, you were out of position. Now let's look at an example of how to play an overpair when you are in position.

Hand in Action

With the blinds at $1,000/$2,000, you raise to $5,000 preflop with J-J from early position. Only the big blind calls. Both you and your opponent have over $150,000 in chips. The flop comes 8♠ 6♦ 4♣. Your opponent checks and you bet out $8,000. He calls.

The turn card pairs the 8.

YOU   **OPPONENT**

BOARD

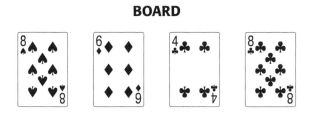

Your opponent checks again. Based on your read of the situation, you don't think your opponent has an 8, yet the safe play in a tournament is to also check. The worst-case scenario is that you allow your opponent a free chance to hit a draw against you. On the other hand, your check on the turn accomplishes several important things:

1. Checking protects you from being bluffed. If you bet the turn and your opponent raises, what are you going to do? Guess? This is precisely the type of situation you want to avoid.

2. Checking induces a bluff on the river. Since you checked the turn, your opponent will often bet the river whether he improved his hand or not. Your check on the turn is a sign of weakness, so if your opponent misses his draw, he might bluff at the river. If the river is a complete blank, your opponent may even value bet with a 4 or a 6 if he perceives it to be the best hand.

3. Checking keeps the pot small in a marginal situation. J-J is a decent hand, but there are a ton of hands out there that could have you beat.

As you can probably tell by now, your mindset with an overpair on the turn should be one of caution rather than excitement. In deep-stack tournaments it's rare that an overpair is in the lead when an all-in pot is played on the turn. As you get deeper and deeper into a tournament it becomes more likely that your overpair is ahead. Certainly in the early stages you should not be too happy about being all in with pocket aces on a board of 2-3-6-7. If you're not up against a set, you just might be up against a straight. In either case, the most you'll have is two cards in the deck to save you.

FUNDAMENTAL TOURNAMENT CONCEPT

There is a grand misconception about what it takes to be a successful tournament player in today's landscape. All you hear about is aggression, aggression, aggression—but it's careful play in marginal situations that separates the world's most successful tournament players from the rest of the pack.

> **IN DEEP-STACK TOURNAMENTS, IT'S RARE THAT AN OVERPAIR IS IN THE LEAD WHEN AN ALL-IN POT IS PLAYED ON THE TURN.**

LOOKING FOR TELLS

While the majority of your energy on the turn should be dedicated to going through the details of the hand, you shouldn't abandon the presence of any physical tells that your opponent is giving off. Even if you don't think you are noticing anything consciously, your subconscious mind works in mysterious ways. If the subconscious mind recognizes something, it will help you make a better decision.

Some call it instinct, intuition, feel or whatever. I believe that it's more like tapping into a vast database that has seen thousands of similar situations and recognizes patterns in behavior. What's difficult about this process is that being in tune with yourself, or having a conversation with yourself that taps into your subconscious mind, isn't an exact science. It doesn't quite work like, "Hey subconscious mind, is he bluffing or what? Should I call him or fold?"

I don't claim to be an expert on the subconscious mind and how it works, but I genuinely believe that sometimes when you look at someone, despite the fact that you don't think you see anything peculiar, you really might be seeing what you think you see. Despite the fact that you can't verbalize what tell you are seeing, it's there.

A perfect example of this is my good friend, Jennifer Harman, who, incidentally, is one of the top players in the world. Jennifer has an innate ability to sniff out bluffs and read weakness in her opponents. She'll often make some excellent, risky calls in high pressure situations, but when you ask her why she called, she might say, "I dunno, cause I figured he was bluffing."

"But, how did you know that, Jennifer? Was it the way he played his hand? Did you pick up a tell? What was it?"

She might reply, "I don't know, something just told me he was bluffing."

What "told her" that an opponent was bluffing was her subconscious mind. It has seen so many hands played that it has become very good at spotting tells and relaying them to her conscious mind. Jennifer does herself a big favor by listening to those "feelings."

FOUR TELLS TO LOOK FOR

There are some things, however, that you can look for on a conscious level that will help you make good decisions. Here are some to keep in mind.

SMALL BALL

1. Early Reachers

Some players have a tendency to reach for their chips prematurely. Be on the lookout for that. If you are planning on betting against one of these players, make sure you take your time and are very deliberate. A few extra seconds and your opponent may give away his intentions before you actually make your bet. Be careful, though, as some of your opponents are actors, and will reach for their chips to discourage you from betting.

2. Speed of Their Action

Pay close attention to how long it generally takes an opponent to call a bet on the turn and you may pick up some patterns. For example, if a player calls quickly on the turn, it could mean that he is on a draw and isn't thinking about whether or not he has the best hand. A quick call could mean something completely different too. A quick call from your opponent may signify that he is trying to discourage you from betting the river, almost like saying, "I got you, man. Don't even think about betting the river because I'm calling you down."

Each tell could have various meanings. It's your job to accurately discern what your opponent is trying to accomplish with his actions.

3. Card Protectors

This one is rare, but if you find yourself up against a player such as I describe, you'll be able to exploit him pretty easily. Basically, you should focus on how well an opponent is protecting his hand. If he normally has a chip on his cards, but this time he doesn't, that could mean he isn't all that interested in this particular hand. Or conversely, if he seems overly protective of his hand, it could signify that he is hanging on to that monster and doesn't want anything to happen to it.

4. Quick Checkers

Paying attention at all times is the best way to pick up on physical tells. Often, players will check very quickly on the turn. That means something. Depending on the player, it could mean that he plans to check-raise you, or is on a draw. It's different with all players, so you should label the action as one way or the other. Every instance is different, and it's your job to figure out which is which. I can't do everything for you!

GIVING AWAY FREE CARDS

Throughout this section, I've stressed the importance of protecting your stack in favor of protecting the pot. As a result of this philosophy, you are going to end up allowing your opponent to see some free cards. It's not the cardinal sin that people often make it out to be. In limit hold'em, it may be true that giving away a free card is often foolish, but in no-limit, it's essential for your survival and will help you avoid several traps where your more aggressive opponents would surely go broke.

It's important to understand that by playing small ball, you will take more lumps and lose more pots than when you are playing big-bet poker. That's the bad news. The good news is that if you are emotionally stable enough to handle some rough patches, playing this way will allow you to stick around longer in the tournaments, as well as ensure that your entire stack will not be at risk very often.

Let's look at a few examples.

Hand in Action 1

With the blinds at $1,500/$3,000, you raise to $8,000 preflop in late position with J-J. The big blind plays back at you, reraising $20,000 more. Both you and your opponent have over $400,000 in chips, so you call.

SMALL BALL

The flop comes 9♣ 7♦ 2♥. Your opponent bets out $30,000 and you call the bet, still unsure as to whether you have the best hand. The turn is the 2♠

YOU   **OPPONENT**

BOARD

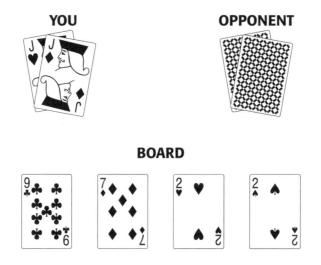

Your opponent checks, leading you to believe that he has an A-K. The standard play here would be to bet around $50,000. But if your opponent is at all tricky, he might be setting a trap for you with A-A or K-K. If he check-raises, it opens up the opportunity for him to bluff you and you'll likely be forced to fold. Instead, let's say that you check, giving away a free card. If your opponent has the A-K, he only has six outs (three aces and three kings) to beat you. Only 14 percent of the time will he catch an ace or a king. At the same time, if your opponent is trying to trap you with A-A or K-K, you give *yourself* a free shot at hitting one of the two remaining jacks.

If the river card is a blank, your opponent will probably bet with A-A or K-K, at which time you can decide whether your J-J is good. If your opponent checks the river, you should look to value bet your J-J. By that point, he may call you with just ace-high since you showed weakness on the turn. If he has a hand such as 6-6 or 8-8, then it's very likely that he'll call a value bet of about $50,000.

That situation reminds me of a story that Gus Hansen once told me about a hand he played against a player he knew very well. It's almost identical actually.

Hand in Action 2

Gus raised with J-J and the big blind reraised him. Gus knew that his opponent was a tight player and probably had A-K or a better pair, so he decided to just call and see what hit the flop.

The flop came 7♣ 2♠ 3♦ and the big blind checked to Gus. Knowing his player, Gus was still suspicious that his opponent was setting a trap for him so he checked behind him. The turn card paired the 2.

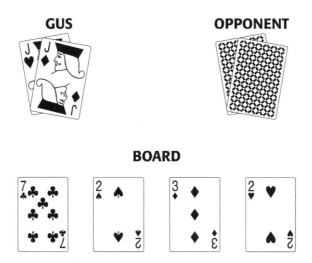

Once again, his opponent checked. Gus figured that his opponent would not check twice with A-A or K-K, so he must have A-K. However, Gus also figured that his opponent would call an all-in bet on the turn with A-K. Further, Gus believed that his opponent would call him on the river with A-K high, whether he made a pair or not.

So, rather than risk a 14 percent chance of going broke on the hand, Gus decided to check what he knew to be the best hand. That way, if an ace or king hit the river, Gus could evade being eliminated from the tournament. At the same time, it wouldn't cost him any value since his read led him to believe that he could get all his chips in on the river when there was no risk of being outdrawn.

This is obviously an extreme example of a situation where a player had a dead read on his opponent, but it helps illustrate the bigger lesson. (By the way, Gus went all in on the river when a 4 hit and his opponent called him with A-K, doubling him up.) That is, it's often better to allow an opponent to outdraw you for free in a smaller pot than it is to play a big pot for your tournament life where you could take a bad beat and be eliminated from action.

MAKING A WEAKER PLAY FOR BIGGER CONSIDERATIONS

A lot of poker theorists are going to strongly disagree with the above paragraph, claiming that the best approach is to maximize your equity in each hand you play, but there are other considerations to think about. Namely, if you are doing great in a tournament by chopping away at small pots and you think you'll be able to continue to do so, why would you risk even a 14 percent chance of going broke? Surely getting all of your money in as over a 4 to 1 favorite isn't a bad thing, but if there is an alternative that helps you avoid risking your whole stack, you should consider making what, for all intents and purposes, is the weaker play.

This concept is hard for a lot of people to wrap their head around. Tournament poker is different from playing in a cash game. When you play for money, all that matters is that you make the play with the highest expected value. But in a tournament, your expected value is directly tied into the likelihood of your going broke and being eliminated from the tournament. It's the reason you always hear the pros say they want to avoid coin flips. It's the reason why a player like Phil Hellmuth may fold pocket tens preflop against a player that he thinks has an A-K, despite the fact that he is a 57 percent favorite. He doesn't want to take the risk of being eliminated 43 percent of the time, because he truly believes that he can build his stack without taking these types of risks.

I agree with him. If you want to be a consistent winner in million dollar events, this is a concept that you need to accept.

RIVER PLAY

INTRODUCTION TO RIVER PLAY

When playing a small-ball brand of poker, your goal with many of the marginal hands you'll be playing is simply to get to the river without investing too high a percentage of your chip stack—unless you actually have a monster hand and want to build the pot to get maximum value for the hand.

Since your table image will likely be one where people suspect that you are bluffing throughout the hand, the river is not the time to make them right. With the small-ball approach, your bluffing frequency should be lower than if you were playing a more traditional style of hold'em. The key reason is simply because people will lean towards calling you more often because you are playing more than your fair share of hands. If you watch some of the world's best no-limit hold'em tournament players, you'll notice that they don't bluff on the river nearly as often as you think. They understand that once an opponent has played a hand all the way to the river, he is likely going to see it through to the end if he has any kind of a hand.

Gus Hansen is an excellent example of a player who personifies the wild, crazy image. But watch his play more closely and you'll see that while he'll raise with hands such as 9-2 and 10-4, rarely will he waste large amounts of chips on the river as a pure bluff. It is an understanding of table image that forces Gus to have the goods on the river if he bets. That is, he has created an image that will get him more action. It's no coincidence that Gus is one of the most successful tournament players of all time. His approach to the game has a lot of merit.

With these river concepts in mind, you should understand that the river isn't a time for wild, sophisticated bluffs, although you can occasionally bluff in the perfect situations. Instead, the river is a time to extract full value for your strong hands, avoid losing more chips than necessary, and induce bluffs from opponents who think you are weak.

GETTING MAXIMUM VALUE

One of the key things to avoid when playing small ball is falling into predictable patterns based on your bet sizes. For example, you don't want your bluffs to be 60 percent of the pot and your value bets to be 80 percent of the pot. In theory, that would work out extremely well if no one paid attention, but in reality your more perceptive opponents will pick up on these patterns and exploit you. They'll reraise-bluff your smaller bets and lay down strong hands against your bigger bets.

The best way to value bet the river with hands you want to get paid off on is to bet the same amount that you'd bet if you were bluffing. Essentially, the size of your bluff bet and the size of your value bet should be close to identical.

I've actually seen some young players apply a version of small ball who made it ridiculously obvious, purely by the size of their bets, when they had a strong hand and were looking for extra value.

Hand in Action

For example, our hero raised from late position to $250 before the flop. With the blinds at $50/$100, the big blind called. The flop came 10♣ 10♠ 8♣. The big blind checked and our hero bet $350. The big blind called. The turn was the 6♦ and again the big blind checked. This time our hero bet $900. The blind called again. The river card was the 2♣.

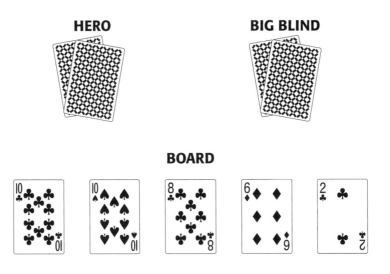

HERO   **BIG BLIND**

BOARD

With $3,050 in the pot, our hero went a little nuts and bet $6,500.

Earlier in the session I noticed that the kid had gotten caught bluffing twice, and on those occasions, his bets were 50 to 60 percent of the pot size. Considering that I knew he was trying to play small pots, he made it too obvious that he had a monster hand. The big blind showed pocket aces and mucked them face up! I'm certain that if the kid would have bet $1,700

SMALL BALL

to $2,200 the big blind would have called him instantly. The kid drastically overpriced the hand and it cost him an extra $2,000 or so.

I've used a blackjack analogy once before regarding small-ball poker, and I'm going back to it one more time to illustrate my point. I'm assuming that most of you have heard of card counting in blackjack, and know that when done properly, card counting can give blackjack players an advantage over the house.

Essentially, it works like this: When the remaining deck is rich with high cards, it is good for the player. When the remaining cards in the deck are mostly smaller cards, it is good for the house. Card counters are notorious for varying their bet sizes based on the "count," the high-low card ratio of the remaining cards in the deck. When the deck is pro-player, they increase their bets; and when the deck is pro-house, they lower their bets.

Almost every card counter in the world gets caught, but many of them get caught quickly because they are too greedy. Similar to our example with the kid trying to make a big payday (he had made a full house on that hand), a bad card counter alerts the house to his favorable situation when he makes drastic changes in his bet sizes. Imagine you were a pit boss in a casino and you have a player betting $10 a hand at the start of a shoe. Then after about six hands, his bets go to $500 for the rest of the shoe. Hmm... you think he might be counting cards?

The key is to make subtle changes to your bet sizes so that they go unnoticed. Therefore, rather than jumping from $10 to $500, maybe you double up and increase to $20 after a win and $40 after another. But you don't vary your bet sizes so drastically that your cover is blown like the hero in our poker hand example who got greedy and overbet the pot.

CORRECT VALUE BET SIZING

In a tournament, the small-ball approach is one where you want to avoid big pots at all costs unless you have the nuts. By default, pots will get bigger when you get to the river, and that puts you in dangerous territory. In fact, small ball works best when most hands *don't* even get to the river, but when they do, one player just makes a small bet and another player may call. The value in this approach to the game isn't to make large value bets in dangerous situations, but instead to nickel and dime your opponents in the marginal situations. And on the rare occasions when you have the nuts, you hook them for a bigger bet along the way.

> **IN FACT, SMALL BALL WORKS BEST WHEN MOST HANDS DON'T EVEN GET TO THE RIVER.**

However, when you do have the nuts, or what you think is clearly the best hand, you shouldn't veer from the small-ball betting patterns that you'll be using throughout the tournament. In fact, you shouldn't bet more than the amount in the pot. There are some very rare cases where you may want to bet more than that, but for the most part, your value bets shouldn't exceed the pot size.

The key to figuring out the correct value bet size is figuring out the strength of your opponent's hand. The stronger you think your opponent's hand is, the more you should bet. Conversely, if you think your opponent has close to nothing, then you want to make it easy for him to justify making a bad call. In extreme cases, you might even want to bet the minimum, even if it represents only 10 percent of the pot!

In a tournament, the amount you bet when value betting should also take into account the amount of pressure your bet will be putting on your opponent. For example, if you make a pot-sized bet that would put your opponent all in, you might scare him away from calling since he desperately wants to stay in the tournament. In a case like that, instead of betting 100 percent of his chips and putting his tournament life on the line, you might want to bet 75 percent of his chips. That way, he may think, "Well, I think I have the best hand here, but even if I'm wrong, I'll still have some chips left to play with." And then you get "some" of his chips!

Let's take a look at three examples and try to figure out what size value bet makes the most sense:

Hand in Action #1

With the blinds at $100/$200 a player from first position makes it $600 to go before the flop. You reraise him from late position to $2,100 with A-A. He calls. The flop comes 2♦ 2♠ 6♣. Your opponent checks and you bet $2,500. He calls. The turn is the 8♥.

Your opponent check-calls $4,000. The river brings the 2♣.

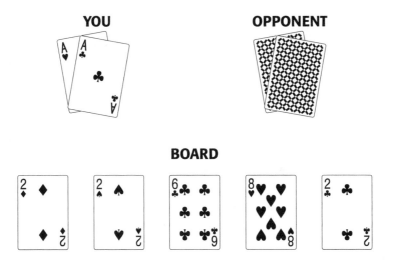

Your opponent checks on the river. Both you and your opponent have $16,000 in chips remaining and there is $17,500 in the pot.

How much should you bet?

1. $4,000

2. $10,000

3. All In

SMALL BALL

Hand in Action #2

With the blinds at $50/$100, you raise preflop to $250 from the button with A♠ 8♠. The big blind calls. The flop comes K♠ 8♦ 4♣. You both check the flop. The turn is the 5♠.

Your opponent checks, and you bet $400. He calls. The river is the K♥.

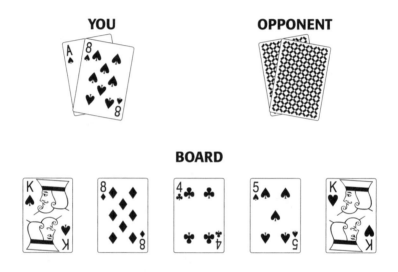

YOU   OPPONENT

BOARD

Both you and your opponent have over $10,000 in chips and there is $1,350 in the pot. How much should you bet?

1. $1,350

2. $550

3. $1,000

Hand in Action #3

With the blinds at $400/$800 and a $100 ante, a player from early position makes it $2,400 before the flop. You call from the button with the 7♣ 8♣. The flop comes K♦ 5♣ 6♦. Your opponent bets $3,000 and you call. The turn is the A♥ and both of you check. The river is the 4♣.

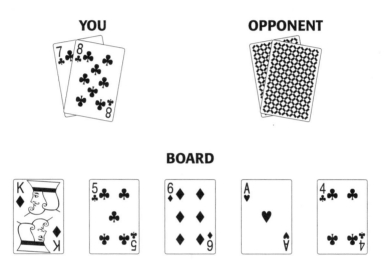

YOU

OPPONENT

BOARD

The 4♣ gives you the nut straight. Both you and your opponent have over $50,000 left in chips and there is $12,900 in the pot.

Your opponent checks to you on the river. How much should you bet?

1. $12,900

2. $8,500

3. $4,000

Let's see how you did.

Answer to Hand in Action 1

"A" is incorrect. It should be clear in this situation that your opponent has a strong hand and has shown a willingness to pay off decent-sized bets. The way the hand has played out makes it look as though your opponent likely has a decent sized pocket pair, so $4,000 is too small a bet in this situation.

"B" is correct. A bet of $10,000 represents a good percentage of the pot. The bet is not so big that it will apply maximum pressure on your opponent, which will increase the likelihood of him paying you off.

"C" is incorrect. It wouldn't be a horrible play, but let's consider what hands your opponent likely has here. He probably doesn't have K-K or you may have heard from him sooner in the hand. His most likely hands are in the range of 9-9 through Q-Q. An all-in call would be a very risky move for his tournament life, and the fact that you've forced him to make that decision could convince him that he's beat. That's not the result you want. If he folds, your bet sizing error could have cost you a nice value bet and call on the river.

Answer to Hand in Action 2

"A" is incorrect. Why bet so much when you have a marginal hand? If he is slowplaying a king, you are costing yourself more than you need to. By betting the whole pot, you decrease the chances that your opponent will make a loose call with bottom pair or even ace high.

"B" is correct. The way the hand played out doesn't look like either you or your opponent has a very strong hand, so any value bet here with second pair and an ace kicker should be considered a very thin value bet. There is no guarantee that your hand is the best one, so by making a smallish bet you accomplish two things:

1. You lose less when your opponent has you beat.
2. You increase the likelihood of your opponent paying you off with a very weak hand such as bottom pair or ace high.

"C" is incorrect. For the same reasons you shouldn't bet the whole pot in this situation, you shouldn't bet $1,000 either. If you are beat, your $1,000 bet will never get your opponent to fold—all it will do is cost you more chips when he shows you 10-10 or K-3. When making a thin value bet with a marginal hand, you don't want to waste that good read by letting your opponent off the hook by overbetting. You know your hand is likely the best hand, so make sure you get something for it.

Answer to Hand in Action 3

"A" is incorrect. If your opponent had a strong enough hand to call a pot-sized bet, what makes you think he would have checked on both the turn and the river? Your opponent likely checked because he didn't like the ace or the king and has a hand like Q-Q. If not that, maybe he has a K-Q and just didn't like the ace. In either case, it doesn't look as though he has A-K, A-A, or K-K, so he just isn't going to call a pot-sized river bet.

"B" is incorrect. Based on the way the hand played out, it should be obvious that your opponent isn't overly strong as he would have been betting on the turn or river. A bet this big will usually convince him that his pair of queens or K-Q is no good, and you'll let him off the hook.

"C" is correct. By making such a small bet in relation to the pot size, you'll be laying your opponent an excellent price to look you up and see if you are bluffing. Also, if he has K-Q, he may believe that you are betting with a pair of kings and have a worse kicker than he has. The only significantly important factor in choosing this bet size is that, in some rare cases, if your opponent is trapping you with A-A, K-K, or A-K, he likely won't be satisfied with earning your $4,000 river bet. He may decide to raise it $12,000, at which point you can reraise again and hope he pays that off as well.

WHEN CHECKING WINS MORE THAN BETTING

Maximizing your profit on the river isn't always about how much you should bet. In certain situations it also is about the following: Is your opponent more likely to call your bet, or bet if you check to him? The standard situation for this ploy is when you have a marginal to strong hand, but think your opponent either has you crushed or has missed his draw. In these types of situations, betting the river won't do you any good because when your opponent has you crushed, he is going to raise you; and when he misses his draw, he's just going to fold anyway.

Hand in Action

Let's look at an example where checking a strong hand might earn you extra value while a bet would be less effective.

You are playing in a $10/$20 blind no-limit cash game and decide to limp in from the small blind with A♥ 3♥. The big blind makes it $60 and you call. The flop comes A♠ 10♠ 4♥. You check. Your opponent makes a continuation bet, as expected, pushing forward $80 worth of chips. You call.

The turn card is the 4♣ and both you and your opponent check. The river is the 8♦.

YOU **OPPONENT**

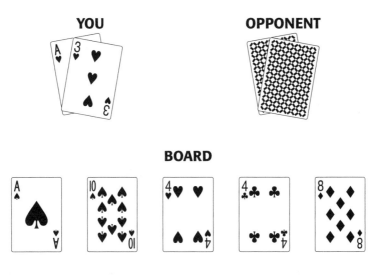

BOARD

It is a close call as to whether betting or checking the river is the better play. Your ultimate decision on how to proceed depends on how you read your opponent. If he doesn't really bluff and you don't think he would value bet a hand such as J-J, Q-Q, or K-K, you should probably bet about $120 and hope he calls.

Most players don't fit that category, however, and would not only value bet a hand such as Q-Q, they may also decide to bluff the river by betting with a hand such as Q-J. Against a player like this, checking will often be the more profitable play. Whereas your opponent won't call a bet, he may see your check as a sign of weakness and decide to take one more stab at the flop.

Eventually your opponents are going to pick up on the fact that you'll often check marginal to strong hands on the river looking to induce a bluff. But that's also something that you should be able to exploit in another way. If your opponents are on to your tendency to check some good hands on the river, they will think twice about making thin value bets against you. Their hesitancy to value bet the river could earn you some free showdowns in situations where you were planning to call a bet.

Hand in Action

For example, suppose you are in the same $10/$20 no-limit cash game. This time a player raises to $60 from middle position. You defend your blind with the A♠ 4♠. The flop comes Q♠ 10♥ 4♥ giving you bottom pair and a backdoor flush draw. You check-call your opponent's $80 flop bet. The turn is the 10♦, and both you and your opponent check. The river card is the 3♣.

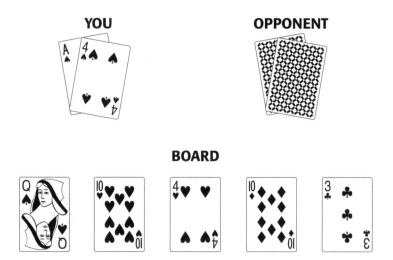

This is a situation where making a bet yourself has little to no value. Although it looks as though you may have the best hand, you'd much prefer seeing your opponent check the river behind you.

Let's say your opponent has J-J. With the 10 pairing on the turn, he can't win if you called with a 10 in your hand, and he also can't beat a queen. If your opponent bets about $150, you very well might call the bet thinking that he missed his straight or flush and has nothing but ace high. If your opponent is perceptive, though, and has caught on to the fact that you have been checking some hands on the river that you could have bet, he may decide not to value bet the river since he may believe that there is little that he can beat if you call.

That's actually the place where you eventually want to get. You want your opponents to think twice about making thin value bets against you. Playing small ball is all about keeping the pots small, especially when you're out of position in marginal situations. Since those situations are much more common than ones where you have a monster hand on the river and look to play a big pot, it's in your best interest to have your opponents play cautiously against you on the river.

Obviously, if your opponents begin to make an adjustment to your play by checking hands that they may have otherwise value bet, you'll have to start betting your own hands for value a little more often. Sadly, your opponents won't habitually do it for you anymore! I'm going to share a real life example of this exact scenario playing out online at PokerStars.com.

BETTING FOR VALUE WHEN YOUR OPPONENTS WON'T

I was playing heads-up with a player who I knew little about other than he was a winning, aggressive player. In the first thirty minutes of play, a pattern kept developing: I would check the river with top pair or middle pair and my opponent would value bet a worse hand. For example, we played the following hand.

Hand in Action

I check-called a flop of J-9-4 with a J-10. The turn card was a 2 and it went check-check. The river came a 3.

SMALL BALL

DANIEL

OPPONENT

BOARD

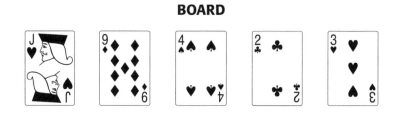

I checked again hoping for my opponent to bluff at the pot. He didn't bluff, but he value bet his Q-9 assuming that it was the best hand.

There was absolutely nothing wrong with his play. That was a pretty standard value bet for him on the river. As you can see, however, my checking the J-10 didn't cost me anything because he would have just called the bet if I had bet the river. The money still went in the middle, but my play sent my opponent a clear message: Just because I check the river doesn't mean I have nothing!

I continued to play that style against him out of position and eventually he made an adjustment. That's precisely what I was hoping for! He had picked up on my tendency to play cautiously on the river and just check-call, which forced him to change his strategy and avoid making value bets with hands that he would normally bet. The adjustment he made actually saved me lots of river bets in situations where I would have called, but didn't have to since he checked. Here is a hand that we played later in the session.

Hand in Action 2

My opponent raised before the flop and I called with a 10-8. The flop came J-10-6. I checked and he made a small bet. The turn was a 7 and I checked again, as did he. The river was another 6.

DANIEL **OPPONENT**

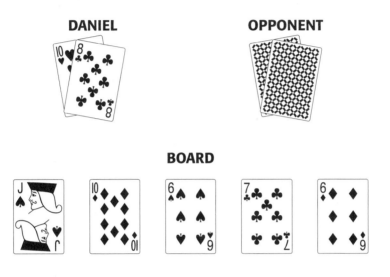

BOARD

It went check-check on the river. I showed my pair and he turned over K-10! This is a hand that he clearly would have bet for value earlier in the session.

The strategy isn't complete, however, without a minor adjustment. Knowing that I've lulled my opponent into checking down marginal hands on the river, I now bet my own hands for value a slightly higher percentage of the time on the river. It's a cat-and-mouse game that you can play on a regular basis, more specifically when playing heads-up. In sticking with the small-ball concept, though, you always want to tame your opponent into keeping the pots smaller, especially when you're out of position. This generally means that you'll be playing cautiously or weak when you're out of position—but that's okay. Remember, your goal is to minimize your losses when you're out of position, and maximize your profits when you're in position.

USING THE DEFENSIVE BET

The goal with the defensive bet is essentially to minimize your losses in marginal situations where you are uncertain whether you have the best hand, but think you have to call an opponent's bet if he bets the river. The idea is to bet a smaller amount than you think your opponent would bet, which will force him to raise you on the river if he is looking for more value on the hand. Most of the time, however, your opponent won't have a hand strong enough to make that play. Even when an opponent suspects that you may be making a defensive bet, he still probably will just call on the river—unless he has the nuts or close to it. Let's take a look at a few examples of how to use the defensive bet effectively.

Hand in Action

With the blinds at $50/$100 before the flop in tournament action, a player raises your big blind to $300. You defend with the A♠ 8♠. The flop comes K♦ 8♦ 3♣. You check to your opponent and he also checks. The turn card is the 6♥. You check the turn, slightly worried that your opponent is trapping you with a king. He bets $450 and you decide to look him up. The river card is the 5♦, putting a third diamond on the board.

YOU

OPPONENT

BOARD

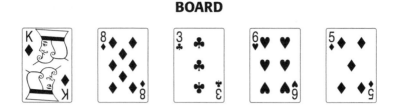

If you are up against an aggressive player who is capable of making large bluff bets on the river, or even a value bet with a hand such as A-K, this might be a good time for a defensive bet since you can now represent a flush. If you bet the river, your opponent is not going to raise you unless he actually hit the flush. Even with a set of kings, your opponent will likely just call on the river rather than raise. However, if you check the river, he'll likely make close to a pot-sized bet with a set.

Since you aren't really sure where you stand in the hand, the last thing you want to do here is face a large river bet. The best way to avoid facing that is to make a defensive bet. With $1,550 in the pot, you could bet as little as $550 on the river. Your river bet really isn't intended to be a bluff at all, but it accomplishes the following:

1. It takes your opponent's big-bluff weapon away from him on the river.
2. It allows you to see the hand through at a cheaper price.

Your opponent isn't likely to fold any hand that beats you for such a small bet, but that's not the goal of making a bet. The bet is designed so that you can minimize your own damage on the hand and not be faced with calling a large river bet in a situation where you would be unsure what to do. The bet simplifies your decision for you.

If your opponent raises, well, you should probably dump your hand as he's likely to have made a flush on the river. Now, there are some players capable of pouncing on a defensive river bet as a bluff, but they are few and far between. Besides, we have a plan for those guys that we'll get to later. But before we move on to that, let's look at some other scenarios where the defensive bet works well.

Hand in Action

With the blinds at $100/$200, you have pocket fives in the big blind and call a $600 raise before the flop. The flop comes 5♣ 6♦ 7♣. You check and your opponent bets $900. You raise the bet to $2,500 and he calls.

The turn card is the 2♠. You bet $3,500 and he calls. At this point, you put him on an overpair, but are unsure. He may have a flush draw or a possible straight draw. The river card is an ugly one, the 4♦.

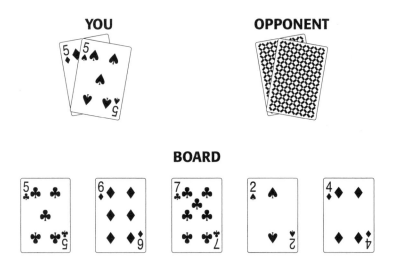

YOU   OPPONENT

BOARD

If your opponent has been calling with an 8 in his hand, he may have just made the straight. Despite that, this is the perfect opportunity for you to make a defensive bet. If you bet on the river and your opponent raises, you'll simply have to fold your set. It's extremely unlikely that he could raise you on the river without the straight, especially since you were in the big blind and could have made the straight yourself.

There is $13,300 in the pot and your turn bet was $3,500. You don't want to bet less than $3,500, but you don't want to bet much more than that either. If you check the river, your opponent may decide to get aggressive and try to steal the pot away from you and bet $12,000 with a missed flush draw. Even though you can beat a bluff, poker is so much easier when you don't have to face such high-pressure decisions for large percentages of your chips. Instead, betting anywhere from $3,500 to $4,500 on the river is the way to go.

In addition to helping you defend against a huge river bet, there is an added benefit to this bet size. If your opponent has A-A, he may decide that you were bluffing with a flush draw and pay you off! If your opponent has an 8 in his hand, he might not even raise you fearing that you won't call unless you also have at least an 8, and you could even have flopped a straight with an 8-9.

Checking isn't a terrible option here, but it's more dangerous. If your opponent makes a big river bet, you'll be forced to play the guessing game. The defensive bet allows you to control the pot size by dictating the amount of the river bet rather than allowing your opponent to decide how big the pot will be. Obviously, the defensive bet is a bet that is always made out of position. If you are in position, there is no need to bet at all in these marginal situations.

The only real danger in using this ploy is that sometimes you'll be facing perceptive opponents who may pick up on your pattern and decide to bluff-raise when you make a defensive bet. As I mentioned earlier, this type of player isn't common, but he does exist and you should be prepared for him. When you think he's aware that you use the defensive bet, you can

SMALL BALL

actually bait him into bluff-raising you by making the defensive bet when you have the nuts!

Let's take a look at an example.

Hand in Action

With the blinds at $200/$400, you raise preflop to $1,000 from middle position holding 10-J. A tough player on the button calls your raise. The flop comes K♦ Q♥ 4♣ and you decide to check the draw to your opponent. He bets out $1,800 and you call. The turn is the insignificant 2♣. You decide to play the hand meekly and check again. This time your opponent also checks. The river is the 9♦.

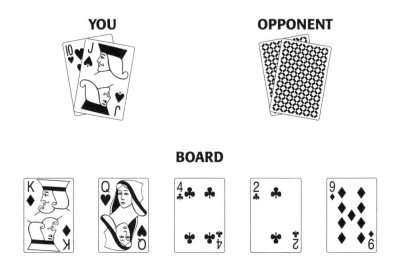

The 9 gives you the nut straight and an opportunity to make a defensive-sized bet, trying to sell the idea that you have a hand such as A-Q. Keeping in line with your real defensive bets, $2,000 is around the right number. That bet size doesn't look like the type of bet you'd make if you have just made the nuts. In that situation, you usually would want to bet more to get full value. However, an aggressive player who may be on to your defensive betting style may see this as the perfect opportunity to represent exactly what you already have!

You see, if he puts you on a hand such as A-Q, or even A-K for that matter, a river raise in this situation is very believable from his perspective. The way he has played the hand, he could easily have the nut straight, and if he does, he'll probably make a raise to $6,000 or $7,000.

Let's say that your opponent has 6-6. He might bet the flop in position to win it right there, but once you call, he knows you have something, so he checks the turn. But on the river, he senses another opportunity to steal this pot. If you bet bigger on the river, you take his play away from him, making him less likely to pounce. If you check, he may decide not to try the bluff since it looks like he'll get called. The $2,000 bet in this situation is the perfect play. He'll call it with a queen or a king, and he may also raise you with absolutely nothing!

As with virtually anything relating to poker strategy, the key to success is learning how to mix up and adjust your play according to your opponent's perception of you and your style. Maximizing value on any particular hand is just as much about knowing your opponent as it is playing the hand fundamentally correctly.

That's actually one of the reasons I have a problem with using absolute terms when it comes to poker. One bet is rarely better than another in every situation. So much of it is dependant on the opponent you are playing. For example, take that last hand we just covered and change the opponent from a tough, aggressive player to a weak player who calls too much on the river. Against that kind of player, a defensive bet would be foolish. Instead, you would want to bet about $6,000 on the river and hope to get a call from a king or a queen. Your defensive bet has little value since your opponent won't raise you on the river unless he has, well, the same hand as you!

The defensive bet is an important weapon, especially in tournament poker. It's a bet that will help neutralize an opponent's positional advantage and allow you to take control of the river with minimal risk. It's a play that's most effective, though, when used sparingly. The situation has to be just right for it to work properly. Knowing when the right time to use it is a skill that should come with experience.

LAYING DOWN HANDS ON THE RIVER

You can't become a great poker player if you never lay down the best hand on the river from time to time. However, you don't want anyone to know that you are capable of making big laydowns, because if you do that, your opponents will attempt more bluffs against you, which will just make things more difficult in the long run. Conversely, the image you'd much rather have is one of a calling station. It's usually an insult when someone pegs you as a calling station, but the rewards of that image should far outweigh the bruising to your ego. When they see you as a calling station, your opponents will be less likely to try creative river bluffs against you. This table image will also make it that much easier for you to make laydowns in situations where you know your opponent wouldn't try to bluff the "calling station."

The real reason that it's difficult to lay down hands on the river correctly is because the pot is generally laying you a good price to call. Allowing the price you are being laid to influence your thought process too strongly will absolutely cloud your judgment, and you'll start coming up with all kinds of excuses to make sloppy river calls.

The Math Player

A specific type of player will often justify making bad calls on the river because the pot odds are correct. He will often neglect to realize that, no, the pot odds aren't right because opponents will beat him in that situation more often than he might convince himself that they will. Let's take a look at an example in which a "math player" makes a bad river call because his thinking on the river is influenced too strongly by the pot odds.

Hand in Action

Math Guy raises preflop to $600 with the A♣ 7♦ with the blinds at $100/$200 and a $25 ante at an eight-handed table. Only the big blind calls the bet. The flop comes K♣ 4♦ 4♠. The big blind checks, so Math Guy makes a continuation bet of $900. The big blind calls. The turn comes with the 9♦ and both players check. On the river, a 6♠ hits. Here is how the situation looks:

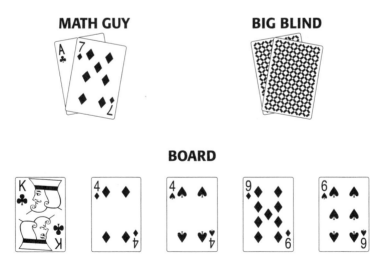

MATH GUY **BIG BLIND**

BOARD

The big blind bets out $400. That's an extremely small bet and, because of that, it only costs Math Guy $400 to win $3,700 if the big blind is bluffing. That means that Math Guy only needs to pick off a bluff one in nine times to show a profit on the call. Those are amazing pot odds, but the problem is this: What hands could his opponent have to play this way that don't beat his A-7 high? No draw was present on the board, so the only way Math Guy can justify making this $400 call is to believe that the big blind has been setting up an elaborate bluff, hoping that a really weak bet on the river (the extra $400) would look strong. The other possibility is that the big blind is making a defensive bet with ace high, in which case he might split the pot provided that his ace high has a low kicker as well.

While it seems that the price is right, in reality the likelihood of that A-7 being the best hand based on the way the hand was played is minimal. So minimal, that not even 9 to 1 is the right price when your best hope is a random berserko bluff or a split pot! This is a rare and extreme example, but it helps illustrate the point that when you are trying to figure out whether a call makes sense, you shouldn't allow pot odds to incorrectly influence you into making sloppy calls. Pot odds should always be an important consideration, but again, don't let it be the only deciding factor in making your final decision to call or fold. Let's look at a likely situation.

WHERE POT ODDS MISREPRESENT A SITUATION

With the blinds at $50/$100, you raise to $250 before the flop with J♣ J♦. A player on the button calls your raise, as does the big blind. The flop comes Q♥ 7♠ 2♠. The big blind checks and you decide to take control of the hand by betting $450 into a pot of $800. The button calls and the big blind folds.

The turn card is the 9♦ and you decide to try to win the pot one more time with a second bullet. This time, you fire out $900 into a pot of $1,700. Again, the player on the button calls. The river card is the K♣, an ugly-looking card. You decide to check to the button since it looks very likely that you are beat.

YOU   **BUTTON**

BOARD

Your opponent bets $1,100. Yuck. There is $3,500 in the pot already, so that means you need to call $1,100 to win $4,600. That's better than 4 to 1 odds that your jacks are the best hand.

Here is what I want you to avoid doing: Do not let your first thought be, "He only needs to be bluffing about 20 percent of the time for my call to be correct." It's a thought you should get to eventually, but I strongly urge you to get out of the habit of that being your *first* thought as it might make you lean towards making a call for the *wrong* reasons.

Instead, go through the hand from the beginning. Your opponent just called you from the button. What type of cards would he do that with? It could be hands such as K-Q, A-Q, 8-8 or 10♠ J♠. Obviously, the type of hand he has depends on the type of player he is. Now, move to the flop. He called you on an uncoordinated board with an overcard to your jacks and three players in the pot. At this point, you can narrow down his hand even further. He may have a flush draw, he could have a pair of queens, he may have a set, or he might have a hand such as 8-8 and is calling because he thinks he might have you beat. He may even have a hand such as 7♣ 8♣ for middle pair. All these hands are possibilities.

On the turn card you bet to protect against having a flush draw or a hand such as 7-8 beat you. When your opponent calls again, you should assume that you are either behind, as your opponent likely has top pair, or that your opponent is drawing to the flush. The 9 on the turn may have even helped him with additional outs and he may have picked up a straight draw as well.

The river is the nightmare card: Another overcard, and it's a spade. By this point, you've narrowed your opponent's most likely hands to:

1. A pair of queens
2. A flush

When a flush card hits *and* your opponent bets, the amount of his bet should be a factor for sure, but you should be better than 90 percent sure that your jacks are not the best hand. So, unless you are getting 10 to 1 odds on the river call, you should still fold despite the fact that it "seems" like you are getting great pot odds on the call.

Your opponent's bet size screams of a value bet hoping to get called. He may have made the flush, or have a hand such as K-Q and hope you'll call with a pair. Either way, calling here would be a mistake. Yes, it's true that a small majority of players are capable of setting up a bluff on the river this way, but it's highly unlikely, and it's not a good situation to try being a hero. Besides, if your opponent were setting up a bluff, his river bet would likely be much larger so that he wasn't giving you such great pot odds on the call. Remember, he doesn't know you have J-J, so if he is trying to move you off a hand such as A-Q or better, he will likely think that a bigger bet is necessary.

You can use your common sense in making laydowns on the river, but for the most part, it's always better to err on the side of paying it off in marginal situations where you don't yet have a read on your opponent's tendencies. The key to being able to make big laydowns on the river, though, lies in your read of your opponent. Without that knowledge, a sexy, monster laydown would be foolish against a player you don't know.

MAKING BIG LAYDOWNS BASED ON READS

I recently made a laydown playing in a $25/$50 no-limit hold'em game online at PokerStars that many people questioned.

Hand in Action

A tight player that I knew fairly well limped in from first position. The button limped and I completed the bet from the small blind with the Q♣ 8♥. The big blind checked and four of us took the flop: Q♥ Q♦ 4♣. I decided to check to the player on the button, as did everyone else, and he bet $150. I obviously thought I had the best hand, but didn't exactly see this as a dream situation because if one of the other players in the pot had a queen, his kicker would likely beat mine. By calling, I figured I would get information from the other players' actions behind me. The big blind folded, but the player who limped in under the gun overcalled. That worried me.

The turn card was the 10♠ and I once again checked, as did both of my opponents. The river card was the J♦.

SMALL BALL

TIGHT PLAYER

BUTTON

DANIEL

BOARD

Rather than bet, I figured no one would call me with a worse hand, so I checked to see what action developed behind me. Besides, that wasn't a great card for my hand as I'd now be losing to an 8-9, A-K, or J-J. The player under the gun bet $400 into a pot of $650 and the button folded. Now, it was up to me. Raising never crossed my mind for even a second. The price the pot was laying me wasn't much of a consideration either—I was getting 2.6 to 1 odds on the call. What I focused on was the situation, the overcall on the flop, and the bet size on the river. Knowing what I did about the player, I knew that for him to overcall on the flop, he had to have a strong hand. I also knew that he was very unlikely to bluff in this situation.

Even though I had three queens, a seemingly strong hand in a small pot like this one, the range of hands I could beat was miniscule. The idea of a split pot was something I deemed impossible. This particular player would never limp in from first position with worse than a Q-10.

The only real hand I could beat was A-A or K-K. There was a possibility that he would limp in before the flop with one of these hands, but because I knew my opponent's tendencies rather well, I didn't think he would even bet the river. Even if he did, he likely would have bet something like $250 or $300. I folded the hand and my opponent showed A-Q for trips with a better kicker. Yeah, me!

The point of sharing this hand helps illustrate situations where you can make laydowns based on the situation and the fact that your opponent's range of hands is very narrow. The goal in poker is to improve to the point where you can put your opponent on one of just a few hands rather than a wide spectrum of hands. The fewer hands you can narrow it down to, the easier it becomes to make good laydowns based on the pot odds you are being laid. For example, had my opponent bet something like $100, even though I was pretty sure I was beat, I would have certainly called that bet as I wasn't that certain!

TELL-BASED LAYDOWNS

Never underestimate tells or your ability to recognize them. You'll surprise yourself if you spend a little more time focusing on the man and what he is doing with his body, his eyes or his hands. It's not easy to spot tells in every player, but some players give off very specific information about the strength of their hand. If you recognize something in particular, it can make the difference between paying off a losing hand, or picking off a bluff with bottom pair.

However, I still think that making a tell-based laydown is something that you should do only after you've already exhausted all of the other information in the hand—what happened preflop, postflop, and on the turn. You also look at things like the players' betting patterns, the situation, and the pot odds. Once you've processed all of that information, then look for a physical tell. Before you get totally confused, it would help to know what exactly to look for. Well, it's likely not something you are magically going to see for the first time. Instead, it's probably something you should have picked up on before you played the particular hand you're playing.

Tells vary from player to player, so simply looking for a guy covering his mouth or clenching his teeth won't tell you very much unless you've seen it before and know what it means. An extreme example is something like seeing an opponent who is chewing gum suddenly stop chewing when you stare him down. That might lead you to believe he's bluffing, but on what basis? Have you seen him do that before? Does he do it when he's bluffing, or does he always do it? That's why paying attention is so important. Reading tells is certainly not a reliable science because each individual has distinct tells that are exclusive to him. Unless you know what you are looking for, nothing you see will necessarily be much good to you.

For example, I recently played in a tournament with an older French gentleman. He made a river bet against me and I stared him down a little bit. He looked extremely comfortable, his body appeared loose, and I couldn't really get a read off him, although it looked like I was beat. But I called him for two reasons:

1. For information
2. Because I had a pretty strong hand myself

Well, that same French guy was in a pot later with another player at the table and made a bet on the river, but this time, his body stiffened, he stared blankly at the flop, and he looked very uncomfortable. The other player folded and the French gentleman showed a bluff. About an hour later, I got my chance with him again. I checked the river to him and he made a pot-sized bet. Because I had some information already stored in my brain, I made a decision based not only on the play of the hand, but also on a physical tell. I had bottom pair and I felt like he was pushing me around. I looked over at him and he didn't look back. His body looked tense, almost like a statue. I called and his hand hit the muck.

That's one of the most fascinating aspects of poker and something that certainly differentiates online poker from live poker. Obviously, this French player could have been using a reverse tell in the hope that I would call him. That is a talent in itself. Playing the physical tell game certainly isn't easy for beginners or online players, but it's something that can give you that extra edge in tight spots when you aren't sure what to do. My French friend was pretty dependable.

Hand in Action
Not twenty minutes later, I picked up K-K on a board of 9-6-3 and bet the flop. He called. The turn was an ace.

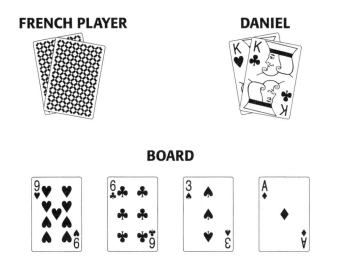

FRENCH PLAYER   **DANIEL**

BOARD

I checked, and he bet. I looked over at him and he smiled right back at me. I folded my K-K and he happily showed me A-6 for two pair.

On that first hand, I made the wrong decision in calling because I had no reliable tells on him. But once I was able to spot something, it allowed me to play flawless poker against him for the rest of the session.

Anyone who informs you that looking for physical tells is overrated is limiting his potential as a player. They are out there, and if you focus, I promise that you will amaze yourself with the subtle things you see.

FIGURING OUT THE CORRECT RIVER BET

Hand-reading skills are essential in figuring out how big your river bet should be, or even if it would make more sense to check the river. Having an idea about what your opponent might have will allow you to gauge how much he is willing to call when you are looking to make a value bet, or even how small a bluff bet you can make when you think your opponent missed a draw.

In situations where you put your opponent on a missed draw, if you plan to bluff the hand, your bet size should be on the smaller side. In case you are wrong and your opponent wasn't on a draw, there is no need to lose more chips than necessary with your bluff. Let's look at an example.

Hand in Action

With the blinds at $50/$100, you raise preflop to $250 in late position with 4-4. The small blind calls the bet and the big blind folds, so you'll see the flop heads-up. It comes 8♥ 9♠ 9♥. The small blind checks to you and you bet out $400. He calls.

The turn card is the K♣. The small blind checks again and you decide to take one more stab at the pot in case your opponent is drawing. You bet $650 and again your opponent calls. You put him on either a flush draw or a hand such as J-10. Since he didn't raise you on the turn a 9 is unlikely. In this scenario, you normally would have put in your last bet on the turn unless a 4 hits the river, in which case you'd make another value bet.

However, the river card is the 8♦ counterfeiting your pair and leaving you to play the board. Here is the situation:

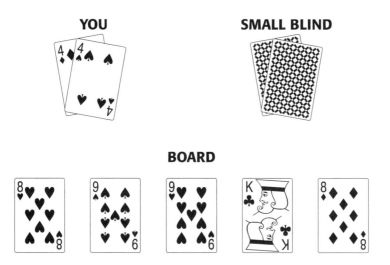

YOU

SMALL BLIND

BOARD

Your opponent checks and you decide that it's very likely that he is also playing the board. A bet here could steal his half of the pot for you. There is $2,700 in the pot and if your opponent has the type of hand you put him on, a big bet simply isn't necessary. He'd be hard pressed to call you with the board on the river, knowing that his best-case scenario is a split pot. Virtually any bet will win you this pot if your read is correct. But you don't want to make the bet smaller than your turn bet because it may be too enticing for your opponent to call. Also, with a slightly bigger bet than your turn bet, you may force your opponent off an ace-high as well. A bet of about $800 should do the trick. A bet that size into a $2,700 pot looks like a legitimate value bet. At the same time, it's small enough so that when you are wrong, the damage to your stack is minimal.

Replaying the Scenario from a Different Perspective

Now, what if that same scenario were slightly different. All of the details are the same—you still figure your opponent for the draw—but this time you actually have an A-9 for a full house. This might be a good time to make what may appear to be a goofy bet of, say, $400. For $400, your opponent might just call playing the board thinking that he is getting a good price on the call. Better still, he may see your goofy bet as a sign of weakness and go for a bluff check-raise.

As I mentioned previously, gauging when it's appropriate to make a goofy-looking bet like this one depends heavily on the type of hand you put your opponent on. If you think your opponent may have an 8 or a king, or is the type of player that always thinks you're bluffing, a bigger value bet would be in order. Against a player like that in this scenario, you'd be better off with a bet of $1,200 to $1,400.

RECOGNIZING SITUATIONS

The best players in the world are all very good at recognizing situations on the river where checking is better than betting. They also are good at using their hand-reading skills to come up with a bet that makes the most sense based on what they think their opponent has. That skill, figuring out your opponent's hand, is the most important factor in deciding how much to bet on the river, or whether it makes more sense to check. Poker isn't as simple as, "Well, I have the top full house and want full value, so I may as well bet the whole pot." Approaching your decisions that way will cause you to lose out on opportunities to gain a little extra value here and there when your opponent might call a smaller bet.

Let's look at a few more examples.

Hand in Action

With the blinds at $25/$50, a player limps in preflop from early position and you limp in from late position with pocket eights. Both blinds call. In four-way action, the flop comes J♥ 10♠ 4♥. All players check and you bet $150 to test the waters. The blinds fold and the limper calls. The turn is the 10♦ and once again, your opponent checks to you. Your read tells you that his most likely hand is a draw so you bet again, $375 this time. Again your opponent calls. The river is the 6♦ and your opponent checks.

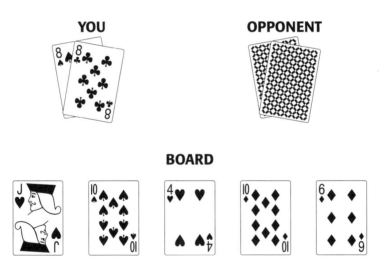

At this point, you figure that your 8-8 is the best hand. How you proceed on the river is completely reliant on your read of your opponent. If you have no read at all, the safest and most logical play is to check behind him and hope that he missed entirely. Things change a little bit, though, when you have some information on your opponent. For example:

- If you know your opponent is tricky, you should check the river.

- If your opponent plays his hands meekly, you should check the river because he may be checking a jack.
- If your opponent thinks you bluff too much and may be betting a busted draw, you should value bet the 8-8! A bet of $500 may get called by a hand as weak as ace-high in this situation. If your opponent has the 6♥ 7♥, for example, he is also very likely to call your river bet.

As you can see, your decision about whether or not a bet makes sense is entirely dependant on your read of your opponent. Let's take a look at another example.

Hand in Action

A player under the gun raises to $600 with the blinds at $100/$200. You look down at pocket aces from the small blind and reraise to $2,100. Your opponent calls. That leaves you with $45,000 in chips while your opponent has $85,000. The flop comes 3♦ 3♣ 7♠. With $4,400 in the pot, you bet $2,500, which should appear to be either a continuation bet with A-K or an overpair. Your opponent calls the bet. At this point, it looks like your opponent must have a strong hand because:

1. He raised under the gun
2. He called a reraise
3. He called you on a bad board

It looks as though he also has a high pair. The turn is the 2♦ and there is now $9,400 in the pot. On the turn, you decide to bet $5,500 and your opponent calls again, building the pot size to $20,400 and leaving you with $37,000 in chips for the river. The river comes with the 3♥, giving you a full house. Here's how it looks:

YOU **OPPONENT**

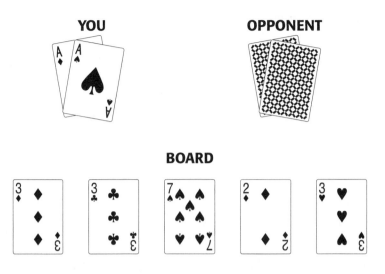

BOARD

Now it's time to decide how much to bet. Before you do that, you must review what you know about the hand and then think about reads you might have on your opponent.

What You Know
- His hand has to be strong to call on the flop and turn; it looks very much like he has a pocket pair.

What You Need to Figure Out
- Is this player capable of making a big laydown if you bet too much?
- Will this player think you may be running a big bluff?
- Is there any chance you're beat?
- What's the most he will call without making him feel like it'll hurt too much?

Against a typical opponent—one that is likely to pay you off with kings, queens, jacks, and maybe even tens, nines or eights—a big bet is in order on the river. With $20,400 in the pot, a bet such as $17,000 would make sense, leaving you with

$20,000. Betting that amount could possibly even sway your opponent into thinking that you bet $17,000 so that you'd still have $20,000 left if your bluff didn't work. The reason a big bet is not only appropriate, but should work in this situation, is because of what you know—your opponent has a strong hand. If you didn't think your opponent was very strong, you'd have to lower your asking price accordingly.

Let's take a look at a more complicated example.

Hand in Action

With the blinds at $100/$200, you raise preflop to $500 from middle position with the A♣ 7♣. The big blind calls you. The flop comes Q♥ 7♥ 4♣ and the big blind bets $800. Still unsure what your opponent has, you decide to take the safe approach and just call. The turn is the 2♣, giving you a backdoor flush draw along with the pair of sevens.

This time your opponent bets $1,800 and now you are starting to suspect that he has a hand such as Q-J or K-Q. You call. The river is the A♥.

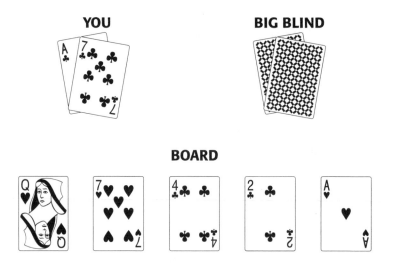

YOU   BIG BLIND

BOARD

Not exactly the card you were pulling for, but still a good card as you now have a two-pair hand, aces up. That card also brought the flush with it, which may scare your opponent. There is $6,300 in the pot and both you and your opponent have $30,000 in chips left. He checks and it's up to you.

What You Know
- It appears that your opponent has a pair of queens. You can't be sure about that, but it looks that way.

What You Need to Figure Out
- Is it likely that your opponent has you beat? If so, you'd check, but that seems weak. It's unlikely that he flopped a set, made a flush, or rivered two pair (aces and queens) and checked.
- Is this player the type that pays off big bets, or would a big bet scare him off? A bet that's too big will scare away most players, even if they suspect you're bluffing.
- What does this player put you on?
- What is the most you can bet to make your opponent feel like he's forced to pay you off?
- Would your opponent go for the check-raise if he made the flush? If that's the case, then you don't want to bet too much.

Pick a number from $2,000 to $2,600, something like $2,200, and make the bet. You'll give yourself a decent chance to win the pot if your opponent happens to put you on the straight draw, 5-6. It's a longshot to get paid off, but a bigger bet than that will minimize your long-term profit against most players. By betting about one-third the pot size, you may convince a player to make a "pot-odds call," even though he thinks he's probably beat. You'd be surprised how often players will find a way to justify making a longshot call on the river when the pots get bigger.

In summary, figuring out the right river bet is heavily dependant on your hand and your people-reading skills. The better you become at this aspect of the game, the better you'll be able to play tricky situations on the river. You simply can't have any success in deep-stack, no-limit games unless you develop the ability to determine the correct amount to bet on the river to the point that it becomes "easy."

CHECKING IN MARGINAL SITUATIONS

Tournaments require an adjustment from playing no-limit cash games. One of the key adjustments that you need to make often comes at the river in marginal situations where you might consider checking rather than looking to squeeze out a value bet. This premise holds true both in and out of position. We'll address both of those situations separately, starting with hands when you are out of position. Here's an example of a hand where you might consider sacrificing value in favor of protecting yourself from playing, and possibly losing, a big pot on the river:

Hand in Action

With the blinds at $50/$100 a player in first position makes it $300 to go before the flop. A late-position player calls and you also decide to call from the big blind with the 4♦ 5♦. The flop comes 6♣ 7♦ Q♣, giving you an open-ended straight draw as well as a backdoor flush draw. You check, the preflop raiser bets $550 and the third player calls. You also call. At this point, each of you has over $15,000 in chips.

The turn card is the K♦, giving you a backdoor flush draw to go along with the straight draw. Fearing that the raiser has a strong hand, you decide not to semi-bluff the turn, so you check. The original raiser bets again, this time firing $1,800 at the pot. The third player calls the $1,800, which means that you are getting very good odds on hitting your hand, so you also call the bet.

The river is the 8♣—you've made your straight.

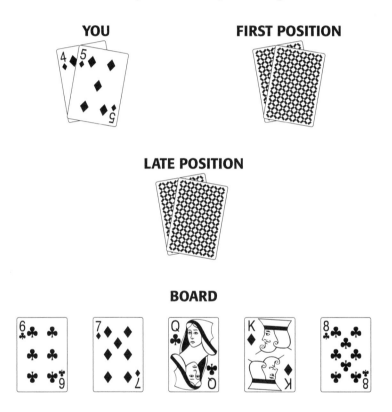

YOU

FIRST POSITION

LATE POSITION

BOARD

The 8 is a good card for you but, obviously, an offsuit 3 would have been much better. Unless the original raiser has been pushing with a draw, it's very likely that you have him beat. However, the real danger lies with the other player in the pot, the one who has just been calling all along—something he might do if he was drawing to either the flush, or maybe even hitting the 9-10 inside-straight draw since the turn card would have given him a double belly-buster straight draw (needing either an 8 or a jack).

SMALL BALL

The pot at this point has $8,000 in it, which is a pretty large pot given that the blinds are just $50/$100. Since you are out of position, you are in no-man's land in terms of being able to get information from your opponents before you have to act.

We learned about a deadly weapon in an earlier section, the defensive bet, and that is certainly an option here, albeit a slightly dangerous one. You have to really know your opponents in a situation like this so that you don't open up the door for an opponent to bluff-raise you on the river. The safest play, especially in a tournament, is to check despite improving your hand by rivering a straight. You would hope that both your opponents also check. If one of them bets the river, you will be put into a difficult situation. If neither player bets, then you will likely turn over a winning hand, despite possibly missing out on a few extra chips if one of your opponents might have called you with a weaker hand.

In this situation, you really have only two viable options: the defensive bet or checking. Once you check, if the player in last position bets, you'll be faced with one of the toughest decisions in poker. You stuck around with a draw, improved your hand to a straight, and now must decide if your opponent is either bluffing or possibly value betting a hand that you can beat. There aren't too many hands that the 4-5 straight can beat that most players would value bet on the river in this situation. It's usually going to be a bigger straight, a flush, a bluff, or possibly three of a kind. Three of a kind, however, is the least likely since there was no raise on the turn. In a three-way pot with a draw-heavy board, most players would look to protect a set so, really, all you can beat if the third player bets is a bluff.

The problem is: What kind of hand would he call the flop with, call the turn with, and then feel the need to bluff with on the river? If he had a queen or a king, he'd likely be happy to check it down and hope it's good. For him to be bluffing in this spot, the only legitimate hand he could have and play that way would be a hand such as 8-9 for a straight draw that paired on the river, or maybe a hand such as the 10◆ 8◆.

When you dig deep into this hand, it should become clear that the result you desire on the river is a street that's checked around. In fact, if you really have a good read on your opponents, this is a situation where you wouldn't need to waste a defensive bet for information, since any bet by an opponent should give you the information you need.

THOUGHTS: IN AND OUT OF POSITION ON THE RIVER

When playing hands out of position on the river where a value bet is questionable, you should always lean towards the side of caution, especially in a tournament, and especially when the pot has become sizeable. Some players who choose a more aggressive style for tournaments may squeeze out some extra value on the river with thin value bets, but in the long run, those types of bets usually end up costing you money.

For one, if you plan on calling a river bet with a marginal holding, you cost yourself money by betting it yourself and thus taking your opponent's possible bluff away from him. Secondly, and more importantly, when you bet marginal hands on the river out of position, you run the risk of being bluffed if your opponent senses weakness or tries to make a play on you. The goal with small ball is to simplify the game a little bit—not depending on crazy, wild river plays, but instead choosing a more passive line that will lead to less trouble.

The situation changes a great deal when you are in position and your opponent has checked to you. At this point you have the opportunity to simply turn your hand face up and win the pot if it's the best hand. By checking, you can no longer be bluffed or outplayed.

FIVE KEY RIVER QUESTIONS

As with any decision you make at the poker table, you should ask yourself a few key questions before you act. For these particular situations—that is, whether to value bet marginal hands in position—you should ask yourself these five questions every time.

1. Will Your Opponent Call?

Before deciding whether you should value bet the river, you first have to figure out if your bet has any value at all. In other words, is there a hand that your opponent will call a bet with on the river? In order to answer that question, you have to replay the details in your mind and try to put him on a likely hand.

The second step is gauging your opponent's tendencies. Is he a calling station? Is he a good player? What type of player does he think you are? So before you do anything, you first must come up with a rough idea of what percentage of the time your opponent will call a bet on the river with the worst hand. If the percentage is very low, a check is probably the best play.

2. Is He Capable of Check-Raising You on the River?

To answer this question, you have to delve into your memory bank and think about this player's betting history. Have you seen him do it before? Is he a tricky player? Once you've answered these two questions, you can compare notes. For example, if the player is unlikely to call with the worst hand, but is also capable of check-raising, then by all means, a bet would be a mistake. Or if your opponent is a calling station that would never check-raise on the river, you are in a situation where a bet likely holds significant value.

3. Will He Check Hands That Have You Beat?

Once again, you need to think about the type of player you are facing. Does he play slightly weak on the river, or is he a player that rarely misses value bets? Does he perceive you as a bluffer? If he does, is he likely to figure that there is more value in checking top pair and letting you bluff than betting it himself? Have you picked up on a pattern that indicates this player will often check some of his stronger hands? If so, you should be wary of making thin value bets against him because that's exactly what he is setting you up to do—make value bets, but ones that only hold value for him!

4. Will He Check-Raise Bluff on the River?

Against a strong, tricky player who is capable of sensing weakness or picking up on the fact that you are trying to make a thin value bet, betting is extremely dangerous. It actually could cause you to lose a pot that you already had won if you had checked. I remember seeing David Chiu use this play against a young, up-and-coming Internet player at Niagara Falls in a World Poker Tour event. David had been playing pretty tight up until that point and Genius28 (his online screen name) surely picked up on that fact.

Hand in Action

Genius28 raised preflop and David called from the small blind. The flop came 4♠ 5♣ 7♠, David checked, and Genius28 took a stab at the flop with a K-Q offsuit. David called. The turn card was the K♦ and both players checked. Presumably, Genius28 may have been a bit worried about facing a set.

The river was the Q♠, giving Genius28 top two pair.

SMALL BALL

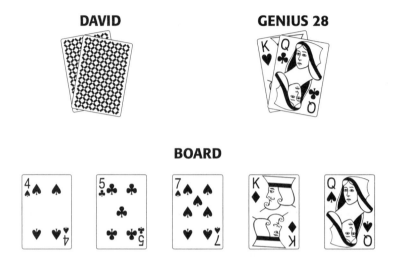

David checked the river once again and Genius28 decided to get some value for his two pair. David looked over at him, and I think he sensed that his opponent was making a value bet. But he probably also figured that if he check-raised the river, the young kid would be hard pressed to call based on David's image and the way he had played the hand. David did check-raise the river, and Genius28 thought for quite a while before folding his two pair face up.

David looked over at the youngster and said, "I only made that play because I knew you were a good player." He turned over the A♠ J♣! Now, I don't fault the kid for making this river bet, but the hand clearly shows the danger in value betting against smart, thinking players who are capable of making sophisticated plays. Instead of picking up a little pot, Genius28 ended up losing the pot, along with a few extra chips with his river bet.

The lesson here is that you really need to be wary of tricky players, especially successful players who likely won't call you as often as you'd like with the worst hand, but may steal some pots away from you when they sense some weakness.

5. Is It Worth It to Bet? Do You Really Need the Risk?

This question essentially sums up all four of the previous questions, but more from the point of view of table composition and chip count, as well as the other key factors. The premise here is to gauge whether you really need to make any marginal plays at all. Or are you in such command of the table that you can wait for better, higher percentage plays to invest your chips?

For example, if the table is letting you get away with highway robbery, stealing pot after pot, you probably don't need to worry about squeezing out a little extra value on the river in a marginal situation since you're able to have your way with your opponents with less risk. There's that consideration, as well as your chip stack. Simply put, if you have a healthy chip stack and your opponent in the hand does too, do you really need to mess with thin value bets against him and put yourself in danger? Conversely, if a thin value bet represents a significant portion of your chip stack, it's likely more important to protect what's in the middle and check it down. That way, you avoid a possible check-raise, as well as maintain your precious chips in situations where you end up value betting the worst hand.

As a general rule, the more precious the chips you'd be value betting are to you, the more you should lean toward taking the safe route and checking it down.

Whether you are in or out of position in a no-limit hold'em tournament, choosing the safer route is usually a recipe for long-term success. The whole small-ball concept dictates a simpler approach to river play so that you don't get caught up in difficult dilemmas for large portions of your stack.

BLUFFING

While bluffing on the river isn't a huge part of the small-ball arsenal, there are certainly some situations where bluffing will make sense for you, especially if your opponents are on to the fact that you prefer playing a more cautious, straightforward style on the river. In fact, unless you are facing an opponent who has at least a little understanding as to your approach to river play, you should probably avoid bluffing entirely.

The best targets for bluffing on the river are smarter players who think they have you all figured out. Those players have been paying attention, and have noticed that while you are entering a lot of pots, you usually have the best hand when you put your money in on the river. More and more great young players are in the game today, players who are capable of thinking at a higher level and who will also fold big hands on the river, especially against small-ball players whose entire strategy is based on playing lots of hands, creating a wild image, and exploiting opponents who buy into the idea that they're crazy players and paying them off on the river. The exploitation happens on the river when the confused player ends up calling a big bet with a marginal hand thinking, "I have to call that guy. He plays every hand!"

On a personal level, adjusting my strategy is something that I was somewhat forced to embrace when younger players—who may have read some of my written material or watched me play on TV or YouTube—stopped falling into my traps. They learned how to play against me by being aggressive with me on the flops. And if I made a big raise on the turn or a big bet on the river, they correctly recognized that, even though they had a strong hand, for a player like me to choose to play a big pot with them at that point, I must have an even stronger hand.

As with any adjustment in strategy, however, there is a counter strategy. This strategy adjustment goes slightly against most small-ball principles and requires even more focus and skill than the standard small-ball goal of projecting the image,

"I'm a wild man, pay me off," followed by the never-actually-bluffing strategy.

I found that the major adjustments players were making against me opened up more opportunities for me to steal bigger pots. The trick to successfully employing this approach is twofold: first, you need to make your bluffs very believable and second, you can't go to the well too many times or it will run dry.

The ability to read your opponent's hand is the most important aspect of successfully bluffing. If you can't figure out the strength of your opponent's hand, you simply won't know when a bluff might work. The best bluffers are players that can sense weakness, and then make a believable play that their opponents buy. The other key to selling a river bluff is your bet size. A bluff on the river usually should represent exactly what a value bet would look like. If you make a bet that's too small, your opponent may decide to make a loose call because the price is right. A bet that's too big may raise suspicions. You want your bluffs to look like you are doing everything you can to get your opponent to call you.

Let's take a look at an example. This hand took place at the 2007 inaugural World Series of Poker Europe event in London that 18-year-old Annette Oberstad won. I was at a tough table with loads of action, with the likes of Gus Hansen and Patrick Antonius.

Hand in Action
With the blinds at $1,200/$2,400, Gus Hansen made it $6,000 to go under the gun. Gus had a monster stack and was playing to form, raising lots of pots from every position with a wide variety of hands. I also had a decent stack and called from the button with the J♣ 9♣.

The flop came K♠ 10♦ 5♦ and Gus fired out a bet of $8,000. I didn't think he needed to have a very strong hand here, so I decided to represent something and hope that Gus folded. I made it a total of $22,000. Gus thought for quite a while, as he often does, which led me to believe that he had a hand such as A-Q or A-J and was trying to work out his pot odds. Either that, or he had a pair smaller than kings. He finally called the raise.

The turn brought the 4♦ and we both checked. I thought a bet here would be too suspicious, as Gus knows that I'm not likely to raise him on the flop with a flush draw; and if I had a king, I would lean toward checking it against him.

The river was a blank, the 8♣.

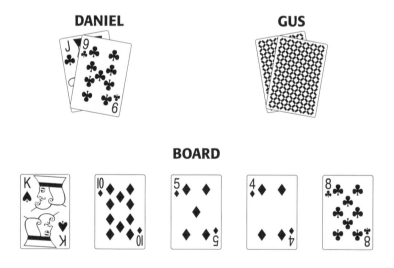

DANIEL   **GUS**

BOARD

Gus checked again. After my acting job on the turn, one that was trying to sell a hand like K-Q, I decided that I needed to take this pot away from Gus because it looked like he couldn't beat a king. Before deciding to bluff, though, our past history and his perception of me was of the utmost importance in helping me come to my decision. I knew that Gus's read on me was that I didn't bluff on the river that much—which was correct, especially against him. I also knew that Gus thought that I would make thin value bets against him on the river, a perception based on countless hands we'd played in the past.

I finally decided to nonchalantly throw out a bet that looked like it was screaming for a loose call. I bet $20,000 despite putting in a raise to $22,000 on the flop! Gus thought for a bit, and then folded what I presumed was an ace high.

I started explaining the hand from the very beginning because all the preceding facts that led to the river were important parts of the story, from Gus's chip stack and loose play to his perception of me. That's how good bluffs work. You don't ever throw in a bluff without any thought, saying, "Well, I can't win if I check." For a good bluff to work, all the facts need to line up—and then you have to make the right bet, because otherwise, you'll get caught.

In the example with Gus, I made a very small river bet, but I don't recommend that line in most cases. This was a specific case where I knew my opponent and was very aware of how he would perceive a bet of that size. As a general rule, your bluffs should mimic your value bets; so, anywhere from 50 to 75 percent of the pot would make sense on the river. Unless, as was the case in my example with Gus, you have reason to believe that a smaller bet might work, or maybe even an oversized bet. The bet size you ultimately choose is solely dependant on how you think your opponent perceives you and what you think will work playing against him.

SUMMARY

In this section, you learned that the river isn't a street where you want to overcomplicate things, that the easiest, less stressful approach is usually the best approach. That has been the theme in almost every section, from checking in marginal situations to paying off river bets.

For the small-ball player, the river is the street where the big pots should go your way more often than not. If that's not the case, then you aren't following the rules properly. It's a street where you want to minimize your own risk and allow your opponents to make the bigger mistakes. In the end, that's what poker is all about, really—capitalizing on other players' mistakes. Sure, it's nice to romanticize about sick bluffs and crazy laydowns, but in the end, the player who wins is the one who plays what appears to be an effortless game, and does not get involved in random, high-fluctuation pots or bluff-rebluff-rebluff situations.

For the small-ball player, the river is a street where you hope to end up with the best hand and choose to play a small pot when you aren't certain about that. It's a street where bluffs are few and far between, but also have a very high success rate. Most importantly, the river is the street where all the hard work you have put in creating that wild image really tends to pay off.

CONCLUSION

I hope this chapter has helped you understand how building a big stack and getting deep in tournaments is relatively easy, provided you have a good system, solid discipline, and of course, decent hand-reading skills.

The small-ball approach is designed to confuse your opponents without taking major risks. It's a style that requires playing a lot of hands, making lots of decisions, while at the same time controlling the pot size so that you can avoid major confrontations in marginal situations.

In this chapter, you learned the correct preflop raising size and the types of hands that work best with the small-ball approach. You then learned how to use position to win pots whether or not you hit the flop. I also instructed you on how to proceed cautiously post-flop in marginal situations, especially when out of position, and listed hands that would help you to avoid going broke unnecessarily. As a byproduct, the small-ball approach will often allow you to pick up extra value when an opponent misinterprets your cautious play as weakness and foolishly tries to bluff you.

Another key concept I emphasized is that by lowering your average bet sizes after the flop, you actually save yourself chips in the long run—chips that you can use to see more flops while you're waiting for that home run flop!

You also learned that big-time bluffs are overrated. Although bluffing is an integral part of the game, it's more effective when done sporadically and targeted to appropriate situations. The safer, more methodical approach that I laid out for you in this chapter will help you consistently build chips in tournaments time after time.

LAST WORDS

LAST WORDS

Daniel Negreanu

I sincerely hope that you got everything you were looking for out of *Power Hold'em Strategy*—and more. The tons of excellent information in this book will help your no-limit hold'em game improve immensely, whether you are an online grinder, a low-limit tournament player, or even an aspiring pro looking to play on the big-time poker circuit. We tried to fit in as many helpful hand examples as we could without creating a 1,000-page monster!

When you apply the advice we've given you to your own game, I have no doubt that you will improve rapidly. Equally important, this book should help you understand the mindset of small-ball players so that when you face off against one, you won't be confused by his approach. Instead, you will be able to exploit him.

If you enjoyed *Power Hold'em Strategy* and would like to further your poker training, www.PokerVT.com is the closest you can get to obtaining one-on-one training with me and several other top players. PokerVT.com (the VT stands for Virtual Training) is an interactive educational site with fresh and regularly updated content.

You'll find the small-ball concepts presented in great detail at PokerVT.com. You also can watch videos of me and other top players playing online. You'll receive a customized course based on your own skill level, with my commentary and analysis from real, live poker hands. Plus, you'll get an opportunity to ask me questions directly. Drop in anytime!

I look forward to seeing you at the tables!

GLOSSARY

GLOSSARY

The glossary is extracted from the poker dictionary, *Poker Talk* by Avery Cardoza, courtesy of Cardoza Publishing,

advertise: Intentionally play weak cards to the showdown to misrepresent one's playing style or skill level, or bluff in a situation in which one is likely to be called, setting the stage for trapping opponents on future hands.

aggressive: 1. A player who frequently bets and raises. **2.** When applied to a game, frequent betting and raising, and thus implying one with big pots.

all in: When a player has all his chips committed to a pot.

GLOSSARY

ante: **1.** Mandatory bet placed into the pot by all players before the cards are dealt; compare with blind. **2.** Put such a bet in the pot.

around back: Sitting in late position.

around front: Sitting in early position.

average stack size: In a tournament, the average number of chips remaining per player, calculated by dividing the number of remaining players into the original starting field and multiplying the result by the per-player starting chip total. For example, if 50 players remain out of a starting field of 200, and each started with $10,000 in chips, then the average chip count would be $40,000.

backdoor: Make an unlikely straight or flush late in a hand by catching successive cards on the last rounds of play. For example, in hold'em, if a player flops J-10-3 to his A-J hand, then catches a king and queen on the turn and river, he has *backdoored a straight.*

bad beat: A loss with a hand that was heavily favored to win.

behind: **1.** Acting or being in position to act after a particular player; being in late position. **2.** Having a lesser holding than an opponent at some point during the play of a hand.

big blind: **1.** The larger of two forced blind bets, posted before the cards are dealt by the player two seats to the left of the button. Compare to *small blind*. **2.** The player occupying this position.

big pair: A pair of jacks or higher.

big slick: Hole cards of A-K.

blank: A card that doesn't appear to help anyone. Also, *brick*, *rag*.

blind: **1.** A mandatory bet made before the cards are dealt by the player or players immediately to the button's left. **2.** The player making that bet.

blinded out: Having lost all one's chips, or a majority of them, to the forced antes and blind bets, that is, without playing hands; what happens to a player who repeatedly folds hands and loses his chips by attrition.

bluff: **1.** Bet aggressively with an inferior hand, one unlikely to win if called, to cause opponents to fold better hands, thus making the bluffer a winner by default. **2.** A bet so made.

bluffing outs: Cards that will allow you to win a pot because you can use them to bluff an opponent off his hand.

board: The community cards in flop hold'em.

bottom pair: A pair formed by combining a hole card with the lowest board card.

GLOSSARY

brick: A worthless card that appears to help no player. Also, *blank*, *rag*.

bubble: In a tournament, the point at which all remaining players will win money except for the next player to get eliminated. For example, with 37 players remaining and 36 places paid, that 37th place is the *bubble*.

bullets: Aces.

bust out: **1.** Lose, usually going broke, in a session. **2.** Exit a tournament. "He busted out on the bubble."

button: **1.** The player occupying the dealer position who goes last in all rounds except the first. **2.** The physical disk, often plastic and labeled "dealer," that indicates the dealer position.

buy-in: **1.** The amount of money a player exchanges for chips to begin a poker session. **2.** The minimum amount of chips required to enter a game.

call: Match a bet on the current round of betting and stay in competition for the pot, as opposed to fold or raise. Also *call a bet*.

call a raise cold: Match a bet and a raise without having yet put any bets into the pot during the round.

calling station: Unflattering term for a player who calls too many bets and rarely raises.

cap: **1.** A ceiling on the number of raises permitted in a round or the amount of money that could be bet either in a round of betting or a hand. **2.** Put in the last raise permissible in a round.

card dead: Condition of being dealt one bad hand after another; essentially getting no good cards to play.

case: The very last one of its type. For example, the *case ace* would be the last remaining ace in the deck. "When Joe bet his case chips and lost, we didn't see him again."

cash game: **1.** A game played for real money. **2.** A non-tournament game. "At the end of the tournament, the players all jumped into cash games."

catch: Get a card that improves one's hand.

catch a piece of the flop: When some portion of a player's hole cards combine with the flop, improving his hand or providing a draw.

catch up: Improve an inferior hand enough so that it is closer in strength to a hand believed to be superior.

change gears: Alter one's playing style during a game from, for example, loose to tight, tight to loose, conservative to aggressive, or aggressive to conservative. Also *switch gears*.

chase: To unwisely call bets or raises on hands that are behind.

GLOSSARY

check: **1.** The act of "not betting" and passing the bet option to the next player while still remaining an active player. Once a bet has been made in a round, checking is not an option. **2.** A betting chip.

check-raise: **1.** Raise in a round after first checking, essentially trapping a player. Also, *sandbag*. **2.** The strategy of checking to induce an opponent into betting so that the bet can be raised.

coin toss: A hand or situation whose winning chances approximate 50-50, that is, one in which neither side has a great advantage over the other. For example, in hold'em, A-K versus two queens is a coin-toss situation.

come over the top: Raise or reraise. "When Billy raised my bet on the turn, I came over the top for all my chips."

complete: Improve a three- or four-card drawing hand to a straight or flush, or improve a two-pair hand to a full house; also, *fill*.

connectors: Two or more cards in sequence, such as 5-6 or J-Q.

coordinated board: A board with flush or straight draws.

coordinated flop: A flop with good straight and flush draws, such as 9-10-J or 7-5-4 of mixed suits, or cards with two or three matching suits.

correct odds: The exact mathematical odds of an event occurring or not occurring. For example, the correct odds against pulling the green chip out of a bag containing one green chip and two red ones are 2 to 1 against.

covered: Have equal to or more than enough chips to meet a bet, usually an all-in bet. For example, on an all-in call, if the winner has $17,000 and the loser less than $17,000, the winner is said to have the loser covered.

cutoff seat: The position to the right of the button.

dead money: **1.** Disparaging term for a player who has little chance of winning. **2.** Money put into the pot by players who have folded and are no longer in competition for it.

defend the blind: In the small or big blind position, call a raise made by an opponent in middle to late position who is suspected of raising to force out opponents so that he can steal the blinds.

dog: A hand or situation that is unlikely to win, and is not the favorite; short for *underdog*

dominated hand: A hand that is greatly inferior to another such that it will lose a great majority of times. For example, K-9 is a *dominated hand* against A-K.

draw dead: Have a hand with more cards to come that is hopelessly beat, no matter what cards are dealt.

"Joe picked up a 9 to complete his 10-J-Q-K straight draw, but was drawing dead to a player already holding a flush."

draw to the nuts: Have a straight, flush, or straight flush draw, that, if filled, will give the player the best possible hand of its type. For example, a player holding A♥ J♥ in hold'em would be *drawing to the nuts* on a flop of K♥ 9♠ 2♥.

dry pot: A bet made into a side pot that currently contains nothing; usually heard as part of the phrase *bet into a dry pot*. **2.** A pot with very little money in it to be won.

early position: Approximately the first third of players to act in a nine- or 10-handed game or the first or second to act in a six- or seven-handed game.

enter the pot: Get involved in a pot by betting or calling.

entry fee: The cost to participate in a tournament, usually collected by a cardroom or casino in addition to the buy-in. For example, in a $1,000 + $30 tournament, the buy-in is $1,000 and the entry fee is $30.

equity: **1.** The amount of money invested in a hand or in a game. **2.** The amount of money in a pot a player would expect to win if the hand were played out over the long run, for example, if the player had a one-third chance of winning a $120 pot, his *equity* would be $40. Sometimes the entire cost of a tournament including buy-in and tournaments fees.

EV: *Expected value.*

even money: **1.** A bet in which either side has about an equal chance of winning. **2.** A bet that pays $1 for every $1 wagered.

expected value: The amount of money likely to be won (or lost) over a specified period of time given the odds of the situation. Often called *EV*, and it can be positive or negative.

fancy play: Checking, betting, or raising in a situation that goes against conventional wisdom, with the purpose of deceiving opponents.

fast: **1.** A game with lots of action. **2.** A player who aggressively bets and raises

favorite: **1.** A hand or situation that is likely to win or perceived to be likely to win; as opposed to *underdog*. **2.** An event that is mathematically likely to occur.

final table: In a tournament, the final table of players, which comes with prestige, especially in major tournaments, and typically includes cash prizes.

flat call: *Smooth call.*

flop: The three community cards that are simultaneously dealt face up upon completion of the first round of betting and can be used by all active players.

flush card: A card that helps make a flush.

flush draw: Four cards of one suit needing one more card of that suit to complete a flush.

four-card flush: A hand containing four cards of the same suit.

four-card straight: A hand containing four cards in sequence, such as 2-3-4-5, needing one more to complete the straight.

free card: A betting round in which all players checked, thereby allowing players to see another card without cost.

full value: Inducing from opponents the maximum number of bets or maximum amount of money possible on a winning hand.

gamble: Play a speculative hand for a big bet.

gap: The missing card in an inside straight draw, for example, 6-7-9-10 for which an 8 is needed to make a straight.

get a piece of the flop: To have one's hole cards combine with the three-card flop to form a potential winning hand, though one not necessarily favored to win.

**get away
from
a hand:** Fold a strong hand against one or more hands that appear to be stronger.

**get full
value:** Maximize the size of the pot by betting and raising with either the probable winning cards or a drawing hand that will win if completed. "Casey jammed the pot on every street to get full value on his set of kings."

**get involved
with:** Play a pot against an opponent or several opponents.

**get
paid off:** **1.** The money a player wins or stands to win. "If I make this hand, I'll get paid off." **2.** Win a pot from a player who calls a bet or raise on the end knowing he has an inferior hand but feels obligated to call due to favorable pot odds or the relatively large amount of money at stake.

**give a
free card:** Check and allow opponents to see another card without having to put any bets into the pot. See *free card.*

go all in: Bet all one's chips.

grind: Play long hours and earn relatively little for the effort.

gutshot: *Inside straight.*

**gutshot
straight:** *Inside straight.*

heads-up: Poker played by two players only, one against the other. **2.** A pot contested by two players.

hit the flop: A hand which is greatly improved by the three-card flop.

hole card: A card held face down by a player, the value of which is hidden from other players. Also *pocket card.*

Hollywood: Show off or act in a grandiose manner, sometimes with respect to trying to influence the actions of opponents during a betting situation.

implied odds: The amount of money that can potentially be won (assuming opponents will make additional bets) compared to the cost of a bet. For example, if a player is contemplating calling a $10,000 bet, and he figures that $90,000 more will be put into the pot, he has implied odds of 9 to 1—that is, he is betting $10,000 to possibly win $90,000. Compare with *pot odds.*

in front: **1.** Being in early position on a hand. **2.** A position that is before another player. "I was in front of Chris and he kept raising me."

in position: Being in late position, that is, being one of the last players to act in a round.

inside straight: **1.** A straight draw consisting of four cards with one "hole," such that only one rank can complete the hand, for example, 2-4-5-6, in which only a 3 can complete the straight. Also *belly buster, gutshot straight, gutshot, one-gapper.*

Compare to an *open-ended straight* or *outside draw*, which has two ranks (eight outs) to complete. **2.** The completion of such a draw. "My set got beat by an inside straight."

in the money: **1.** In a tournament, to finish among the top players and win cash. The terms *money finish* and *cashed* are related.

Internet player: **1.** An individual who plays poker on the Internet. **2.** A derogatory term used by cash and tournament competitors for players who have learned their poker skills on the Internet and are viewed as poor players.

isolate: Raise with the intention of creating a heads-up situation.

keep someone in line: Raise or reraise an aggressive player to keep him from bullying and controlling play.

kicker: The highest side card to any hand of one pair, two pair, three of a kind, or rarely, four of a kind hand. For example, a player holding 3-3-5-7-A has a pair of threes with an ace kicker. In hold'em, with competing pocket cards of A-J and K-J on a flop of J-Q-3-J-4, the pot would be won by the A-J hand, the three jacks with the ace kicker beating the three jacks with the king kicker.

last to act: The player who acts last in a betting round.

late position: The last two or three seats in a nine- or 10-handed game, or the last or next-to-last player in a game with five to seven players.

leak: **1.** A weakness or "hole" in a player's game. **2.** An activity away from the poker tables that drains one's bankroll, such as craps or sports betting.

legitimate hand: A hand that is of reasonable strength, as opposed to a bluff, in which the hand held is weak.

limp: Call a bet, that is, not raise, as a way to enter the pot cheaply, or, if the first player to make a bet, open for the minimum. Also, *limp in*.

limper: A player who makes the minimum permitted bet as a way to enter the pot.

long run: The concept of expected results occurring over a large number of trials.

longshot: A hand or situation that will rarely win or occur.

loose: **1.** A player who plays many hands and enters many pots. **2.** When applied to a game, a collection of players who play many pots.

loose-aggressive player: A player who not only plays many hands, but plays them aggressively with frequent bets and raises.

maniac: A player who bets and raises recklessly.

marginal hands: Hands that are borderline profitable, with long-term expectations of about break-even when played, thus being about equally correct to play as to fold.

maximum value: To induce from opponents the most bets possible on a winning hand, often used as part of the expression, "get maximum value."

middle position: **1.** The middle three or four seats in a nine- or 10-handed game or the middle position in a smaller game. **2.** In a pot contested by three players, the second to act.

min-raise: To raise the minimum amount possible.

miss the flop: When a player's starting cards are not improved by the three community cards of the flop. "Jack's 3-3 missed the A-9-9 flop and he folded when T-Mart pushed in $2,000."

money manage- ment: A strategy used by smart players to preserve their capital, manage their wins, and avoid unnecessary risks and big losses.

monster: A very big poker hand.

move in: Go all in on a bet or raise, putting all one's chips at stake.

GLOSSARY

moves: Fancy plays: bluffs. "Watch out for B-Man; he's got lots of moves."

muck: **1.** Fold. "He bet and I mucked." **2.** The place on the table where discarded cards are placed. "Throw that piece of cheese in the muck."

multiway: Three or more players competing for a pot.

negative expectation: When a player or a hand is mathematically favored to lose in the long run, as opposed to positive expectation.

nit: Tight player who takes no chances, and is thus, very predictable. Even tighter is a *supernit*.

nuts: The best possible hand given the cards on board; usually expressed as *the nuts*.

odds: **1.** The mathematical expression showing the percentage chance of an event occurring, typically expressed in numerical format such as 5 to 1 or 3 to 2, with the chances of the event not occurring listed first, and the chances of it occurring, listed second. Odds of 5 to 1 is also expressed as *5 to 1 against*, which means that out of six times, one would expect the event not to occur five times and occur once. **2.** The betting odds established for such situation, that is, what someone booking the situation would pay.

offsuit: **1.** Cards of different suits. For example, *K-Q offsuit* means a king and a queen that are not of the same suit. Also, *unsuited*. **2.** A card of a different suit than a potential flush draw. "An offsuit king came on the river."

online poker: Poker played on the Internet as opposed to "live" poker, in which players are actually seated together at a physical table. Also, *Internet poker*.

on the bubble: In a tournament, the point at which all remaining players will win money except for the next player to get eliminated. For example, when there are 37 players remaining and only 36 places are paid. See *bubble*.

on the button: The player who occupies the dealer position and has the dealer button in front of him.

on tilt: A player who has lost control of his emotions due to a bad loss or succession of losses and is playing recklessly. The term is borrowed from what happens to a pinball machine when it is shaken too violently and no longer operates properly. Also, *steaming*.

open-ended straight: Four consecutive cards to a straight (not including an ace, which would make it a one-ended straight) such as 8-9-10-J, such that a card on either end will make a straight, as opposed to an *inside* or *one-ended straight*.

outflop: Make a better hand on the flop than an opponent.

out of position: **1.** Being in the disadvantageous position of acting before opponents. **2.** In early position, with one or more active players after.

outs: Cards that will improve a hand that is behind enough to win a pot. For example, a hand of 7-7-9-9-K has four outs against a completed straight, the two remaining sevens and nines, which will make a winning full house, while a player who needs to complete a four card flush draw to win, has nine outs, the remaining suited cards in the deck.

overcard: A hole card higher in rank than any board card. For example, if a player holds A-10 and the flop is K-J-6, the ace is an overcard.

passive: **1.** A player who rarely raises. **2.** A game that has little or no raising, and thus relatively small pots.

play a rush: Play more hands during a winning streak in the belief that winning begets winning.

play back: Raise or reraise an opponent's bet or raise.

pocket cards: The initial cards a player is dealt.

pocket pair: A pair as one's hole cards.

position: **1.** A player's relative order of acting compared to opponents, particularly with respect to the number of players acting after his turn. **2.** Specifically good position, that is later and better than opponents. "When you're on the button, you have position and can open with more hands."

positive expecta-tion: A player or a hand that is mathematically favored to win in the long run, as opposed to *negative expectation.*

pot-committed: To bet so much of one's stack, usually around half or more of one's chips, that in effect, a bettor has decided to commit all his chips to the pot if he is raised.

pot odds: The amount of money in the pot compared to the cost of a bet. For example if $50 is in the pot, and a player needs to call a bet of $10 to play, he is getting pot odds of 5 to 1. Compare with *implied odds.*

preflop: The action that occurs after players receive their starting cards and before the three-card flop is dealt.

premium hand: One in a group of the best starting hands in a poker game.

put a player on a hand: **1.** Deduce an opponent's hand by his betting and playing actions. **2.** Assume that a player has a good hand. "When he kept raising, I put him on a hand and folded." In this sense, also *give credit to.*

rag: A worthless card not thought to help anyone; brick.

rainbow: Cards of different suits. "The flop came 10-J-K rainbow."

GLOSSARY

represent: Bet or raise on cards that appear to indicate a particular hand or type of hand but not actually have that hand. For example, to bet out on a board of four diamonds, as if a flush were held, but not actually hold one.

river: the fifth and last community card dealt or its betting round (or both considered together).

rock: A tight player, one who bets only with premium hands, that is, infrequently.

satellite tourna- ment: A one-, sometimes two- or three-table tournament in which the winner gains entry into a larger-buy-in tournament for a fraction of the cost. For example, $10,000 buy-in tournaments often feature $1,000 satellites preceding the event. Sometimes, a second- and third-place cash prize is awarded as well. With more than a few tables, it becomes a *supersatellite*. With one table, also *single table satellite, one table satellite*.

second nuts: The second-best possible hand given the cards on board. Also see *nuts*.

semibluff: Bet or raise with a hand that is perceived to be second-best or worse but has two ways to win, either by forcing opponents out, or if that fails, by improving to a winner with a fortuitous draw. For example, in hold'em, raising to force out opponents with a hand of 8♠ 7♠ on a board of Q♠ K♠ 6♦, a hand that will likely lose if called, but which could win if another heart is dealt.

set: A three-of-a-kind hand made with a pair in the hole and one on board.

Set mining: Calling a raise hoping to flop a set.

Short buy-in: To buy in to a game for a minimal amount, much less than is allowed.

short-handed: A game played with less than the full or typical number of players. In hold'em, a game played with six or fewer players.

short stack: **1.** A player who has relatively few chips in comparison to opponents. **2.** In a tournament, the holder of relatively few chips compared to opponents such that the player is in serious jeopardy of losing them all.

show a hand down: Reveal cards after all the betting has been completed on the last round.

showdown: The final act of a poker hand, the point at which remaining players reveal their hands to determine the winner of the pot.

shut down: Discontinue aggressive betting and check or sometimes fold when a scare card comes or an opponent plays back.

side game: A cash poker game played at the same time as a tournament, and sometimes filled with both weak players who bust out early and with the pros who gather like vultures to feed on the remains.

GLOSSARY

slow down: Discontinue betting or raising by checking or calling instead.

slowplay: Bet a strong hand weakly—by checking, calling, or conservative betting—to disguise its strength and keep opponents in the pot.

small ball: A term borrowed from baseball, a strategy that relies on seeing a lot of flops cheaply to either win a big pot by connecting with unusual hands or a small pot by outplaying weaker opponents without risking too many chips.

small blind: **1.** The smaller of two forced blind bets in hold'em posted by the player immediately to the left of the button before the cards are dealt. **2.** The player occupying this position.

smooth call: Call a bet when you hold a really strong hand (and a raise would also be correct). Also, flat call.

solid player: A player with fundamentally good poker skills.

stack size: **1.** The total number of chips a player has on the table. **2.** In a tournament, the relative number of chips a player has compared to other players.

steal: Bet or raise with an inferior hand that would probably lose if played to the showdown, with the goal of forcing opponents to fold so that the pot can be won by default.

steal the blinds: On the first round of betting, bluff opponents out of a pot no one has entered so that the blinds (and antes, if any) can be won without a fight.

stone cold bluff: A bet made with the intention of forcing all opponents to fold, one which has almost no chance of winning if called.

straddle: **1.** Before the cards are dealt, an optional raise for two times the big blind made by the player seated to his left, which gives the straddler the option of last action on the first round of betting. Often called *live straddle*.

suited: Pertaining to two or more cards in the same suit.

suited connectors: Cards that are of consecutive rank and in the same suit, such as 8♦ 9♦.

super-satellite: A low buy-in tournament featuring multiple tables, in which the top finishers win seats into a large-buy-in tournament for a fraction of the cost. For example, $200 supersatellites typically precede $10,000 events and allow players with smaller bankrolls to earn a shot at the big event.

tell: An inadvertent mannerism or reaction that reveals information about the strength of a player's hand.

tight: **1.** A player who plays only premium hands and enters few pots. **2.** When applied to a game, a collection of players who play few pots and give little action.

tight-aggressive: A player who plays few hands, but when he does, he plays them aggressively.

tilt: See *on tilt*.

top kicker: **1.** The side card to a pair, two pair, three of a kind, or quad hand being higher than the side card of an opponent with an equivalently ranked hand. For example, with a board of K-J-8-7-2, if you have A-K and your opponent has K-T, you both have two kings, but your ace is the top kicker. **2.** The side card being the highest possible card, usually an ace.

top pair: **1.** In flop games, a pocket card that combines with the highest board card to form a pair. **2.** Having a higher-ranked pair than an opponent.

trap: Induce a player to invest more money in a situation in which he is an almost sure loser.

trap hand: A hand that, if played, has a high risk of incurring a major loss of chips.

trash: Worthless cards or a hand with little potential for winning without a bluff.

tricky play: Checking, betting, or raising in a situation that seems contrary to the apparent or logical play, with the purpose of fooling opponents into thinking one has a hand of a different nature.

trouble hand: A hand that, if played incorrectly, can lead to disastrous losses.

true odds: When the payout on a bet is exactly equally to the likelihood of that event occurring.

turn: The fourth community card in Texas hold'em..

uncoordinated board: A board that has no flush or straight draws, such as Q-7-3 or 10-5-2 of three suits.

underdog: See *dog*.

unraised pot: **1.** A hand in which there were no raises in the first round of betting. **2.** A round with no raises yet made.

unsuited: Cards of different suits. See OFFSUIT.

value bet: A wager made for the purpose of increasing the pot—as opposed to having opponents fold—with either the best cards, cards that have a good chance of winning but may not be the best, or a drawing hand that would likely win if completed.

GREAT CARDOZA POKER BOOKS
ADD THESE TO YOUR LIBRARY - ORDER NOW!

POKER TOURNAMENT FORMULA 2: Advanced Strategies for Big Money Tournaments *by Arnold Snyder.* Probably the greatest tournament poker book ever written, and the most controversial in the last decade, Snyder's revolutionary work debunks commonly (and falsely) held beliefs. Snyder reveals the power of chip utility—the real secret behind winning tournaments—and covers utility ranks, tournament structures, small- and long-ball strategies, patience factors, the impact of structures, crushing the Harringbots and other player types, tournament phases, and much more. Includes big sections on Tools, Strategies, and Tournament Phases. A must buy! 550 pages, $24.95.

DANIEL NEGREANU'S POWER HOLD'EM STRATEGY *by Daniel Negreanu.* This power-packed book on beating no-limit hold'em is one of the three most influential poker books ever written. Negreanu headlines a collection of young great players—Todd Brunson, David Williams. Eric Lindgren, Evelyn Ng and Paul Wasicka—who share their insider professional moves and winning secrets. You'll learn about short-handed and heads-up play, high-limit cash games, a powerful beginner's strategy to neutralize professional players, and how to mix up your play and bluff and win big pots. The centerpiece, however, is Negreanu's powerful and revolutionary small ball strategy. You'll learn how to play hold'em with cards you never would have played before—and with fantastic results. The preflop, flop, turn and river will never look the same again. A must-have! 500 pages, $34.95.

POKER WIZARDS *by Warwick Dunnett.* In the tradition of Super System, an exclusive collection of champions and superstars have been brought together to share their strategies, insights, and tactics for winning big money at poker, specifically no-limit hold'em tournaments. This is priceless advice from players who individually have each made millions of dollars in tournaments, and collectively, have won more than 20 WSOP bracelets, two WSOP main events, 100 major tournaments and $50 million in tournament winnings! Featuring Daniel Negreanu, Dan Harrington, Marcel Luske, Kathy Liebert, Mike Sexton, Mel Judah, Marc Salem, T.J Cloutier and Chris "Jesus" Ferguson. This must-read book is a goldmine for all serious players, aspiring pros, and future champions! 352 pgs, $19.95.

INTERNET HOLD'EM POKER *by Avery Cardoza.* Learn how to get started in the exciting world of online poker. The book concentrates on Internet no-limit hold'em, but also covers limit and pot-limit hold'em, five- and seven-card stud, and Omaha. You'll learn everything from how to play and bet safely online to playing multiple tables, using early action buttons, and finding easy opponents. Cardoza gives you the largest collection of online-specific strategies in print—more than 6,500 words dedicated to 25 unique strategies! You'll also learn how to get sign-up bonuses worth hundreds of dollars! 176 pages, $9.95

TOURNAMENT TIPS FROM THE POKER PROS *by Shane Smith.* Essential advice from poker theorists, authors, and tournament winners on the best strategies for winning the big prizes at low-limit rebuy tournaments. Learn proven strategies for each of the four stages of play—opening, middle, late and final—how to avoid 26 potential traps, advice on rebuys, aggressive play, clock-watching, inside moves, top 20 tips for winning tournaments, more. Advice from Brunson, McEvoy, Cloutier, Caro, Malmuth, others. 160 pages, $14.95.

NO-LIMIT TEXAS HOLD 'EM: The New Player's Guide to Winning Poker's Biggest Game *by Brad Daugherty & Tom McEvoy.* For experienced limit players who want to play no-limit or rookies who has never played before, two world champions show readers how to evaluate the strength of a hand, determine the amount to bet, understand opponents' play, plus how to bluff and when to do it. Seventy-four game scenarios, unique betting charts for tournament play, and sections on essential principles and strategies show you how to get to the winners circle. Special section on beating online tournaments. 288 pages, $24.95.

Order now at 1-800-577-WINS or go online to: www.cardozabooks.com

FREE BOOK!
TAKE ADVANTAGE OF THIS OFFER NOW!

The book is **free**; the shipping is **free**. Truly, no obligation. Oops, we forgot. You also get a **free** catalog. **And a $10 off coupon!!** Mail in coupon below to get your free book or go to www.cardozabooks.com and click on the red OFFER button.

WHY ARE WE GIVING YOU THIS BOOK?
Why not? No, seriously, after more than 27 years as the world's foremost publisher of gaming books, we really appreciate your business. Here's our appreciation back! Take this free book as our thank you for being our customer; we're sure we'll see more of you!

THIS OFFER GETS EVEN BETTER & BETTER!
You'll also get a **FREE** catalog of all our products—over 200 to choose from—and get this: you'll also get a **$10 FREE** coupon good for purchase of any product in our catalog!

Our offer is pretty simple. Let me sum it up for you:
1. Order your **FREE** book
2. Shipping of your book is **FREE!***
3. Get a **FREE** catalog (over 200 items—and more on the web)
4. You also get a **$10 OFF** coupon good for anything we sell
5. Enjoy your free book and **WIN**!

*U.S. customers only. Sorry, due to very high ship costs, we cannot offer this outside the U.S. However, we still have good news for foreign customers: Spend $25 or more with us and we'll include that free book for you anyway!

CHOOSE YOUR FREE BOOK
Choose one book from any of these books in the Basics of Winning Series (15 choices): Baccarat, Bingo, Blackjack, Bridge, Caribbean Stud Poker and Let it Ride, Chess, Craps, Hold'em, Horseracing, Keno, Lotto/Lottery, Poker, Roulette, Slots, Sports Betting, Video Poker.

Or choose from these five books: Internet Hold'em Poker, Crash Course in Beating Texas Hold'em, Poker Talk, Poker Tournament Tips from the Pros, or Bobby Baldwin's Winning Poker Secrets.

When you order by Internet, enter the coupon code **DANIEL** to get your free book

GREAT CARDOZA POKER BOOKS
ADD THESE TO YOUR LIBRARY - ORDER NOW!

HOLD'EM WISDOM FOR ALL PLAYERS *By Daniel Negreanu.* Superstar poker player Daniel Negreanu provides 50 easy-to-read and right-to-the-point hold'em strategy nuggets that will immediately make you a better player at cash games and tournaments. His wit and wisdom makes for great reading; even better, it makes for killer winning advice. Conversational, straightforward, and educational, this book covers topics as diverse as the top 10 rookie mistakes to bullying bullies and exploiting your table image. 176 pages, $14.95.

MILLION DOLLAR HOLD'EM: Winning Big in Limit Cash Games *by Johnny Chan and Mark Karowe.* Learn how to win money consistently at limit hold'em, poker's most popular cash game, from one of poker's living legends. You'll get a rare opportunity to get into the mind of the man who has won ten World Series of Poker titles—tied for the most ever with Doyle Brunson—as Johnny picks out illustrative hands and shows how he thinks his way through the betting and the bluffing. No book so thoroughly details the thought process of how a hand is played, the alternative ways it could have been played, and the best way to win session after session. *Essential* reading for cash players. 400 pages, $29.95.

THE POKER TOURNAMENT FORMULA *by Arnold Snyder.* Start making money now in fast no-limit hold'em tournaments with these radical and never-before-published concepts and secrets for beating tournaments. You'll learn why cards don't matter as much as the dynamics of a tournament—your position, the size of your chip stack, who your opponents are, and above all, the structure. Poker tournaments offer one of the richest opportunities to come along in decades. Every so often, a book comes along that changes the way players attack a game and provides them with a big advantage over opponents. Gambling legend Arnold Snyder has written such a book. 368 pages, $19.95.

HOW TO BEAT SIT-AND-GO POKER TOURNAMENTS by Neil Timothy. There is a lot of dead money up for grabs in the lower limit sit-and-gos and Neil Timothy shows you how to go and get it. The author, a professional player, shows you how to reach the last six places of lower limit sit-and-go tournaments four out of five times and then how to get in the money 25-35 percent of the time using his powerful, proven strategies. This book can turn a losing sit-and-go player into a winner, and a winner into a bigger winner. Also effective for the early and middle stages of one-table satellites.176 pages, $14.95.

HOW TO BEAT INTERNET CASINOS AND POKER ROOMS *by Arnold Snyder.* Learn how to play and win money online against the Internet casinos. Snyder shows you how to choose safe sites to play. He goes over every step of the process, from choosing sites and opening an account to how to take your winnings home! Snyder covers the differences between "brick and mortar" and Internet gaming rooms and how to handle common situations and predicaments. A major chapter covers Internet poker and basic strategies to beat hold'em and other games online. 272 pages, $14.95..

I'M ALL IN: High Stakes, Big Business, and the Birth of the World Poker *Tour* by *Lyle Berman with Marvin Karlins.* Lyle Berman recounts how he revolutionized and revived the game of poker and transformed America's culture in the process. Get the inside story of the man who created the World Poker Tour, plus the exciting world of high-stakes gambling where a million dollars can be won or lost in a single game. Lyle reveals the 13 secrets of being a successful businessman, how poker players self-destruct, the 7 essential principles of winning at poker. Foreword by Donald Trump. Hardback, photos. 232 pages, $24.95.

7-CARD STUD: The Complete Course in Winning at Medium & Lower Limits *by Roy West.* Learn the latest strategies for winning at $1-$4 spread-limit up to $10/$20 fixed-limit games. Covers starting hands, 3rd-7th street strategy, overcards, selective aggressiveness, reading hands, pro secrets, psychology, and more in an informal 42 lesson format. Includes bonus chapter on 7-stud tournament strategy by Tom McEvoy. 224 pages, $19.95.

DOYLE BRUNSON'S EXCITING BOOKS
ADD THESE TO YOUR COLLECTION - ORDER NOW!

SUPER SYSTEM *by Doyle Brunson.* This classic book is considered by the pros to be the best book ever written on poker! Jam-packed with advanced strategies, theories, tactics and money-making techniques, no serious poker player can afford to be without this hard-hitting information. Includes fifty pages of the most precise poker statistics ever published. Features chapters written by poker's biggest superstars, such as Dave Sklansky, Mike Caro, Chip Reese, Joey Hawthorne, Bobby Baldwin, and Doyle. Essential strategies, advanced play, and no-nonsense winning advice on making money at 7-card stud (razz, high-low split, cards speak, and declare), draw poker, lowball, and hold'em (limit and no-limit). This is a must-read for any serious poker player. 628 pages, $29.95.

SUPER SYSTEM 2 *by Doyle Brunson.* The most anticipated poker book ever, SS2 expands upon the original with more games and professional secrets from the best in the world. Superstar contributors include Daniel Negreanu, winner of multiple WSOP gold bracelets and 2004 Poker Player of the Year; Lyle Berman, 3-time WSOP gold bracelet winner, founder of the World Poker Tour, and super-high stakes cash player; Bobby Baldwin, 1978 World Champion; Johnny Chan, 2-time World Champion and 10-time WSOP bracelet winner; Mike Caro, poker's greatest researcher, theorist, and instructor; Jennifer Harman, the world's top female player and one of ten best overall; Todd Brunson, winner of more than 20 tournaments; and Crandell Addington, no-limit hold'em legend. 672 pgs, $34.95.

CARO'S GUIDE TO DOYLE BRUNSON'S SUPER SYSTEM *by Mike Caro.* Working with World Champion Doyle Brunson, the legendary Mike Caro has created a fresh look to the "Bible" of all poker books, adding new and personal insights that help you understand the original work. Caro breaks 36 concepts into either "Analysis, Commentary, Concept, Mission, Play-By-Play, Psychology, Statistics, Story, or Strategy. Lots of illustrations and winning concepts give even more value to this great work. 86 pages, 8 1/2 x 11, $19.95.

ACCORDING TO DOYLE *by Doyle Brunson.* Learn what it takes to be a great poker player by climbing inside the mind of poker's most famous champion. Fascinating anecdotes and adventures from Doyle's early career playing poker in roadhouses are interspersed with lessons from the champion who has made more money at poker than anyone else in history. Learn what makes a great player tick, how he approaches the game, and receive candid, powerful advice from the legend himself. 208 pages, $14.95.

MY 50 MOST MEMORABLE HANDS *by Doyle Brunson.* This instant classic relives the most incredible hands by the greatest poker player of all time. Great players, legends, and poker's most momentous events march in and out of fifty years of unforgettable hands. Sit side-by-side with Doyle as he replays the excitement and life-changing moments of the most thrilling and crucial hands in the history of poker: from his early games as a rounder in the rough-and-tumble "Wild West" years—where a man was more likely to get shot as he was to get a straight flush—to the nail-biting excitement of his two world championship titles. Relive million dollar hands and the high stakes tension of sidestepping police, hijackers and murderers. A thrilling collection of stories and sage poker advice. 168 pages, $14.95.

ONLINE POKER *by Doyle Brunson.* Ten compelling chapters show you how to get started, explain the safety features which lets you play worry-free, and lets you in on the strategies that Doyle himself uses to beat players in cyberspace. Poker is poker, as Doyle explains, but there are also strategies that only apply to the online version, where the players are weaker!—and Doyle reveals them all in this book.192 pages, illustrations, $14.95.

BOBBY BALDWIN'S WINNING POKER SECRETS *by Mike Caro with Bobby Baldwin.* The fascinating account of 1978 World Champion Bobby Baldwin's early career playing poker against other legends is packed with valuable insights. Covers the common mistakes average players make at seven poker variations and the dynamic winning concepts needed for success. Endorsed by superstars Doyle Brunson and Amarillo Slim. 208 pages, $14.95.

MIKE CARO'S EXCITING WORK
POWERFUL BOOKS YOU <u>MUST</u> HAVE

CARO'S MOST PROFITABLE HOLD'EM ADVICE *by Mike Caro.* When Mike Caro writes a book on winning, all poker players take notice. And they should: The "Mad Genius of Poker" has influenced just about every professional player and world champion alive. You'll journey far beyond the traditional tactical tools offered in most poker books and for the first time, have access to the entire missing arsenal of strategies left out of everything you've ever seen or experienced. Caro's first major work in two decades is packed with hundreds of powerful ideas, concepts, and strategies, many of which will be new to you—they have never been made available to the general public. This book represents Caro's lifelong research into beating the game of hold em. 408 pages, $24.95

MASTERING HOLD'EM AND OMAHA *by Mike Caro and Mike Cappelletti.* Learn the professional secrets to mastering the two most popular games of big-money poker: hold'em and Omaha. This is a thinking player's book, packed with ideas, with the focus is on making you a winning player. You'll learn everything from the strategies for play on the preflop, flop, turn and river, to image control and taking advantage of players stuck in losing patterns. You'll also learn how to create consistent winning patterns, use perception to gain an edge, avoid common errors, go after and win default pots, recognize and use the various types of raises, play marginal hands for profit, the importance of being loved or feared, and Cappelletti's unique point count system for Omaha. 328 pages, $19.95.

CARO'S BOOK OF POKER TELLS *by Mike Caro.* One of the ten greatest books written on poker, this must-have book should be in every player's library. If you're serious about winning, you'll realize that most of the profit comes from being able to read your opponents. Caro reveals the the secrets of interpreting *tells*—physical reactions that reveal information about a player's cards—such as shrugs, sighs, shaky hands, eye contact, and many more. Learn when opponents are bluffing, when they aren't and why—based solely on their mannerisms. Over 170 photos of players in action and play-by-play examples show the actual tells. These powerful ideas will give you the decisive edge. 320 pages, $24.95.

CARO'S FUNDAMENTAL SECRETS OF WINNING POKER *by Mike Caro.* Learn the essential strategies, concepts, and plays that comprise the very foundation of winning poker play. Learn to win more from weak players, equalize stronger players, bluff a bluffer, win big pots, where to sit against weak players, and the six factors of strategic table image. Includes selected tips on hold 'em, 7 stud, draw, lowball, tournaments, more. 160 pages, $12.95.

CARO'S PROFESSIONAL POKER REPORTS

Each of these three powerful insider poker reports is centered around a daily mission, with the goal of adding one weapon per day to your arsenal. Theoretical concepts and practical situations are mixed together for fast in-depth learning. For serious players.

11 DAYS TO 7-STUD SUCCESS. Bluffing, playing and defending pairs, different strategies for the different streets, analyzing situations—lots of information within. One advantage is gained each day. A quick and powerful method to 7-stud winnings. Essential. Signed, numbered. $19.95.

12 DAYS TO HOLD'EM SUCCESS. Positional thinking, playing and defending against mistakes, small pairs, flop situations, playing the river, are just some sample lessons. Guaranteed to make you a better player. Very popular. Signed, numbered. $19.95.

PROFESSIONAL 7-STUD REPORT. When to call, pass, and raise, playing starting hands, aggressive play, 4th and 5th street concepts, lots more. Tells how to read an opponent's starting hand, plus sophisticated advanced strategies. Important revision for serious players. Signed, numbered. $19.95.

THE CHAMPIONSHIP SERIES
POWERFUL INFORMATION YOU <u>MUST</u> HAVE

CHAMPIONSHIP NO-LIMIT & POT-LIMIT HOLD'EM *by T. J. Cloutier & Tom McEvoy.* The bible for winning pot-limit and no-limit hold'em tournaments gives you all the answers to your most important questions: How do you get inside your opponents' heads and learn how to beat them at their own game? How can you tell how much to bet, raise, and reraise in no-limit hold'em? When can you bluff? How do you set up your opponents in pot-limit hold'em so that you can win a monster pot? What are the best strategies for winning no-limit and pot-limit tournaments, satellites, and supersatellites? Rock-solid and inspired advice you can bank on from two of the most recognizable figures in poker. 304 pages, $29.95.

CHAMPIONSHIP HOLD'EM *by T. J. Cloutier & Tom McEvoy.* Hard-hitting hold'em the way it's played *today* in both limit cash games and tournaments. Get killer advice on how to win more money in rammin'-jammin' games, kill-pot, jackpot, shorthanded, and full table cash games. You'll learn the thinking process for preflop, flop, turn, and river play with specific suggestions for what to do when good or bad things happen. Includes play-by-play analyses, advice on how to maximize profits against rocks in tight games, weaklings in loose games, experts in solid games, plus tournament strategies for small buy-in, big buy-in, rebuy, add-on, satellite and big-field major tournaments. Wow! 392 pages, $29.95.

CHAMPIONSHIP OMAHA (Omaha High-Low, Pot-limit Omaha, Limit High Omaha) *by Tom McEvoy & T.J. Cloutier.* Clearly-written strategies and powerful advice from Cloutier and McEvoy who have won four World Series of Poker Omaha titles. You'll learn how to beat low-limit and high-stakes games, play against loose and tight opponents, and the differing strategies for rebuy and freezeout tournaments. Learn the best starting hands, when slowplaying a big hand is dangerous, what danglers are (and why winners don't play them), why you sometimes fold the nuts on the flop and would be correct in doing so, and overall, how you can win a lot of money at Omaha! 296 pages, illustrations, $29.95.

CHAMPIONSHIP HOLD'EM TOURNAMENT HANDS *by T. J. Cloutier & Tom McEvoy.* An absolute must for hold'em tournament players, two legends show you how to become a winning tournament player at both limit and no-limit hold'em games. Get inside the authors' heads as they think their way through the correct strategy at 57 limit and no-limit starting hands. Cloutier & McEvoy show you how to use skill and intuition to play strategic hands for maximum profit in real tournament scenarios and how 45 key hands were played by champions in turnaround situations at the WSOP. Gain tremendous insights into how tournament poker is played at the highest levels. 368 pages, $29.95.

CHAMPIONSHIP HOLD'EM SATELLITE STRATEGY *by World Champions Brad Dougherty & Tom McEvoy.* Every year satellite players win their way into the $10,000 WSOP buy-in and emerge as millionaires or champions. You can too! Learn the specific, proven strategies for winning almost any satellite from two world champions. Covers the ten ways to win a seat at the WSOP, how to win limit hold'em and no-limit hold'em satellites, one-table satellites, online satellites, and the final table of super satellites. Includes a special chapter on no-limit hold'em satellites! 320 pages, $29.95.

HOW TO WIN THE CHAMPIONSHIP: Hold'em Strategies for the Final Table, *by T.J. Cloutier.* If you're hungry to win a championship, this is the book that will pave the way! T.J. Cloutier, the greatest tournament poker player ever—he has won 60 major tournament titles and appeared at 39 final tables at the WSOP, both more than any other player in the history of poker—shows how to get to the final table where the big money is made and then how to win it all. You'll learn how to build up enough chips to make it through the early and middle rounds and then how to employ T.J.'s own strategies to outmaneuver opponents at the final table and win championships. You'll learn how to adjust your play depending upon stack sizes, antes/blinds, table position, opponents styles, chip counts, and the specific strategies for six-handed, three handed, and heads-up play. 288 pages, $29.95.

Order now at 1-800-577-WINS or go online to: www.cardozabooks.com

POWERFUL WINNING POKER SIMULATIONS
A MUST FOR SERIOUS PLAYERS WITH A COMPUTER!
IBM compatible CD ROM Win 95, 98, 2000, NT, ME, XP

These incredible full color poker simulations are the best method to improve your game. Computer opponents play like real players. All games let you set the limits and rake and have fully programmable players, plus stat tracking, and Hand Analyzer for starting hands. MIke Caro, the world's foremost poker theoretician says, "Amazing... a steal for under $500... get it, it's great." Includes free phone support. "Smart Advisor" gives expert advice for every play!

1. TURBO TEXAS HOLD'EM FOR WINDOWS - $59.95. Choose which players, and how many (2-10) you want to play, create loose/tight games, and control check-raising, bluffing, position, sensitivity to pot odds, and more! Also, instant replay, pop-up odds, Professional Advisor keeps track of play statistics. Free bonus: Hold'em Hand Analyzer analyzes all 169 pocket hands in detail and their win rates under any conditions you set. Caro says this "hold'em software is the most powerful ever created." Great product!

2. TURBO SEVEN-CARD STUD FOR WINDOWS - $59.95. Create any conditions of play; choose number of players (2-8), bet amounts, fixed or spread limit, bring-in method, tight/loose conditions, position, reaction to board, number of dead cards, and stack deck to create special conditions. Features instant replay. Terrific stat reporting includes analysis of starting cards, 3-D bar charts, and graphs. Play interactively and run high speed simulation to test strategies. Hand Analyzer analyzes starting hands in detail. Wow!

3. TURBO OMAHA HIGH-LOW SPLIT FOR WINDOWS - $59.95. Specify any playing conditions; betting limits, number of raises, blind structures, button position, aggressiveness/passiveness of opponents, number of players (2-10), types of hands dealt, blinds, position, board reaction, and specify flop, turn, and river cards! Choose opponents and use provided point count or create your own. Statistical reporting, instant replay, pop-up odds high speed simulation to test strategies, amazing Hand Analyzer, and much more!

4. TURBO OMAHA HIGH FOR WINDOWS - $59.95. Same features as above, but tailored for Omaha High only. Caro says program is "an electrifying research tool...it can clearly be worth thousands of dollars to any serious player. A must for Omaha High players.

5. TURBO 7 STUD 8 OR BETTER - $59.95. Brand new with all the features you expect from the Wilson Turbo products: the latest artificial intelligence, instant advice and exact odds, play versus 2-7 opponents, enhanced data charts that can be exported or printed, the ability to fold out of turn and immediately go to the next hand, ability to peek at opponents hand, optional warning mode that warns you if a play disagrees with the advisor, and automatic mode that runs up to 50 tests unattended. Tough computer players vary their styles for a great game.

---

6. TOURNAMENT TEXAS HOLD'EM - $39.95

Set-up for tournament practice and play, this realistic simulation pits you against celebrity look-alikes. Tons of options let you control tournament size with 10 to 300 entrants, select limits, ante, rake, blind structures, freezeouts, number of rebuys and competition level of opponents. Pop-up status report shows how you're doing vs. the competition. Save tournaments in progress to play again later. Additional feature allows quick folds on finished hands.